Advance Praise
The Taste of Many Mountains

"Both a personal voyage of discovery and a description of how researchers have come to understand Fair Trade, *The Taste of Many Mountains* sheds light on the long journey that coffee makes from small holder farms in Guatemala to the barista. The story captures key elements of our research on the impact of fair trade coffee and addresses profound questions about global poverty."

— CRAIG MCINTOSH
Professor of Economics,
Graduate School of
International Relations and
Pacific Studies, University of
California at San Diego

"Coffee lovers are on a continual quest for the great cup of coffee. Dr. Bruce Wydick is on a simultaneous quest to understand how some of those great coffees are nurtured and grown by some of the world's poorest farmers. And that begins the story, the mystery, and the twists in *The Taste of Many Mountains*. The noble lives of the growers he portrays who farm the hillsides of Guatemala could only be developed by the heartfelt, firsthand knowledge of a researcher who has lived in their midst, agonized with their struggles, and admired their characters. Anybody who wants to 'do good' needs to read *The Taste of Many Mountains!* An excellent novel in its own right—it also explodes the illusion of easy answers and cliché responses to the challenges of globalization and alleviating poverty. Dr. Wydick's first novel is brewed perfectly for his readers—full of rich body with double-shots of insight."

— SANTIAGO "JIMMY"
MELLADO
President & CEO Compassion
International

"Pack your bags, join a colorful international research team of graduate students, and head to the Guatemalan highlands as an economic sleuth—or read this book. It will transport you into the world of cutting edge economics and into the lives of people far away whose stories are surprisingly interwoven with our own. This book is a wonder: simultaneously thought-provoking and educational, entertaining and gripping, and deeply moving."

— CHRIS AHLIN
Associate Professor of
Economics, Michigan State
University

"What actually works to reduce poverty in poor countries? A distinguished development economist uses the unusual format of a well-written, emotion-packed novel, weaving together careful history and sophisticated economics, to show the ordinary reader what works and what does not. Gripping, enlightening, and very readable. A must read."

— RON SIDER
founder of Evangelicals for
Social Action

"Bruce Wydick's story is a tale of discovery, a quest to Central America to find out how the coffee trade really works. While sympathetically portraying a range of perspectives about international economics, wealth, and poverty, the book is also a meditation on how we know anything about the workings of the economy."

— DEAN SCRIMGEOUR
Assistant Professor of
Economics, Colgate University

"*The Taste of Many Mountains* will amuse, confuse, and perhaps displease its readers. While a novel about economics graduate students would seem to many to be, at best, an effective treatment for insomnia, this book is both engaging and thought-provoking. Anyone who is interested in reducing poverty in developing countries would learn much from this book, and those who think they already know how to achieve this goal are likely to learn the most."

— PAUL GLEWWE
Professor, Department
of Applied Economics,
University of Minnesota

"Bruce Wydick takes us to the coffee plantations of rural Guatemala, traces the production path to the lattes we sip each day, and asks some penetrating questions: Why do coffee growers' children remain shoeless despite the success of the Fair Trade scheme? Why does a bout of bad weather profit these impoverished farmers more? What can we truly do to ensure they're paid a living wage? A detective story and an economics lesson in one, *The Taste of Many Mountains* is an engaging read on one of today's critical justice issues."

— SHERIDAN VOYSEY
writer, speaker, broadcaster,
and author of *Resurrection
Year: Turning Broken Dreams
into New Beginnings*

"Bruce Wydick successfully mixes adventure, mystery, and economic analysis in his novel. His book will generate great discussions in an introductory Economic Development class or a Latin American studies course. Students with little or no exposure to life in a developing country will get a compassionate view of the origins of something we often take for granted: a cup of coffee."

— EMILY CONOVER
Assistant Professor of
Economics, Hamilton College

"Building on a dominant, tangible ritual of modern society—coffee drinking— Bruce has crafted a thoughtful story of economic and personal discovery. The narrative is rich in economic principles, filled with insights into the richness and process of doing research fieldwork, and packed with perspectives on poverty and global markets."

— TRAVIS LYBBERT
Associate Professor of
Agricultural and Resource
Economics, University of
California at Davis

The Taste of Many Mountains

Bruce Wydick

THOMAS NELSON
Since 1798

NASHVILLE   MEXICO CITY   RIO DE JANEIRO

Published in Nashville, Tennessee, by Thomas Nelson. Thomas Nelson is a registered trademark of HarperCollins Christian Publishing, Inc.

Published in association with the literary agency of The Agency Group, Ltd.

Thomas Nelson, Inc., titles may be purchased in bulk for educational, business, fund-raising, or sales promotional use. For information, please e-mail SpecialMarkets@ThomasNelson.com.

Any Internet addresses (websites, blogs, etc.) and telephone numbers in this book are offered as a resource. They are not intended in any way to be or imply an endorsement by Thomas Nelson, nor does Thomas Nelson vouch for the content of these sites and numbers for the life of this book.

Publisher's Note: This novel is a work of fiction. Names, characters, places, and incidents are either products of the author's imagination or used fictitiously.

Library of Congress Cataloging-in-Publication Data

Wydick, Bruce, 1954–
  The taste of many mountains / Bruce Wydick.
    pages cm
  ISBN 978-1-4016-8992-6 (paperback)
  1. Coffee growers—Guatemala—Fiction. 2. Coffee industry—Fiction. 3. Globalization—
Fiction. 4. Guatemala—Fiction. I. Title.
  PS3623.Y36T37 2014
  813'.6—dc23   2014007192

Printed in the United States of America

14 15 16 17 18 19 RRD 6 5 4 3 2 1

The taste of many mountains
imbued my coffee cup.
But I knew not of where it came
before I drank it up.

Author's Note

THE COFFEE MARKET IS A COLLISION BETWEEN THE RICH world and the poor world. I consider this as I sit at a breezy café in Berkeley, watching the coffee next to my laptop getting cold.

The price I paid for the cup of coffee sitting in front of me represents a tiny fraction of the income coffee consumers like me in rich countries earn every day. But it equals the daily wage of a coffee laborer in the developing country where the coffee is grown. As a development economist, I am familiar with the data: the wages of the coffee drinkers around me are more than a hundred times greater than that of the man, woman, or child who picked the coffee beans used to make this drink.

Coffee is produced in what many call the Third World for consumption in the First World. The contrasts between these worlds are painfully manifest in the statistics. Consider the economically average person in the top ten coffee-consuming countries. Since we are on the subject of coffee, I'll call him Joe: Joe Average. The counterpart to Joe, the economically average person in the top ten coffee-*producing* countries, I will call Joaquin. The first difference between Joe and Joaquin is their difference in income. Because Joe's income is many times higher than Joaquin's, Joe can consume more of just about everything than Joaquin. This includes some things that he needs—like housing, food, and health care—as well as things that he doesn't, like his chrome-plated espresso machine.

Joaquin's children are much less healthy than Joe's children. In fact, they are about ten times more likely than Joe's children to die before they reach the age of five. And if Joaquin's children live past age five, there is a one in six chance that they will be chronically malnourished. The chances that Joe's children will be chronically malnourished are essentially nil.

I consider the many people I have met in Guatemala like Joaquin who cultivate coffee for a living. Many can barely spell their name. Indeed, one out of five adults in the coffee-producing world is illiterate, with the rate far higher among coffee laborers themselves. Among the Joes of the coffee-consuming world, adult illiteracy is rare, less than 1 percent. And almost four in five adults use the Internet in Joe's world, while fewer than one in five use it in Joaquin's world. The digital divide between Joe and Joaquin is a digital chasm.

Compared to the coffee-consuming world, the coffee-producing world is also a violent world. Joe has never lived through a civil war. They are tragedies he reads about that affect poor people in poor countries who live across oceans. Indeed, *not one* of the top two dozen coffee-consuming countries has experienced a civil war in the last fifty years. Joaquin's family has probably endured a civil war, for in the last fifty years, civil wars have afflicted most of the large coffee-producing nations: Colombia, Côte d'Ivoire, the Dominican Republic, El Salvador, Ethiopia, Guatemala, India, Peru, Rwanda, Uganda, and Vietnam.

Civil wars are sparked by the harsh inequalities in the coffee-producing world: prodigious land ownership among the privileged few mingled with the cheap labor of the uneducated masses. These glaring inequalities in the coffee-producing world brew a deep-rooted social discontent that in sequence provokes repression, government brutality, and, all too often, war.

⁓

Coffee was discovered not in the rich world, but in the poor world. Scientists have traced the *coffea arabica* plant to the Kaffa province of southwest Ethiopia, a region that remains one of the world's poorest. Indeed, there is evidence from this area dating to the sixth century AD that Ethiopian warriors mixed ground-up beans from the coffea arabica with animal fat. Rolling the concoction into little balls, they created a low-tech energy blob they consumed before going into battle.

One of the early coffee legends from Ethiopia recounts the tale of a young Ethiopian goat herder named Kaldi, who was surprised to discover his goats frolicking friskily after consuming the fruit from a wild bush. Probably bored with his pastoral duties, Kaldi decided to try the fruit himself, and was quickly overcome with a newfound vivacity and exhilaration. When rumors of the stimulatory effects of the plant reached the head of a nearby monastic order, the monk began to ingest the fruit himself, and stumbled upon the idea of boiling it in water to create a hot drink that would keep his monks from falling asleep during evening prayers (apparently easier than making his prayers a little more exciting).

In the sixteenth century coffee spread from Ethiopia to Egypt and to the Arabian Peninsula, specifically near present-day Yemen. Shortly after, it spread to Europe, making successful forays into different European countries, particularly the Netherlands, Italy, France, and England. By 1650 Oxford had its first coffeehouse, and a year or two later the first coffeehouse opened in London. Puritans in England took readily to the new drink because it seemed to be widely adopted as a substitute for opium and alcohol, both of which they detested. It was regarded by many at the time as a "sobering beverage" and a "mighty nutrient for the brain."

By the mid-eighteenth century, thousands of coffeehouses across Europe in cities such as Marseilles and Venice were becoming centers of conversation among merchants, businessmen, and civic-minded intellectuals. In many urban centers, the coffeehouses became places where locals from all walks of life could go to read a newspaper, catch up on political gossip, or discuss the latest enlightenment philosophies. In England, coffeehouses were sometimes called "penny universities" for the education they offered to their customers at the price of a one-penny admission. Many prestigious institutions evolved from these coffeehouses in Britain, including the Royal Society, which began as a gathering of students at the Oxford Coffee Club. The great financial house Lloyds of London began as a coffeehouse catering to merchants involved in overseas trade.

But Europeans quickly discovered that their home continent was unsuitable for coffee-growing. As a result, the crop would be introduced for cultivation almost entirely in European colonies. The Dutch introduced coffee cultivation in Java in 1696, perhaps the first instance of coffee being cultivated in a European colony for eventual consumption in Europe. Around this time a pattern became established: coffee would be consumed in the rich world and culti-vated in the poor world.

How did coffee come to Guatemala? It is claimed that the beans used to begin coffee cultivation in much of Latin America and the Caribbean came from a solitary plant. In 1714 the Burgermeister of Amsterdam bestowed on King Louis XIV of France the gift of a single coffee plant, a descendant from a Dutch coffee estate in its colony in Java. The king treasured the seedling and had it planted in the Royal Garden in Paris. Realizing that the crop could be cultivated more successfully in the colonies, the French naval officer Gabriel Mathieu de Clieu was given one of the few surviving descendants of that plant to bring to Martinique, where the king desired to establish overseas French coffee cultivation.

The ship encountered myriad obstacles in its quest across the Atlantic. Attacks by Tunisian pirates and ferocious storms threatened the boat. There was a scuffle aboard the ship between de Clieu and a jealous rival, when at one dramatic moment, a branch of the coffee plant was torn off. At another point in the voyage, the sailing ship stalled for weeks without wind in the Doldrums, and the crew was running so low on water that it had to be rationed. Faithful to his duty, de Clieu allocated part of his ration to the fragile plant.

Just a few years after the 1726 planting of de Clieu's coffee seedling in Martinique, twenty million coffee plants were growing on the Caribbean island, and Louis XIV appointed de Clieu governor of the Antilles region. And so it was from de Clieu's original plant that many coffee plants were ultimately taken to cultivate other parts of Latin America and the Caribbean.

It is believed that somewhere between 1750 and 1760, Jesuit missionaries, desiring to bring opportunities for agricultural prosperity to the native Indians, began to import coffee plants from the Dominican Republic and Cuba to their missions in Central America. One of their first destinations: Guatemala.

—

This book is a work of fiction, but it is based on a true story of a group of graduate students who embarked on a journey that crossed two worlds to follow a trail of coffee beans, from a peasant farmer in Guatemala to a café in San Francisco. The assignment we gave them was to calculate the profit made at every stage. What the researchers and students involved with the project discovered from this journey was a story that was too compelling not to tell.

Although many of the major characters resemble students I have worked with and people I have encountered in the course of my research, they (and most of the minor characters in the book) are fictional. Yet most of the events recorded in the story are true in that they are taken from actual experiences and from stories that have been recounted to me in the hundreds of interviews I have carried out over the years of my fieldwork in rural Guatemala.

The chasm between the world in which coffee is consumed and the world in which coffee is grown is not easily grasped through the recitation of economic facts and figures, summaries of academic studies, and policy briefs. The crossing of these two worlds must be experienced. And it is my hope that you will experience this crossing through the eyes of my students, as they themselves experienced it. The tension around globalization and poverty is observed through the lives and experiences of characters rather than through an orderly pedagogy. I want to involve readers in the plight of characters affected by global issues rather than merely present the more general and esoteric theories that are the preferred medium of economists. I want to engage readers in this crossing of two worlds as much as I want to inform.

The coffee market is a microcosm of the intersection of economies and cultures that accompanies economic globalization. It illuminates the disparities between the rich world and the poor world, and yet creates a space in which these two worlds meet to carry out business. In the coffee market, the rich meet the poor, and awareness grows of the chasm that separates them.

On one side are lives too often ripped apart by poverty and violence;

on the other side are lives more often blessed with peaceful prosperity. And as our awareness of the chasm grows, we yearn for quick solutions that would create an economic bridge across it, to somehow assuage the dissonance we feel in our conscience created by these contrasts.

The development of mechanisms that bridge the economic chasm between the First World and the Third World (rather than merely relieve guilt in the First World) may well be the most critical research problem in social science. The struggle to bridge the chasm often pits left against right, the dispassionate scientist against the vociferous advocate, heartfelt emotion versus reason and evidence. I wanted to tell a story that illuminates the breadth of this chasm and illustrates the struggle of those who seek to bridge it. This book is my attempt.

CHAPTER 1

Guatemala, May 12, 1983

The young Mayan woman fled from her adobe house to take refuge in a neighbor's barn. Her worn sandals flip-flopped as she ran frantically and awkwardly across the muddy grass of the small village, the small bundle on her back shrouded in a nest of colorful blankets. Glancing over her shoulder, she hastily unhitched the wooden latch, opened the door, and scanned the dilapidated barn for a hiding place. Sliding herself between a feeding trough and the barn wall, she covered herself with straw. She lay on her side, nearly hyperventilating, in muffled silence. The only sounds now were the synchronous rhythms of her wheezing lungs and the pounding pulse inside her head, disrupted by the sporadic rat-a-tat-tat of machine gun bursts. Sweat poured down her head, chest, and back. Her sanctuary smelled of animal dung, old hay, and the dusty pine boards of the barn's old walls.

Governments at peace with their people are much alike, but genocidal governments are each maleficent in their own way. The human depravity that characterized the massacres of the Quiché, one of the twenty-three indigenous groups in Guatemala, in the genocide of the 1980s was no more and no less ruthless than Pol Pot's killing fields in Cambodia. But these massacres lacked the twisted creativity of Hitler's death camps. In Guatemala soldiers with guns unloaded from pickups into indigenous villages and shot everyone.

After hearing of massacres in neighboring areas, they had confronted Father Dias, the local priest, asking him how God could allow such things. The priest had explained that God's Spirit spoke to the conscience of all people to dissuade them from wrong. But if one disobeyed the voice long enough, it would slowly recede until he no longer could distinguish goodness from evil, until his conscience was defiled and he was no longer able to experience shame. It was only in this way that the young woman could begin to understand what was transpiring in her village.

She peeked through a crack in the wall of the barn. Could she be seen? She saw a group of young women being forced into a line by the troops. Two nervous-looking recruits with sunglasses and automatic weapons stood in front of the women. The soldiers were also young, maybe even still teenagers, and she understood that they had been given a heavy responsibility. They had been given the responsibility of no longer experiencing shame. The women were shaking, crying, one clutching the arm of her friend Mildred, who was trying to plead with the recruits in Spanish.

Virtually all of the women had been friends since childhood. Together they had picked coffee in the fields each November and December in the cool morning mist, through the afternoon sun, and until dusk. They would bring a stack of tortillas wrapped in a cloth to last the whole day. And as they would pick, they would eat and chat together for hours, their delicate fingers effortlessly flowing over the coffee cherries as they slid the red and orange ones off into a sack tied on their waist, careful to leave the yellow and green ones for the second harvest. They talked about parents, school, and boys. And each year as they grew older together, the conversation returned to the latter with greater frequency and enthusiasm than the year before.

Mildred was always the brave one. One time in the fields, Mildred had caught the small son of the foreman stealing coffee cherries from the sack of one of the other women, who was away relieving herself. Many in the village would have let the boy go, pretending they did not see, for the foreman was the right-hand man of the plantation owner. A willingness to confront transgression, especially in the family of a superior, is not characteristic of the Quiché. But Mildred had scolded the boy, and she had scared him. If she caught him again, she would thrash his rear so long and hard he wouldn't sit for a month. And he did not steal from the workers again. Yes, Mildred would be the one to stand up to the soldiers.

But as the young woman watched through the crack in the barn, she saw an officer with a pistol begin to walk toward Mildred.

—

Angela

San Francisco, April 5, 2007

Angela arrived at her professor's office for a special meeting. Taking a deep breath, she tapped lightly on the door. Through the beveled glass, she caught a shadow of movement that beckoned her in. She felt the perspiration on her hand as she twisted the old brass doorknob and entered the office. Today there would be final news on her fieldwork assignment for her thesis.

"Please have a seat, Angela." Her professor hastily cleared some ungraded papers off a space on the couch next to his desk so that one of the cushions was visible. Displays of indigenous art from the developing world filled the shelves of the office. Above a messy desk, an enormous world map took up most of the space on the wall. Pins in the map described the location of ongoing research projects around the globe.

He sat in his desk chair and looked at her. "I have a research project for you in Guatemala."

Angela raised her eyebrows and felt a surge of excitement.

"It's sitting on my desk."

Angela looked and saw nothing extraordinary except the desk full of more ungraded papers, a stapler, and an old coffee mug with an uncommonly high steam vapor rising above it.

"I share at least one heartfelt conviction with millions of others in the world," he said as he reached for the mug and swallowed contentedly from it, "and it is that without a cupful of Juan Valdez's Best before nine a.m., the day is off to a bad start—almost by definition." He paused and looked up at Angela. "And for some consumers, if it's not fair trade, it's not ethical . . . almost by definition. But does it matter?"

4

Angela grinned. "You got my attention, Prof." She could sense where this was going.

The professor smiled. "The project is part of an impact study on fair trade coffee for which we just received funding with some researchers over at Berkeley. As you probably know, fair trade attempts to guarantee coffee growers a minimum price for their crop in exchange for promising to comply with some basic labor and environmental standards."

He pressed his fingertips together under his chin, making eye contact with her over his bifocals. "It's funded by the US Agency for International Development. Our government has an interest in preventing another outbreak of civil war in Central America. Seems to feel a little guilty about its involvement in the last ones." He swallowed another mouthful from his mug and then added, "We know that these wars are incubated in the economic disenfranchisement of the rural poor . . ."

She finished the sentence for him. ". . . many of whom are coffee growers."

Her professor nodded. "Correct. Profits of the multinational coffee conglomerates have never been higher. But coffee growers remain impoverished. USAID is engaged in a concerted effort trying to find ways to augment their incomes."

"And fair trade coffee is one way?"

"The expansion of fair trade marketing channels is one possibility," he affirmed. "But we need to find out if fair trade coffee is worth expanding."

Angela knew that her part was next. Her professor continued. "We want you to follow a bag of coffee beans from peasant coffee growers in Guatemala to the coffee drinker in the States, tracing the path of the beans through all the intermediate links in the chain: local buyers, processors, fair trade exporters, roasters, and retailers—calculating the profit made at every stage."

"Like how the $3.50 some guy pays for a latte gets divided between everyone who touches the beans?"

"Precisely."

Intriguing, but it sounded like a big job. "Do I have help?"

He took another sip. "Of course. You'll be part of an excellent team that will include two top doctoral students from Berkeley, Sofia Cavallera and Richard Freeland. Rich is being temporarily diverted from another project in Guatemala and Sofia is already there working on another aspect of the study." Angela smiled—a chance to work with doctoral students at Berkeley. She had even seen Sofia present at a conference in the spring. It had been an impressive paper.

The professor reclined back in his chair, happy to see Angela's interest. "You are from Guatemala originally, if I remember correctly?" He toyed with the earpiece of his bifocals in his teeth.

Angela hesitated. "Well, kind of. My mom and dad are from north of LA. I was adopted."

"Ever been back?"

"No, actually. Suppose I've been looking for an excuse the last few years." Angela gazed at the world map. "Especially since studying international development, I've kind of wondered what life would have been like if . . ." Angela returned eye contact.

". . . if your life would have been lived in Guatemala instead of Simi Valley?"

"Yes, Prof."

"Do you know where you were born?" he asked.

"Somewhere in the northwest highlands, I think."

"That's coffee country, Angela. In fact, you'll be based in the highlands, in Huehuetenango." He smiled. "I believe this summer you will learn about much more than the distribution of profits in the coffee value chain." Angela returned his smile a little self-consciously. She tucked a lock of her dark brown hair behind her ears.

The project was more than she ever could have hoped for: working with outstanding researchers and a chance to explore the place of her birth for the first time. She got up to leave.

"Angela, there's something else. I've also asked Alex to be part of the team."

He might as well have told her that at every moment during the trip, she was to be accompanied by an untamed chimpanzee. "Alex?" The soaring helium balloon that had ascended so high the last few minutes had just been pricked and had descended back to earth.

"Prof," she pleaded. "Alex is a left-wing nutcase."

"Perhaps, but one with a keen interest in fair trade coffee. He's a good student, Angela, quite smart actually. And he's even learning something about economics. I think he'll work well with you . . . if you can forgive him for his behavior in the debate." He looked at her wryly.

"Thanks, Prof. We'll see." She shook hands politely and left the office with emotions that could not have conflicted more sharply.

Angela walked down the stairwell and passed the classroom where the infamous Debate had taken place early last semester in their international trade class. It caused her to reflect on the event, which to this point she had endeavored to exorcise from her mind. In a deliberation over the merits of globalization, Alex had used a presentation that unfairly relied on emotional manipulation and pictures of physically abused multinational factory workers that, by some miracle, captured more votes from the inexperienced class than her rigorous presentation of Ricardian comparative advantage. At least for that day, the activist had triumphed over the scientist. But even more than this, Angela resented his insinuations that she cared less about the poor in the developing world than he did. The difference between them, at least as she saw it, was her commitment to what well-constructed theory and a scientific evaluation of the evidence might bring to the subject.

On top of this, Alex had recently dated her housemate for a few weeks, quickly dumping her for a relationship with a cute little college sophomore that lasted again only so long. Alex was able to do this, because even Angela admitted that at least on the surface he was tall, boyishly attractive with a cute accent, and far too charming for his own good, or anyone else's. Her housemate cried all night on the couch. His looks, his manner, and the way he used them to satisfy his own ends only magnified her antipathy toward him. Yes, Alex Van Vleck was an ideologue and a flake, and the thought of three months working side by side with him was a vile one.

But even Angela could see how their personalities and motivations had swept them from opposite angles into the same research project. For different reasons, it was too interesting for either of them to resist: For him it would be a way to validate the efforts of those who circumvented exploitative corporate coffee conglomerates. She, on the other hand, was genuinely curious about the impact of fair trade coffee. And there was that further curiosity she shared with many adopted children, of wanting to see and explore their origins. Only added together did it marginally outweigh the bane of a summer full of Alex.

—

Just before midnight on June first, the twin engines of United Airlines flight 805 from San Francisco to Guatemala City droned through the darkness that enshrouded northern Mexico. As she tried to sleep, Angela's head kept drooping off to the side, waking her up again. It was a vicious cycle, afflicting her at a time she knew she needed sleep.

Alex was sleeping soundly in the seat next to her, wearing a bulky, inflated neck support he bought on a whim at an airport gift shop. Angela grew more irritated as she watched him sleep, partly because she was frequently irritated with Alex anyway, and partly because the neck brace made Alex's jaw hang open while he was sleeping. It gave him a cadaverous look, like a slain gangster in a movie, shot dead but still sitting upright. A thin line of drool leaked from the corner of his mouth. His longish blond hair and a facial expression that more or less permanently projected cynicism, even when parked in neutral, completed the picture. His satisfied snore only slightly trailed the engines of the 767 in the competition to keep Angela awake.

A flight attendant passed by with the drink cart and stared just momentarily at Angela. *"Jugo o café quisiera Usted?"* she asked, quickly identifying her as one of the Guatemalan passengers and asking for her preference in Spanish. Angela also could sense that the stewardess was staring at the conspicuous birthmark on her left cheek.

"Jugo, por favor," replied Angela in the cleanest accent she could produce. She turned her head so that her cheek was no longer in the attendant's line of vision, a habit she had cultivated from long years of trying to avoid unwanted stares.

Angela Lopez-Williams was adopted as an infant by Kevin Williams and Maria Lopez of suburban Los Angeles. Although her mother was Mexican-American, Angela had grown up with mostly English-speaking friends, in a mostly English-speaking neighborhood, and attended mostly English-speaking schools. Yet she knew that she was an artifact of globalization, the product of two worlds.

Angela knew that to the casual observer, with her stature on the short side of average, bronze complexion, and dark brown hair, she looked as Guatemalan as any native, to the point that she would often draw initial conversation in Spanish. But as she grew older, even when her mother spoke to her in her native tongue, she had developed a lazy, teenage habit of answering her mother in English. As a result, she never developed full fluency with the language. And she found that when she did speak Spanish, she realized her accent had been poisoned over the years with a rounded North American drawl that lacked the stiletto-like precision of a native speaker. It frustrated her. But she didn't want to be a Latina anyway. But maybe she did; it kind of depended on the day.

Once when she was a little girl, her mother told her that her family was just like the coffee she used to make at the café, *cafe con leche*, coffee with milk and two spoons of sugar to make it extra sweet. Her mother's unwavering kindness helped, at times.

Unable to sleep, she unbuckled her seat belt, walked down the aisle, and opened the latch to the cramped toilet. She splashed warm water on her face. Drying it with a paper towel, she looked in the mirror at the large birthmark in the shape of a spotted crescent that ran from the corner of her left eye, across her cheek, and down to her chin. When she was a toddler, the doctor told her mother it might fade away after a few years. It never did.

Angela dwelled on it more when traveling to a new place because in new places one met new people, and the conspicuousness of it always made first meetings awkward. During conversation, she had become sensitive to when someone's angle of eye contact with her moved almost imperceptibly away from her own eyes toward her cheek.

This was always more of a problem relating to people in the Latino community, a culture that often makes physical irregularities fair game for frivolous nicknames. There was that time, that stain in her memory, when her high school offered a Spanish literature class, where they were reading Cervantes's *Don Quixote de la Mancha*. A group of Mexican sophomores sitting together in the back of the class pounced on the word *mancha,* also the word for "blemish" in Spanish. Jonathan Dias stood up and pointed at her: *"Y aqui tenemous Angela de la Mancha!"* They all hooted with unabated laughter, high-fives slapped all around the group. Humiliated, she had quickly looked to the teacher, Mr. Pérez, for support. Instead she saw the faintest smile edge up the corner of his mouth. In that split second, before he regained his composure to begin a ritually ineffectual round of reprimanding, it was obvious that he found the remark humorous too. It had become lodged in her mind like an inoperable bullet.

It caused her to forsake her Latin identity for some time, determining never to visit the country of her birth—or any place like it. She favored vacations with her father's extended family. At school she retreated into a world of books, history, and mathematics. She found it was a world in which she thrived, and was lauded for her efforts. It was a space in which people were rewarded for the quality of their ideas and the crispness of their proofs, where irregularities and cultural contradictions became irrelevant. It was a safe hiding place, the refuge of so many bright but socially marginalized teenagers who later emerge as society's great thinkers and scholars.

And well before graduation, colleges began throwing scholarships at her.

In high school Angela viewed Latin America as a corrupt, dirty place with (worst of all) mediocre universities. But at UCLA she began to return in small steps: a Latin American history class here and there, attendance at a few club meetings with a friend. But now as the plane continued its voyage through the night over the Petén jungle of northern Guatemala, she walked out of the restroom, leaned over and looked out of the cabin window, and wondered how many of her relatives might be below her, asleep in the silent darkness. She returned to her seat. The warm water on her face had made her sleepy, and she finally began to nod off.

Her slumber was interrupted by the bing of the seat belt sign. "Alex—almost there." Angela nudged him. Alex awoke slowly, made some strange contortions with his mouth, and licked his dry lips.

He looked at Angela. "Were you wanting to sleep on my shoulder?" he asked, grinning. He projected his morning breath in her direction from about a foot away, an arguably socially normal distance for many Europeans, but inside the personal space of most North Americans. "Don't be a creep," Angela shot back, self-conscious and trying to back away while still seat belted. "My head kept bobbing when I was trying to sleep, and despite all my internal powers of concentration, I think it accidentally landed on that bony shoulder of yours a couple of times. Almost gave me a black eye."

Alex grinned again. "I told you that you should have bought one of these blowing-up things in the airport. Certainly you would have much less crankiness if you would have had some sleep."

Seeing Alex awake, the perky stewardess offered him a last chance at the beverage cart. "Juice, coffee, tea?" she asked in English.

Alex become more serious. "Are you brewing bird-friendly coffee?" he inquired. Angela cringed and tried to escape by burying her head in the in-flight catalog of eccentric gadgets as she sipped her juice. Her eye caught a bizarre ad for a solar-heated doggie waterbed.

"Pardon?" asked the perky flight attendant, blinking and smiling profusely, yet deeply confused.

"Is it bird-friendly certified—the coffee you are at the moment serving?" clarified Alex.

Her smile became more strained and awkward. "Er . . . I don't know . . . what is that, sir?"

"It is coffee specifically cultivated for protecting natural habitats of endangered bird species," he replied in a monotone Dutch accent.

"Oh . . . how wonderful," she replied, trying to accommodate.

"At least is your coffee fair trade?"

"Hmm . . . I don't think so. I'm sorry, sir."

"In that case, no thanks," replied Alex, ending the exchange abruptly. The flight attendant seemed happy to wheel her beverage cart to the next passenger row.

"Didn't feel like engaging in a little global exploitation at the moment?" inquired Angela.

"No, not at this moment I do not," affirmed Alex, unfazed. "Nor at any moment."

Another twenty minutes went by, and the plane touched down and taxied along the tarmac to the gate, with the flight attendant giving instructions over the plane loudspeaker in nearly flawless English and then in flawless Spanish. Angela felt another quick tinge of jealousy. Why hadn't she taken Spanish class more seriously?

They ambled down the gate into the terminal, the darkness outside beginning to give way to dawn. The walkway was of well-worn linoleum, probably built during an earlier, more hopeful era when Guatemala had great plans for its place in the world. The aged terminal was both adorned and scented by the smashed cigarette butts on the floor, flung there by nicotine-starved passengers getting their fix after a long, smokeless flight. They passed by drug-sniffing dogs as they progressed uneventfully through immigration and customs.

In the arrival area, they were greeted by several dozen enthusiastic new friends who offered them taxi rides in Spanish, some even trying in broken English. "Hey, meester, you and wife want ride to Antigua?" shouted a small, round man with a wispy mustache.

"Hey, I'm not his wife," Angela shot back to wispy mustache over the crowd. "Alex, let's figure out what we're doing." She was feeling a little overwhelmed with their newfound popularity, which she suspected was related to their ignorance about local public transportation rates.

"Well, we're meant to meet Sofia at nine o'clock in Antigua," said Alex.

Angela shouted across the crowd to wispy mustache in English, "Hey—how about twenty-five dollars to take us to Antigua?" Others vied with wispy mustache to accept the offer, but he had been first.

"No problema," he replied as he fought his way through the crowd. "My car is over here. You two, come." He motioned to them to follow him as he strode victoriously to his taxi.

"You overbid," noted Alex as they walked to the car. "He accepted your offer *much* too readily. You should have ground the little taxi drivers down to the lowest price they were willing."

Angela knew Alex was baiting her, but she retorted anyway. "Don't think I'd care to ride in a car with the guy who'd win that bid," she replied. "Ever heard of adverse selection? The only guy who accepts a low price like that is probably a kidnapper or something. Alex"—she looked at him with her best serious expression—"I probably just saved your life."

"In that case I will reward you by permitting you the front seat." He squeezed into the back of the cramped two-door Toyota where he sat with his legs bent up close to the hair that flowed over his ears.

Angela asked the driver in Spanish, "How far is Antigua?"

"Pues, not far, maybe forty minutes," he replied.

Alex gave his nascent Spanish its first test-drive. Intending to ask the driver if he was from Guatemala City, he instead asked smoothly, "Sir, are you in Guatemala City?"

Wispy mustache stared at Alex in the rearview mirror with a look that seemed to be asking himself why they allowed these long-haired hippies high on drugs to enter his country. "Yes, and you are too, my friend," the driver said, gave him a condescending grin, and shook his head.

Angela laughed and gazed outside the passenger window to see the dawn shedding its light on a new day in Guatemala City. So this was home.

CHAPTER 2

Angela

GUATEMALA CITY IS ONE OF THOSE HOMELY AND CRIME-
infested cities that looks better in the dark but is safer in the daytime.
And as the beat-up taxi sputtered out of the small international airport
through the city's spartan downtown, Angela watched as concrete
houses and potholed streets became illuminated by the peach-colored
haze of the new morning. Old Blue Bird school buses filled the streets,
pressed into service after their retirement in the United States, violating the early morning sky with noisy cloudbursts of diesel. Purchased
as castoffs, they had been driven down through Mexico and sold to the
urban public transit system. Sturdy iron racks were welded on top to
haul passengers' wholesale goods and agricultural produce to urban
markets. Despite having been repainted with colorful designs, faded
black letters on the sides of the buses testified to a former life, reading "South Milwaukee Unified School District" and "Chattanooga
Detention Facility." The buses were already jammed with passengers
headed to market at dawn.

The taxi rattled its way up the mountain grades on the Pan-
American Highway as it left Guatemala City behind in the distance.
Angela noticed that the billboards offering discounted cell phone

plans and cable TV service became fewer and farther between. The gritty blight of urban sprawl began to give way to small farms with vegetables, cash crops sown in tidy rows. After a short time they turned to the south and began to descend from the Pan-American into Antigua, the old capitol. After a few miles the taxi entered the city and clattered along the narrow, cobblestone streets, the sound waves generated by the noise of its loose bolts and aging muffler ricocheting off the exterior walls of the pastel stucco buildings.

They passed by colonial-style houses with black iron lanterns hung off the sides of their facings and finally under the clock tower of the beautiful yellow Santa Catalina Arch. The contrast between Antigua and sooty Guatemala City could not have been more stark. While the latter remained one of the unsightly capital cities of Latin America, Antigua, with its Spanish Mudéjar architecture, could have been confused with seventeenth-century Seville. Signs for Spanish-language schools were ubiquitous as were their perky North American and European pupils, busily walking from guesthouse to coffee shop to language lesson. Finally, at shortly past eight a.m., they pulled up to a tree-lined street that bordered the central square.

Angela paid the driver, and she and Alex walked with their backpacks to a café on the square. A waiter approached them, and they ordered breakfast and coffee. Their table looked directly onto the square. Angela and Alex sat and watched Antigua begin a new day. Even this early in the morning, older locals were starting to congregate near park benches. A flock of about twenty young children in tidy uniforms pranced to school along a path that cut diagonally across the central square. A teenage couple, also in school uniform, sat on a bench and caressed each other's hair. The warm smell of *elotes*, the fried corn on the cob sold by vendors in the central square, filled the sunny morning air.

While they were waiting for their breakfast, a young shoe-shine boy approached.

The boy pointed to Alex's feet. "Your shoes are full of dust."

Alex politely rejected the offer: *"No gracias, amigo."*

The boy ignored the refusal, opened his shoe-shine kit, and began to work on Alex's loafers. The other shoe-shine boys gathered round to see the big fish that the boy had landed. They formed an inquisitive huddle around the table just as the waiter arrived with their breakfast: eggs, tortillas, beans, and goat cheese. *"Vayanse, chicos."* The waiter half-heartedly motioned the boys away with a faint wave of his hand, but the command lacked both spirit and authority. The boys retreated a few steps, but with no other potential customers in sight, gradually returned as soon as the waiter turned his back to go inside the kitchen.

Angela looked at the food on her plate, suspecting the boys hadn't eaten breakfast that morning. "Want a tortilla?" Angela asked.

"Si!" they replied, and Angela divided her tortillas among the boys. She had never been a big breakfast fan anyway and was also feeling slightly woozy after lack of sleep on the red-eye flight and the bumpy ride to Antigua.

At that moment a woman in her late twenties walked up to their table. She was Latin American, but almost certainly not Guatemalan. She wore turquoise earrings and a blue blouse, but also a backpack, heavy jeans, and leather boots. She was just slightly plump, with fair skin and perfectly straight brown hair. A black unibrow over her dark brown eyes made her resemble a graduate-student version of Frida Kahlo wearing narrow, thick-rimmed academic glasses. "Sofia Cavallera?" asked Angela. There was a twinkle of affirmation in the brown eyes.

"I see you've made a few *amigos*," remarked Sofia. "Yes, Antigua, the town where the resistance of the tourist's unshined shoe is futile."

She turned to Alex. "Alex, your professors warned me about you in their e-mail," she laughed.

Angela had also learned quite a bit about Sofia since receiving the assignment. She had graduated first in her enormous undergraduate class at the University of Buenos Aires with a double major in mathematics and economics. She had been accepted enthusiastically by most of the highest-ranking economics programs in the United States, including the two most renowned, MIT and the University of Chicago. Already she had two papers from her dissertation forthcoming in prestigious economics journals.

Sofia had earned an early reputation as a kind of economics "detective." Her research agenda was disarmingly simple. She sought to determine whether programs in developing countries collecting large sums of money from governments and ordinary people actually worked. A more difficult question than one might imagine, it required both a creative mind and masterful use of statistical methods. Moreover, her easygoing demeanor concealed how ruthlessly efficient she was at uncovering the truth.

Angela had heard one particular story about Sofia through her advisor, who had sat next to her in a seminar given at Berkeley. A well-known but rather blustery researcher from the World Bank, Garrison Blumenthal, had come to present an academic paper. His work had "revealed stunningly large effects" from an electrification program the Bank had piloted in several countries. Basing their decision largely on Blumenthal's celebrated results, the Bank planned an expansion into more countries the following year. The seminar that day was packed with an enthusiastic crowd of professors and their graduate students, crammed into a room that was far too small for the big event. Unfortunately for Blumenthal, the crowd included Sofia, who had been working on the same data. Using a newer and more incisive econometric methodology, her findings had revealed that essentially all of the "stunningly large effects" Blumenthal had "revealed" were attributable to a fatal underlying bias in his empirical technique.

It took awhile after Sofia raised her hand in the seminar for Blumenthal to finally call on her. But when he did, and she graciously but decisively unloaded the bad news, Blumenthal's expansive forehead underwent a series of spectral transfigurations. An ashen-white upon the initial ingesting of the remarks was followed by an alternating fiery red and cabernet purple during a series of increasingly defensive yet decreasingly effective rebuttals, by which time the Berkeley faculty had seen Sofia's point and began to help Blumenthal conceptualize his error. The cabernet slowly faded to a light olive as the last of his counterarguments withered in the dense humidity of the crowd, at which point he interrupted his failing confutation with a request for directions to the men's room.

The World Bank's expansion of the program was put on hold.

Sofia's recent research had been funded under the same USAID coffee grant that supported the fieldwork of Angela and Alex. She had been collecting data in Guatemala for several months as part of the study, focusing on the economic impacts of fair trade coffee.

While Angela had heard about Sofia's reputation, her lack of pretension made it hard for Angela to feel intimidated for very long. And she felt honored to have Sofia leading their little traveling research group. "Sofia, what's the plan?" Angela inquired.

"Well, I thought we could head right out to our research site in Huehuetenango. We can meet Richard when we get there, and we're not going to get much done here in Gringo-tenango." Just as she said this, a gaggle of awkward-looking Americans ambled by with their Spanish teachers on the way to a tourist museum. "Shall we take the chicken bus? It only costs about two dollars."

"Two bucks? For a four-hour ride?"

"Yep. And worth every centavo. You'll see."

In truth Angela felt a little wary of the chicken bus, but in the end she rationalized that it might be a good way to begin to get to know Guatemala. "Sounds like a bargain," she replied, feigning enthusiasm and ignoring the butterflies that had just hatched from their little cocoons in her stomach. "Lead the way."

They hopped on one of the souped-up old Blue Bird school buses that had "Huehue" painted in colorful cursive script above the front windshield. "Hang on to your stuff inside," said Sofia. "Touristy-looking backpacks have a way of getting off the bus before their riders."

They sat in some seats toward the back and waited as the bus began to slowly fill up. A few twentysomething tourists got on board, but mostly it was Guatemalan indigenous people of all ages. A mother with three young children handed a large burlap *costal* full of goods to the driver's assistant, who heaved them up to the iron rack on the bus's roof where another assistant tied down the bulky items.

Angela watched as a teenage girl talking on her cell phone settled into a seat near the students. Her eye was captured by the young girl's colorful *huipil*, the hand-embroidered blouse worn by Mayan women of all ages. The huipil was decorated with embroidered birds, pieces of fruit, and flowers—a decorative bouquet that lay like a garland around her sweet, round face. An old man, probably in his late seventies, dressed in the traditional Mayan clothing worn by older men, slowly settled himself into the seat behind the teenage girl, directly across the aisle from Angela.

The old man stared across the aisle of the bus at Angela, flashing metal teeth that were the victims of decades of amateur dental work. *"Buenos dias, mi amor,"* he cooed with seasoned octogenarian charm. *"Una flor de primavera."* Angela had become his spring flower. His breath was seasoned with some type of peppermint liquor.

"Angela, you have a new admirer," said Alex with a snicker.

"Should we leave you two alone?" added Sofia with eyebrows raised.

Angela regained her composure and responded in Spanish. "This is my friend Sofia. She's older and much more *mature* than I."

The old man slowly redirected his gaze toward Sofia. He smiled a long, romantic smile. "Ah . . . *muy bien.*" Sofia laughed and rolled her eyeballs, but Angela was content that at least the old man's affections had become divided between the two of them.

After nearly twenty minutes of waiting for the bus to fill up, the driver launched ahead about half full but began to add more and more passengers as they left town. The man who had been lifting people's belongings on the roof rack stayed behind in Antigua, so whenever the bus stopped, people jumped on with bags full of vegetables, meat, grain, slain animals, and cages full of preslain ones. A woman climbed on board with an armful of bean sacks, a sleeping infant tied to her back under a blanket, and a stack of tortillas wrapped in yellow cloth balancing on her head. She clutched the hand of a lethargic toddler who looked badly in need of a tissue.

As the bus bounced along the cobblestone streets to the outskirts of Antigua, Angela sat mesmerized by the colorful, rolling bazaar of animals, vegetables, and humanity with all of their respective noises and smells. Salsa music blared from the bus driver's radio, and the inside of the bus smelled like a collage of farm products. So these were her people. She felt like she should be feeling a little more comfortable in the local atmosphere than she actually did. Wasn't this all supposed to be in her blood?

She and Sofia soon gave up their seats to a pregnant woman and her mother, and they stood in the aisle, pressed fully against the other passengers, holding their backpacks against their chests.

The bus pulled onto the two-lane Pan-American Highway, traveling slowly at first when climbing to elevation, but then at magnificent speed when it reached a downgrade. Every so often the bus stopped along the Pan-American to gather a few more passengers on its way to Huehue. They approached a roadside stop, where half a dozen preteen boys waited for the bus. There was no longer room for more passengers, even standing in the aisle, but somehow four of the boys managed to jam their way in. The other two ran to the back of the bus and climbed onto the ladder that led up to the large steel rack on top.

"Are those kids actually going to ride on that thing down the highway?" Angela asked.

"Unfortunately, I think so," responded Sofia.

The bus picked up to forty, fifty, and then sixty miles per hour, the boys still hanging on the ladder smiling and waving through the window to the graduate students standing in the aisle, now pushed toward the back of the bus by the crush of incoming passengers. The bus headed toward a sharp mountain corner and one of the boys dangled by one arm and one leg off to the side of the ladder, letting the bus whip him through the breeze around the turn. Fortunately, no car met them coming the other direction. The second boy giggled and then began to fight for the same spot on the ladder so he could try it on the next turn.

"Wow," was all Angela could manage to say.

"Angela, are you feeling ill at ease in your native homeland?" inquired Alex.

"Hey, Alex, why don't you hop outside and play on the rack with the *chicos*," she retorted.

With a grind of the transmission, the driver commanded the moaning diesel engine of the bus into high gear. The raucous engine noise forced him to turn up his already blaring salsa music to full volume so that it could be heard more clearly. It seemed to Angela that the bus driver was in a much greater hurry along this road than he should be, or that a road this twisty should allow. Traveling at an intrepid velocity around blind corners, the bus caught up to a minivan from behind. After several minutes of perilous tailgating, the bus pulled into the oncoming traffic lane on the Pan-American to pass on a downgrade. The tension mounted inside Angela as the aged Blue Bird could muster only enough horsepower to slowly inch ahead of the minivan.

Glancing between some of the passengers standing in the aisle, Angela could make out a gray car approaching in the distance from the opposite direction. She looked down through the window aside the bus to see the minivan driver glance up at the bus driver. The look on his face made it clear that being passed by a full bus was presenting an open challenge to his masculinity. His lower jaw seemed to protrude slightly as he determinedly redirected his focus toward the road. To Angela it seemed like instead of allowing the bus to pass, he might actually be speeding up. As the bus inched ahead of the minivan, its diesel engine screamed in protest as the bus driver continued to ask for more on the accelerator pedal. Angela glanced over at Alex. Even Alex's face now began to reveal genuine concern.

Eager to see if the driver was going to pull off the pass, the boys hanging on the back ladder swung out to the side to catch a view down the highway, returning quickly to the relative security of the ladder when they saw the ever-less-distant oncoming vehicle. Angela's left hand clung to the seat next to her, and her right hand clutched her backpack around her chest. Her hands began to sweat and her fingernails drilled holes into the green vinyl of the old bus seat. With the oncoming car less than a hundred yards away, the minivan driver finally acquiesced. This allowed the bus to slip ahead of him in the right lane by about two feet, just as the oncoming car blew by them a split second later, clearing the front of the bus by no more than fifteen feet. Angela looked and saw that the expression on the old man's face had remained a straight-ahead stare, completely unchanged and stoic, an unfazed veteran of Guatemalan bus travel. The boys on the rear ladder laughed with delight, mockingly waving *adios* as they pulled away from the minivan driver behind them.

"*Schijten*, that was a close one," said Alex. Sofia glanced at Alex's pallid face. "You okay, Alex?" she laughed. She then looked down on the bus seat at the small holes in the vinyl from Angela's fingernails that were surrounded by a liquid handprint of sweat. Then she looked above the driver's window, where someone had painted in bold script: *Jesus Conduce Este Bus*, or "Jesus Guides This Bus."

Sofia pointed to the sign. "See, guys, there was nothing to worry about after all."

CHAPTER 3

Alex

AFTER THREE AND A HALF HOURS, THE BUS PULLED INTO
Cuatro Caminos, a transfer point outside where the Pan-American
turns sharply to the north, intersecting with the north-south highway
in the west that runs from Quetzaltenango north to Huehuetenango
and then toward the Mexican border. The bus stopped, and the passengers got out to switch buses, buy something to eat, or use the toilets.
These were the only options, for there was nothing else people did at
Cuatro Caminos. The students hopped off the bus with their packs,
hoping to find something for lunch.

Cuatro Caminos was not the cleanest place one might search for
a bite to eat. Stationed on the intersection of the two highways were
countless fruit and vegetable vendors and outdoor butchers selling
mysterious cuts of meat hanging from hooks over countertops. One
woman was selling chicken feet that were packed more than two feet
high in an unrefrigerated glass case. An Exodus-like plague of greenish
flies frenzily feasted on the garbage tossed aside by vendors and passengers and on many of the food items for sale. The morass of vendors
and constant departure of smoke-belching buses gave Cuatro Caminos
a constant reek of garbage and diesel.

Alex felt the need for a restroom and began to search. After a surprising length of time, he found a "pay *baño*" behind one of the food vendors. He handed a few coins to the teenage girl managing the baño, and she reciprocated with a roll of toilet paper. He walked into a kind of outhouse, which featured a fantastically soiled commode surrounded by rotting plywood walls nailed crudely together. In a short time, he returned to the bus with the ashen countenance of a man who had visited Hades and needed to work through it. "You'll never believe the disgusting place I just went," he announced to the women in a shaky voice, yet one that was nevertheless eager to relate the experience.

"Oh yes, I think we would," replied Angela. "Spare us the details."

"No, seriously. I'm not kidding you guys. The corporation that runs this bus system invests none of its profits in sanitation. Do you want to know how very bad that toilet was I just visited?"

"Actually, not at all," said Angela. "We genuinely do not want to know what you saw in the baño. We don't want to know how it smelled, what you did, or the hurdles you overcame in doing what you had to do . . . not anything about it, really. But whatever it was like, I'm sure it enhanced your solidarity with the oppressed."

Sofia laughed and excused herself as she searched for bananas, which she had told them were reasonably safe.

Alex scowled, forced to reflect in solitude about the human degradation he had endured in the baño.

A few moments later, he headed toward one of the vendors. "Angela, I am having chicken feet. You should try some."

"I'm not going to eat any of this stuff," said Angela.

"Suit yourself," he replied. "But don't you think that we should make better attempts to blend with the local people, to sample native foods?"

"Oh, you're already blending in great, Alex. I can hardly tell you apart from anyone here." It was Angela's turn to scowl, and she quickly left to join Sofia.

Alex purchased the chicken feet and hopped back on the bus. He tried one of them, nibbling a little of the meat right below the talons. A little chewy, but the taste of the salty meat was pleasing. He kept the rest in their plastic bag and put it in his backpack, perhaps for later.

As he waited for the others, his mind recalled what was now infamously referred to as simply The Debate among the students in their program. Randomly paired with Angela, he knew that she understood far more about economics than he did—after all, it had been her undergraduate major and not his. While Angela had been an economics undergraduate at a top American university, he had majored in the "social sciences" at University of Groningen in the Netherlands. He knew he could not compete with her knowledge of economics.

But he could compete on other grounds. He remembered what one of his rhetoric professors in the Netherlands had told the class— debates are frequently won in the more fertile ground of the heart rather than in the head. To Angela's expected presentation of the standard economic model, he planned a counterattack that harnessed not his nascent grasp of economic theory, but several gut-wrenching anecdotes of overseas sweatshop abuses by multinational corporations. He was proud of his sequence of examples, for each was more horrific than the next: pictures of abused local workers in multinational corporations with photos of facial injuries, dismembered limbs, and locked doors that kept underpaid workers from leaving a factory. He was particularly proud of a slide showing body burns on a factory worker in Indonesia who had been working with hot plastics to make baby dolls for American children. A picture was indeed worth more than a thousand words—wasn't that the English idiom? And certainly more than a half hour of long-winded theories and statistics.

It provided proof of the negative impact of globalization on the overseas poor. Solid proof.

He thought about how he had made some in the class cry for the plight of the workers and laugh with scorn at the multinational corporations, each within a few minutes of each other. And fortunately for him, the debate was scored by the class. Alex had swayed many and achieved a mighty victory. He learned later through one of her friends that it was the first B+ that Angela had earned since high school. He reflected back on it, pleased with his strategy and performance.

CHAPTER 4

Angela

NEW PASSENGERS BOARDED THE BUS TO HUEHUE, AND THE diesel engine grumbled back to life. Giving a final cry of "Huehue!" the conductor slapped the side of the bus twice with his palm, and with a magnificent blast of its earsplitting horn, it rolled away.

As it turned northward from Cuatro Caminos, the bus steadily gained elevation, rising from 7,500 feet to over 9,500 feet. They were driving in the clouds, and the air of the western highlands became chilly and moist, even in the afternoon. It started to rain. The bus was less crowded now, and they were able to sit. Alex slept in the seat in front, and Angela sat in silence next to Sofia. Angela was leaning her forehead against the bus window as Sofia rested her chin on her backpack that she held on her lap. They gazed through the droplets on the window at the bittersweet contrasts of Guatemala: the lush countryside dense with adobe houses and endless acres of lush, green coffee plants; rows of corn, or *milpa*, sown alongside black beans; the ornate, multicolored, handwoven clothing adorning the women performing backbreaking tasks that should have been carried out by machines, or at least animals; the lack of clean water amidst the abundance of rainfall; malnourished children playing in the mud in front of their homes with a wealthier child's broken toys.

Angela looked thoughtfully at the rural landscape of her native country. Her thoughts turned to the civil war, which had ended little more than a decade before, and whose theater had been concentrated in the very area in which they were traveling. At UCLA she had written a term paper on the conflict in her Latin American studies class. The results of her research had been grim: up to 200,000 dead or disappeared, most notoriously in Huehuetenango and the adjacent Quiché province.

Though she didn't think of herself as much of a revolutionary, she was beginning to understand how people living in this kind of destitution could be driven to violence. But there had been no reconciliation, no admission of guilt, no government apologies for the massacre. There was little official acknowledgment, let alone sympathy, in this country toward the rural villagers who found themselves caught between the guerrillas and the Guatemalan army with its civil patrols, threatened by both with death if they failed to align with the proper side. Yet every so often a new mass grave was discovered, full of the skeletons of indigenous peasants, frequently women and children, who had given in to the pressure of the wrong group, or were merely accused of doing so. How many of these skeletons pulled out of the ground had been her relatives or their friends, neighbors, the people they saw every day, bought food from, or who taught their children in school?

Angela continued to stare out of the bus window, now noticing a small adobe hovel not more than twenty-five yards from where they were stopped to pick up some passengers. Chickens and pigs sifted through the garbage in the front. Children in ragged clothes were playing soccer with a half-deflated plastic ball. Another nearby child caught her attention, a little girl who appeared to be mentally disabled. "Sofia, look."

But Sofia was already watching.

The little girl was wearing a raggedy top and no pants, and she had mud streaked down her legs. Trying to play with the others, she began to tire, and would sit down to rest. Some of the other children laughed because when she tried to sit down in the grass, a couple of the chickens would come up and peck at her. Scared, the little girl began to cry, but seemed to lack the energy to get up. The other children laughed again as an aggressive chicken pecked at her thigh. The little girl screamed and weakly tried to swat at the chicken, which was too fast for her. She must have spilled some food on herself when she was eating, Angela thought, and the chicken was pecking at it. The process repeated once again. Sofia and Angela glanced at each other, not knowing what to say. The scene was beginning to make Angela sick. The bus slowly pulled away, rounding a corner, and Angela strained to look, but everything was lost from view.

The disquieting image lingered in her mind as the bus rumbled on through the highlands. Angela continued to stare out the bus window covered with rain droplets. Images of poverty passed minute by minute over the reflection of her own face in the window: shoeless children playing in the mud, peasants tending rainy coffee fields, mothers carrying firewood and children at the same time, protecting themselves and the wood from the rain by wearing trash bags with holes cut for their arms.

Her mind was shifting back and forth from her growing subjective emotion and feelings to the objective and the academic, and then back again. Each piece of passing village scenery provided another window into a parallel life, a life that by some stroke of fortune she was chosen not to lead. *This is my life,* she thought. *I am a young mother walking in the rain, carrying firewood and my baby back to my little adobe house with the dirt floor. My husband toils futilely in the maize field, and my children are malnourished and play barefoot in the mud.*

Then back to the academic: *How is this possible, for such abject poverty to exist in a land so rich in soil and natural wealth? Both economic and political freedom seem to exist here now as much as in most other places. What keeps the system from working for these people? What keeps it working for me?* Angela pondered these questions alone in silence for some time.

And then she decided to break the silence. "Sofia, why are these people so poor?" she asked, turning from the window to the Argentinean economist with the long brown hair seated beside her. It was an academic question that, as of this very moment in Angela's life, had become intensely personal.

She turned to Angela. "You mean why are rich countries rich and poor countries poor?" Sofia had probably pondered questions like this for several years now. "Yes . . . the puzzle behind all of the puzzles. I wish I had an easy answer to that question, but I don't."

"Do you have a complicated one?" said Angela, almost happy to hear that she hadn't missed some pat answer while dozing off in class at UCLA.

"I suppose I do," Sofia replied as she gazed out of the window at the same village scenes passing by, "but it probably won't totally satisfy you. At least it doesn't satisfy me."

CHAPTER 5

The young woman slowly sat up from her place in the straw. She tucked her hair back underneath her beautifully embroidered *cinta*, which had been dislodged as she had hidden herself, and peered again outside through the crack in the barn wall. Several more women were being rounded up in the group about fifty meters away, as Mildred and two other women attempted to negotiate with the officer who had approached them. The officer did not want to listen, and he appeared to intentionally turn his head in the other direction. Another soldier pushed one of the women back so hard that she tripped over her sandals, falling to the ground backwards; she was helped up by one of the other women. The soldiers were adding more women from the village to their group. Some held their babies, and many of the women were crying, pleading with the members of the *Patrulla Civil*, the local civil patrol, who led them to the group. One of her neighbors was being forcibly dragged across the ground by the arm.

The young woman's thoughts turned to her husband. He had been working a field about a half mile from the village. Would he be safe? Would he try to come for them? She hoped he would not.

She must not be discovered, for if she were found hiding, she knew what the soldiers would think. Why would she have been hiding if she were innocent of cooperating with the guerrillas? Only a guilty person would be hiding from the soldiers.

But, of course, the guerrillas *had* come into the village.

At least seven or eight had been shot and had bullet wounds. They needed help. They told the villagers their story. Many of their platoon had died in a firefight with the army, and they needed food and medicine. Like everybody in the village, she was afraid when the guerrillas came. The army had poisoned the water supply of one village just for providing cups of water to the guerrillas. She had even heard that they had cut out the tongues of some accused of speaking to the guerillas, as an example to prevent future collaboration.

But what would the guerrillas do to them if they did not help? They did not threaten, but they had guns. And it was understood that the villagers would help them because they had guns. And even though they were afraid of the guerrillas, they were also angry at what the army had done to the Quiché in other villages. So could it be so wrong to offer emergency help to those who were fighting the people who had done such things? Yes, she and Mildred had offered bandages and water to some of the injured guerrillas. But did not Father Dias say this was the Christian thing to do? Did not Christ say he was with those who gave a cup of water in his name? Yet she was afraid.

Yes, indeed she was afraid, for she knew that the soldiers would pressure people at gunpoint to tell them who in their village had helped the guerrillas. They would even threaten to kill that person's children if they did not tell. And she knew that if they threatened to kill her child, she would tell, even if it was Mildred, even her best friend. Was it worse to give away a close friend than one's own child? This made her afraid, for she could not blame the others if they had to make that decision. For this reason, she was glad only Mildred knew that she was hiding in the barn.

―

Angela

June 2, 2007

On its way to San Pedro Necta, the bus needed to ascend about two thousand feet through a twisty mountain road featuring several dozen unusually steep switchbacks. After their ascent they reached the rim of a giant gorge. Sofia caught Angela's attention and pointed down to a small town at the bottom of the gorge. "That's it," she said.

Angela stared down through her window at San Pedro Necta as the bus began its similarly twisty descent. The first landmark that caught her eye was the cemetery, which lay uphill a few hundred yards from the town on the north slope of the gorge. It had to be the most cheerful-looking cemetery she had ever seen, its bright tombstones and crypts colored with the pastel palette of an Easter egg basket.

Angela, Alex, and Sofia dropped their bags in front of the check-in counter at the Hotel Chinita, the only real lodging in town, so far down the scale that it didn't even make the roughest of low-budget backpacker guides. At three dollars per night, it would create the smallest of dents in the students' grant funding. The hotel smelled strongly of must and faintly of burro manure.

"House sweet house," proclaimed Alex as he breathed in deeply.

"Any sign of Rich?" asked Sofia. It was evening now. They were supposed to meet the fourth member of their team at the hotel. Richard Freeland, Sofia's classmate from Berkeley, had been spending time in Guatemala on an internship with the World Bank, studying the impact of a tropical fruit export project the Bank had financed south of Quetzaltenango. "Let me try him on his cell."

Fortunately, cell phone service in Guatemala was outstanding, even better than in the United States. A few years earlier, some European telecommunications companies discovered that boatloads of money could be made connecting remote rural villagers with one another in developing countries like Guatemala, especially among those who had never benefited from landline service. It also made field research a lot easier.

Sofia ended her call. "He's on his way over," she announced. "I caught him at the *cantina* having a drop with the locals. I'm going to pick up a few things down the street before the shops close. I'm sure you'll recognize him. Ever watch *Seinfeld* reruns?"

Angela nodded and grinned. She loved *Seinfeld* reruns. Alex had no clue what she was talking about.

"George Costanza. Even huskier, but with a thick Southern accent."

"Are you kidding?" said Angela, laughing.

About five minutes later, a prematurely balding, thirty-something-year-old American wearing an untucked Hawaiian shirt and khaki slacks sauntered confidently through the front door of the hotel. His skin tone was naturally pale, and his nose and the top of his head were in an incomplete phase of sunburn recovery, still very red. He was on the short side for an American, but still well above the average for Guatemala. Unlike most of his classmates at Berkeley, Richard Freeland was from the South—Georgia. Angela learned from Sofia that he had attended Emory University as an undergraduate, where he was valedictorian and president of the college Republicans. And when he announced at the family dinner table that he would be attending graduate school at Berkeley, his father apparently choked on a fried chicken wing.

Like Sofia, Richard was skilled in econometrics and was doing a master's degree in statistics as well as a PhD in economics. He also had taken a specialized field in international trade. It made him an ideal collaborator for the study, and his advisors, who were also Sofia's, had urged him to take a couple of months' leave from his internship to join the coffee project.

"Y'all's tummies enjoy the bus ride?" He grinned as he introduced himself. He pronounced "ride" kind of like "rod," and Angela looked over at Alex, who seemed momentarily confused about what he meant by the bus rod. "Welcome to Guatemala, you two. Call me Rich, but don't ask me for money," he said, chuckling, as he greeted Angela and Alex, shaking her hand a little too firmly. Angela guessed it was probably not the first time Rich had used that one. But his eyes looked straight into hers when he greeted her, not straying over to the birthmark, which she appreciated. There were two categories Angela had for people when first meeting them, people who noticed and people who didn't, something of course that she always kept as a secret. Rich helped them with their backpacks.

After checking in, they headed to dinner. "Rich, have you done any advanced scouting on the dining establishments of San Pedro Necta?" Sofia asked.

"Yes, ma'am," he affirmed. "We've got the *award-winning* tortillas and beans at the little *comedor* down on that corner. We've got the second-place *runner-up* tortillas and beans down the block a stone's throw or two that direction over there. And last we've got the *booby-prize* tortillas and beans across the street that made me retch my freakin' guts out last night."

"What does this mean, *booby-prize?*" asked Alex, sounding intrigued. Angela laughed inwardly and looked over at Rich.

"Well, young man, that depends entirely on context," drawled Rich, tongue-in-cheek, glancing charmingly at the two women, now both grimacing. He put his arm around Alex's shoulder. "I'll give you the subtle nuances man-to-man when we're alone. For now let's just say ..."

"I vote for the first one," interrupted Sofia, before things got out of hand.

"Me too," replied Angela, and a consensus quickly formed.

"This project may become quite the effective weight-loss program," Angela commented to Sofia as they headed out the door.

The little comedor was filled with the aroma of hot oil and an active grill. They all opted for the award-winning tortillas and beans, which indeed were outstanding, some with chicken and others with *planchada*, the thinly cut grilled steak. Angela had a Coke. "The Coke tastes different here," she remarked.

"That's because it's made with real sugar, and not that corn syrup crap they defile it with in the States," explained Rich.

"Why is it that they must utilize corn syrup?" inquired Alex.

"Because protectionist morons in my beloved country prioritize the interests of a few thousand sugar producers at the expense of three hundred million sugar, uh—I mean corn syrup—consumers." Rich tended to chew with his mouth open as he explained. In order to suppress a grin, Angela tried focusing on her plate as she listened to him. "Because of protectionism, the price of sugar in the United States is multiple times the price it rightfully should be as determined by the market. Since the 1980s they have substituted corn syrup in soda and just about everything else you can think of—Mars bars, gumdrops, the fake maple syrup you put on hotcakes, just about everything that's fun to eat, and some that's not. But here you're gettin' the real sugar."

"This steak tastes different too. It's really good," commented Angela again.

"Same thing. Up in the States it's all corn-fed beef. Down here the cows eat grass, but really all kinds of stuff lying around that comes natural to 'em. My Guatemalan mama who owns the little Sheraton where I stay down here fed me with a bull she slaughtered that seemed like it mostly just roamed around eatin' the trash in the backyard. Didn't have a gun, so she had to hit it over the head with the curly end of a crowbar."

Angela winced and watched Rich dig his fork aggressively into another healthy piece of *planchada*. He continued. "That trash-fed beef surely tasted different—but I'll tell you—not bad at all. Back home it's all corn, corn, corn. Makes fatty meat. Beef I ate here was real lean. Not gonna help my hair grow back, but might deflate the old spare tire a smidge."

They finished their dinner and then retired to the musty charms of the Hotel Chinita. Rich and Alex took one of the two rooms and Sofia and Angela took another down the hall. Angela tossed her backpack on the cheap linoleum floor and flopped down on the hard mattress.

"Ouch."

"Yes, the mattresses here are a little . . . er . . . on the firm side," remarked Sofia.

"By choice, or because they can only afford to fill them with sand bags?"

"You know, I haven't figured that one out yet."

Angela dug into her pack and put on some sleeping clothes, flicking off the plastic switch on the bare bulb next to her bed. She knew it was time to sleep, but something was still bothering her, the unanswered question.

"Sofia, about what we saw today . . . why? I know I'm probably being too persistent, but why is there so much poverty in places like this?"

"Again, I don't have a satisfying answer to that question."

"Try me. I just might be satisfied."

Sofia turned out her own light and lay in a sleeping bag that she had thrown on her bed. She gazed upward where some lights from the town illuminated the pine boards that made up the ceiling. "Well, it seems to be related to a couple of basic things, one being how people in society organize themselves."

"You mean institutions? That always sounded kind of boring."

"Trust me, it's not boring. Understanding them is something people win Nobel prizes for."

"I guess I don't really get it," said Angela.

"The rules of the game that a society makes for itself. Institutions either encourage people to make a living by creating or doing things that benefit other people, or by siphoning off what other people have earned doing just that. In rich countries it's mainly the former, and in poor countries it's more of the latter. When people learn that the rewards of creativity and hard work are mostly confiscated, they don't bother. So a lot of people say that it's *all* about the institutions."

Sofia stopped. Angela figured that Sofia wanted to go to sleep, but she'd had a cup of coffee after dinner, her bed was hard, and she was surprisingly wired even though it had been a long day. *So my relatives are poor because their rules of the game aren't any good*, she thought.

"So what's the other part of it?" Angela asked. There was another pause.

Sofia turned her head on the pillow back to face her. "Well, probably another part of it has to do with things like the aspirations people have for their lives and their identity. Sometimes it's hard for, say, the son of a peasant to see himself as capable of being anything other than a peasant. But if your dad was a doctor or an engineer, then you might have higher aspirations."

Angela thought about herself for a moment. "My dad was a doctor, at least my American dad. I have plenty of aspirations, but I think also plenty of identity issues."

"In what way?" Sofia asked, now sitting up and resting on her elbow.

"Well, you know that I was actually born here, maybe like even right around this region somewhere. But my dad in my adoptive family in the States is Anglo and my mom is Mexican.

"Can I tell you a story?"

"Sure." Sofia listened.

"One day, I think I was in the sixth grade, at some family reunion in LA my uncle, Tio Juan, he dared me to put a handful of *chiltepin* peppers in my *tomales*."

"Wow, that was really mean," commented Sofia.

"I think he was doing this to get me to prove I was a real Latina. But when I bit into those *tomales*, my mouth turned numb, and this blazing fire filled my throat. Sofia, it was so bad. I tried to hold back the tears and be a real Latina, I honestly did, but I ran screaming to the bathroom in front of my mom's whole big Mexican family at the table. I heard my mom cuss out Tio Juan really bad in the back room. He apologized later—I don't think he meant to do any real harm—"

"But he did."

"Yes . . . I suppose he did."

"I'm sorry, Angela."

"Thanks for listening . . . Good night, Sofia." There was silence again for a minute or two. Angela thought Sofia had gone to sleep, but Sofia suddenly turned toward her.

"*Buenas noches, amorcita. Que Jesús te lleva a los angeles,*" she said to Angela, as if to a child. "My dad was a pastor of a small church back in Argentina, and he used to tell us that to say good night when we were little. It can only be said to a genuine Latina."

Angela smiled, and a small tear slid down the birthmark on her cheek and fell onto her pillow. And then she fell asleep.

The next morning they began their research. The professors in California had set up a contact with a local fair trade coffee cooperative in San Pedro Necta. A representative from the cooperative, José-Ernesto, also a local coffee grower, met them at their hotel. Angela and the others greeted him. He was short and friendly, with the winsome smile of a serenading mariachi singer. He wore a small cowboy-type hat made of straw. A white collared shirt fit tightly over a little mound of a beer belly that partially eclipsed a large silver belt buckle underneath it. He welcomed the team enthusiastically, flashing his golden smile, "José-Ernesto Vasquez *a sus ordenes*," a humble Guatemalan greeting literally translated as "at your orders."

They learned that the local cooperative in San Pedro Necta was affiliated with Café Justicia, a fair trade cooperative that works with coffee growers across Guatemala. Their plan was to work with the local cooperative, obtaining a sample of growers with access to both fair trade and conventional channels for selling coffee into the world market. From the sample the students would carry out farm-level surveys to estimate the local growers' average costs of production per sack. Then, after obtaining coffee prices received by farmers via the different marketing channels, they would be able to gain some kind of understanding of local profitability in coffee production, both in fair trade and conventional channels.

The students walked with José-Ernesto as he led them to the local cooperative office, located only a few blocks from the hotel. "What kind of coffee do growers cultivate here?" Angela asked José-Ernesto as they walked. She was only a moderate coffee drinker and, probably among all the students, knew the least about it. The others listened as they negotiated the uneven sidewalks bordering the cobbled streets of what might be called downtown San Pedro Necta.

He smiled and seemed to appreciate her inquisitiveness. "You see, there are two principal varieties of coffee. One, *robusta*, is a cheap and less flavorful variety that comes from the *coffea canephora* plant. It is harvested in parts of Brazil, Vietnam, India, and central Africa. The main advantage of robusta is simply that it can be grown in areas hostile to *arabica* cultivation. Robusta also contains significantly more caffeine than arabica, so it is useful to make highly caffeinated espressos."

"Which, by the way, I highly recommend for turbo-charged performance on econ exams," interjected Rich as he smiled at the others, most of whom uttered murmurs of affirmation, confirming the effectiveness of the robusta-laced espresso.

José-Ernesto continued, "In contrast, virtually all of the coffee grown in Guatemala is arabica, a highly flavorful bean that comes from the plant *coffea arabica*. Arabica is also cultivated in other high-altitude regions in East Africa, Colombia, higher areas of Brazil, and the Andes. Indeed, the hard-bean arabica grown in this area is some of the most flavorful coffee in the world. Climate and elevation are nearly perfect."

They arrived at the local cooperative office, a one-room facility housed in an aging multiuse commercial building.

José-Ernesto reached for a file lying on one of the many dusty shelves from which he extracted a stapled document. *"Aqui está la lista,"* he explained, handing them the list of local coffee growers.

To obtain their sample, they needed to choose about 250 borrowers from the list. It was time to randomize. Using a variety of randomization techniques, they were able to select 249 growers. They needed one more. Sofia spoke up.

"Okay, everybody tell me the last digit of the day of the month that is your birthday."

"Seven," piped Angela.

"My number is two," shouted Alex.

"Hey, Dutch Boy, that's *my* birthday number," interjected Rich, pretending to complain.

"Ocho," said José-Ernesto, having understood the question with the little English he knew.

"Okay, we have 7, 2, and 8," announced Sofia. "Is there a member whose number ends in 728?"

Angela quickly checked over the list. "Nobody."

"How about anyone whose last three numbers contain those digits?" Sofia asked.

Angela and Alex pored down the list. Rich saw it first. "Here's a guy whose last number ends in 278, Fernando Ixtamperic. How do you pronounce that? Ick-stamper-ick?"

"Ish-tamper-ique," José-Ernesto corrected him.

"José-Ernesto, do you know him?" asked Sofia in Spanish.

"Sí, I think so. He lives up near Seis Cierros."

"That a convenient place to start as any?"

"Claro," José-Ernesto nodded. There were several other growers from that area on the list as well.

"Well, señor," said Rich, "show us the way."

CHAPTER 6

Fernando

June 4, 2007

A TINY SHAFT OF WARM LIGHT CUT THROUGH THE MORNING chill of the Mayan highlands, passed between old wooden window shutters, and landed on Fernando's cheek. In the distance the old diesel engine of his neighbor's corn grinder protested its early summons to work and then rumbled to life, gradually moving Fernando from the haze of a blurry dream to the certainty of morning. The light and noise stirred him and opened his eyes, which slowly focused on an insect crawling across the adobe wall adjacent to his bed. The insect stopped momentarily, feelers twitching. Disadvantaged by his sleepy stupor, Fernando fumbled unsuccessfully for his slipper to swat it, and the insect scurried into a small hole in the wall. The rustling of the blankets awakened Fernando's wife, Juana, who sat on the side of the bed for a few moments, then got up to collect sticks for a fire.

The house smelled like the memories of ten thousand fires, each kindled between three rocks on the floor. An iron grill balanced on top of the rocks. Cooking utensils were scattered on the dirt floor, mingled with a few cheap plastic toys and empty coffee sacks. On one of the adobe walls hung an outdated calendar with Pepsi advertisements. Near the calendar hung a colorized black-and-white picture of Fernando's grandparents in an inexpensive frame, and next to it dangled a penmanship ribbon won by Juana in second grade. On the walls next to the fire pit were some roughly hewn shelves on which Juana stored jars of beans, peppers, and spices.

The four adobe walls surrounding the dirt floor were built a generation before by Fernando's father, Emilio, who had inherited the land from Fernando's grandfather, Basilio. It had taken most of the entire dry season for Fernando's parents to finish the house with the help of other family and friends. The building process had involved weeks of fabricating hundreds of adobe bricks from mud mixed with straw. But the house was sturdy and had lasted nearly thirty-five years. The outside walls were finished with *repello*, a whitish plaster made with silty mud and lime.

Outsiders often romanticized the adobe houses as a quaint feature of the indigenous Mayan culture. But like most in their village, Fernando and Juana were not enamored with their adobe house. The dirt walls attracted insects, and Fernando had spotted a particularly dangerous one, a *chinche* or "kissing bug," which hid in adobe walls and was drawn to the breath of unsuspecting sleepers. After withdrawing blood from the facial area, the chinche left a fecal droplet containing deadly parasites, sometimes causing heart failure in its victim years later.

Aside from their hospitality to insects, the walls crumbled in earthquakes, like the one in 1976 that struck Guatemala before dawn. That earthquake killed 23,000 people, many as they slept next to adobe walls. Many houses in Huehuetenango had been flattened. As soon as families had money, they replaced the adobe with concrete block and converted the old house into a pig barn or chicken coop. For Fernando and Juana, this kind of architectural transformation always seemed to lie just out of reach.

A corrugated iron roof, its underside coated with soot, kept the house mostly dry during rainstorms—mostly dry until several years ago when rust began to create little holes in the roof. Coffee prices were low that year, and afforded no surplus for the likes of new roofing sheets. And the lower the prices sank, the more rain poured through the little holes in their roof until there were so many holes that they ran out of buckets, and the dirt floor of their house became a mud floor. On the bad days Fernando would lie in his bed, not wanting to get up because he didn't want to walk through the mud, and he would curse the rain, and the holes in the roof, and the *coyotes* who showed up at his field to offer him nothing for his coffee. But Juana would always comfort him, and rub his aching back, and tell him that God would provide for them, and that next year would certainly be better, which it was occasionally.

Juana began to light the sticks she had collected from the forest. She had collected this wood the day before. Like many Mayan women, she spent many hours a week collecting firewood, walking several miles with a *carga* of wood on her back, often eighty pounds or more of kindling, lassoed together with cord. A leather strap attached to the cord was placed around the forehead to absorb some of the weight off the lower back. Sometimes friends passing by in a truck would stop, help remove her load of wood, and allow her to ride in the back with her bundle. Most days she would walk the entire way.

She felt the residual warmth in the fire pit from last night's fire. Bending down, she blew skillfully on some smoldering coals hidden underneath the ashes while adding a handful of dry sticks. After several minutes of Juana's coaxing, a small fire began to crackle. Over the rocks she placed the iron grill on which to prepare their breakfast: tortillas, beans, and coffee.

Fernando, needing to relieve himself after waking up, trekked in his bare feet to the middle of the milpa, or cornfield. Milpa as family toilet was a common practice that simultaneously circumvented the costs of plumbing as it fortified the crops. One time a public health official came to the village and warned against the practice. He had even brought a movie projector to show them a cartoon that illustrated how flies land on the exposed human feces and carry diseases to food sitting on the dinner plates of neighbors. In this way, he explained, when one person became infected with an illness such as amoebic dysentery or hepatitis, the disease could spread throughout the village. Most of the villagers enjoyed the cartoon and agreed that disease was a problem in the area. They also agreed that old habits are sometimes hard to change.

Fernando returned to the house after stopping to talk with a neighbor, another coffee grower who related the latest coffee price news to him.

"*Son tacaños los compradores...,*" he muttered to Juana as he entered the house. The price that the cheapskate *compradores* were offering on advanced sales had fallen again from the week before.

Juana sighed, assuring him it had to be better by harvest.

After breakfast she began to gather clothes to wash in the creek, and Fernando returned to the field to finish yesterday's chore, applying mulch to the coffee plants. The sun rose in the sky and as the shadows grew shorter, the line of sweat down the middle of Fernando's back grew longer, reaching down toward his belt.

Near midday, Juana called to him in the field in her musical voice, "*Mi amor!*"

"*Qué es Gordita?*" he called back. "Little Fatty" ... it was one of those endearing terms used by the Mayans that would never be employed successfully between North American spouses.

Some young people from the United States wanted to interview him. Interview *him*? It was time for lunch anyway. He approached the house, greeted by a member of his fair trade cooperative who introduced the students: Sofia, Richard, Alex, and Angela. They had come to ask him some questions about coffee farming, his family, his life. Would that be okay?

Fernando was curious at the students' interest in him. Some of his young grandchildren and nephews gathered around to listen to the interview with a newfound respect for their elder relative, who must be very important to have attracted such attention from foreigners.

CHAPTER 7

Angela

HE WAS THE FOURTH GROWER ON THE LIST THAT DAY. Fernando shook hands with the men first. *"Fernando Ixtamperic, a sus ordenes."* He was short, but about medium height for a Guatemalan. His sinewy frame and chiseled features did not belie the perceptible acuity that lay behind the face. There was something in the face—was it curiosity or wisdom?—that separated him from the other growers they had met.

He then greeted the women. Sofia extended her hand, and he shook it, then he greeted Angela warmly. Angela noticed that when she shook his hand, it was so calloused it felt rough like a brick. Then she inwardly cringed as Fernando lingered perceptibly on her birthmark. Although it was just for a moment, it quickly made both her and the others uncomfortable.

Sofia broke in. "Angela is from Los Angeles but was born in Guatemala. She is now returning for the first time."

"Bienvenidos, pues." Fernando smiled at her as he regained his composure.

Angela surveyed the house. It was the first home that day they had actually entered. *So this is how people live,* she thought. She looked at the beds lying against the walls of the main room. She could see that a small family slept together in the one room, the same room where Juana, his wife, prepared the meals, and where the students were sitting and talking with him. A wobbly wooden table furnished the middle of the one-room house. One of the four legs hovered awkwardly over a depression in the dirt floor. She watched as Fernando pulled together some wooden chairs from various parts of the room and arranged them around the table. The chairs were old, tiny, and had perfectly straight backs. Fernando placed his straw cowboy hat on one of the beds and ran his hands through his sweaty hair.

Juana shooed some little chicks out of the house that were being chased around by two of their toddler grandchildren, diverting the joyful little parade outside. Juana smiled at Angela, and she smiled back.

Angela had watched Sofia administer the survey questions for the previous growers and had volunteered to administer the questions this time. Fernando's operation was one of a large handful that had been randomly selected for one of the in-depth case studies, which were intended to provide a more comprehensive picture of the economic welfare of a local coffee grower.

Angela tried to sound very official, although inside she felt like she was opening a portal into a secret world that she entered with some trepidation, but at the same time one she yearned to explore. "Please describe your family. Do you have children?"

Fernando and Juana, both in their late thirties, had four children. They had been married when Juana was sixteen and Fernando was seventeen, about average in their village. While their two youngest, Lourdes, eighteen, and Ema, the baby of the siblings at nine, still lived with them, the oldest, Mirabell and Bartolo, were each married and living nearby. Fernando seemed happy to share background information about his family.

"How long have you been a coffee grower, Fernando?" Fernando's first language was *Mam*, a Mayan dialect almost completely unrelated to the dialects of Quiché and Kaqchikel more common to the region, but spoken in several areas in the western highlands, and by a number of families in the village. His Spanish had a Mam accent, but it seemed clear that he had more education than the average person in their village. The fact that Spanish was a second language for both of them made her feel more comfortable.

"*Pues*, since I was about fifteen years old," he replied.

"Is that when you started helping pick the coffee?" Angela asked for clarification.

"No," said Fernando, grinning. "I started to pick when I was three. When I was fifteen, my parents forced me to leave school so I could help on the plantation most of the time. I didn't want to leave school, but my father became ill. They needed my help. I had plans to be the first in my family to attend *preparatoria. Pero, no.* Juana stopped attending school in the third grade."

"How many *cuerdas* of coffee do you have now?" asked Angela, who had been instructed by Sofia to use the common Guatemalan property measurement. A cuerda was about a sixteenth of an acre, or about four hundred square meters. This was only an approximation because cuerdas came in curiously variable sizes across Guatemala. It was an adjustable measurement. Still, it was the most familiar.

"*Pues*, about sixty," replied Fernando. His was an average-size plot for the area, about 2.5 *hectares.*

"Which members of your family work the field?"

"During the harvest, just about everybody, even the little ones."

"What about other times?"

"Just Juana and me."

They came to questions about his children and grandchildren, and Fernando began to reflect on the sacrifices he had made for his children. All of the older ones had finished high school, the younger one, Ema, still continuing. He and Juana had insisted on it, and were obviously proud of the educational achievement of their children.

Angela watched as little Ema approached her mother, who was standing behind watching the interview. Juana bent down and Ema whispered something in her ear. Juana looked back at her and nodded happily, getting up and walking toward the kitchen. A few moments later Juana approached the table and invited the students and José-Ernesto to stay for *comida*, lunch, the big meal of the day.

The students responded enthusiastically. Rich whispered to Angela, "I'm so starved, my belly must think my throat's been cut." It had been a long hike up to Seis Cierros.

Juana spread a red-and-yellow cloth over the modest table, and they all scrunched around it to share the meal. Ema sat next to Angela and began to ask her questions about *Disneylandia*.

"You have seen him?" she asked Angela with wide, dark brown eyes. *"Ratón Mickey!"*

Then the comida appeared: tortillas, beans, and *atol*, a traditional Mayan drink made with rice water, sweetened with honey and a pinch of cinnamon.

Over lunch Fernando explained to the students that some of his friends and relatives from the village had fled to California during the civil war. Most were still there.

"You all come from California?" he asked the students.

"Yes, all of us attend graduate school there," said Sofia.

"Do you know Miguel Hernando Jeatz Ixtamperic?"

"No, señor, haven't had the pleasure," replied Rich.

"Have you met Jacquelin Maria Mendez Ixtamperic?"

"I don't think so," said Sofia, checking the other faces just to make sure.

"Gloria Eliana Vasquez Batz?"

"Unfortunately, um . . . no." The students shook their heads and then glanced at each other, grinning a little bit by this point. There were nearly forty million people in California, four times the size of Guatemala.

"*Quiren café?*" asked Juana. Did anyone want coffee?

"*Gracias,* señora," Rich said. He pronounced it slowly with a Southern drawl, so that it came out like "grassy-ass." It made Angela giggle along with Juana and Fernando, but for different reasons. Angela noticed that Rich was fairly fluent in Spanish but had a horrendous accent, a combination of qualities that seemed to endear him to Guatemalans.

"*Bien hecho,* Juana. This java's strong enough to float a boat anchor. But as tasty as any I've had. Loving it." Rich gave his cup another loud, healthy slurp.

"This is your own coffee, Fernando?" asked Angela.

"*Sí,* grown from the plot behind the house. We always keep a little for ourselves. Juana roasted it in a pan over the fire last night."

Even Angela could tell that the quality of the coffee was supreme.

"The best in the world, at least that is what we San Pedro growers like to brag to one other," smiled Fernando.

Alex turned to the other students in English again. "To me this doesn't make some sense. If coffee here is so great, why are these people so poor? Certainly they are being exploited."

Angela's immediate reaction was to write off Alex's remark simply because it came from Alex and it involved the word "exploitation." Yet as she considered it, she had to admit that the whole thing was a little strange. Why should growers who happened to be sitting on some of the world's best coffee terrain, cultivating some of the highest quality beans, be living in a mud hut with a dirt floor—especially when the grower was a member of a fair trade cooperative?

Sofia concurred there was an incongruity here, a mystery needing to be explored. She turned to the other students and said quickly in English, "Even though the quality of the beans is high, it seems like the profits to the grower could be getting squeezed by some competitive force along the value chain. Let's focus on what happens to the beans after they leave the grower. I think we may find some clues there.

"José-Ernesto, can you give us an overview of what happens to the beans after they leave the grower?" Sofia asked him in Spanish. After washing down a mouthful of tortillas with some coffee, he was happy to explain as the students listened for clues to the economic mystery.

"You see, a one-hundred-pound bag of roasted coffee beans actually begins as about 780 pounds of coffee cherries, which here we call 'rojitos.' This is what coffee growers harvest from plantations just like this one. But the bean—actually usually two beans—lie inside a little husk that has to come off. So either the grower or his buyer puts the coffee cherries through a process that removes the little husks. Of course the grower gets more money for his coffee if he does it himself. They are put through a pulping machine that pops the beans out, leaving only the two beans from each coffee cherry, so 780 pounds of coffee cherries shrinks down to 156 pounds of what we call *pergamino*, or 'parchment' coffee.

"The parchment, the little white skin that covers the beans, is removed when the beans are milled. Sometimes the beans are polished at this point too, but to be truthful with you, that doesn't make them taste much different. At this point they also get graded and sorted by size, and from your original 780 pounds of cherries, you now have 125 pounds of 'green' coffee. But you don't want to do this until the beans are only a couple of weeks away from being exported, otherwise it spoils the taste if they sit green for too long. Green coffee is important because it's this price of green coffee that gets quoted on your New York Board of Trade in the States."

José-Ernesto grew ever more enthusiastic as his explanation

progressed. Juana's coffee was very strong, and the caffeine was kicking in. The more coffee he drank, the more animated he became in talking about it. Moreover, his knowledge of coffee was encyclopedic. Angela thought to herself that this portly little man must have as much firsthand knowledge about coffee as anyone on the planet. José-Ernesto scanned the table for questions with the mannerism of a college professor looking over his reading glasses at his class while leading a seminar. Seeing none, he continued with the coffee chain.

"After this comes roasting, which is usually done after the beans are exported to the consuming country, like *los Estados Unidos* or *Europa*. Roasting heats the beans to four hundred or five hundred degrees, and the oil inside the beans, the *caffeol*, begins to come out and makes the beans brown and gives them their aroma and flavor. Roasting removes another 20 percent or so of water weight, and this leaves you with 100 pounds of pure, roasted coffee."

"My money says that's where Señor Fernando's profits are going," Rich commented to the other students in English. "Profit probably captured at the roaster level. Few roasters, many growers. Buyers' market."

"Then from the roasters to the supermarket?" asked Angela.

"Yes, or Starbucks, Peets, or anywhere else," said Rich. "Mmmm . . . this sure is good, Juana. *Muy sabroso,*" he added. A love of fine coffee was one of the few values he shared with the other citizens of Berkeley.

"What about fair trade coffee?" asked Alex.

José-Ernesto flashed the students a sparkly smile, again revealing his golden dental work, eager to respond to their barrage of questions. He narrowed his eyes as he considered his response. "With fair trade coffee certified by the Fair Trade Labeling Organization, and TransFair, the certifier for the North American market, international growers receive a minimum of $1.31 per pound for arabica green coffee and $1.01 for robusta."

"A price floor," Rich summarized.

"Exactamente," agreed José-Ernesto. "When the coffee crisis hit a few years ago, the price dropped to less than half of this fair trade price, and selling under fair trade was a big advantage to growers. It helped many growers make it through the crisis. But when the world price of coffee is higher than this, being able to sell at the fair trade doesn't bring much of an advantage."

This confused Angela. "Wait a minute. You mean now that coffee prices are above the fair trade price floor, when someone in the US buys coffee that is called 'fair trade' it doesn't pay the grower any more than regular coffee?" She realized that she had inadvertently stumbled on an important piece to the puzzle.

"Well, in addition to the $1.31 per pound, there is a premium of ten cents per pound added that is to be used by the producer associations for investment back into the association or into the local community. This means that the final price is always ten cents higher than the world price. Moreover, if the coffee is certified as organic, there is an additional premium to the grower of twenty cents extra. But you are right, when the world price of coffee is above the fair trade price floor, the added benefit to growers of fair trade over conventionally marketed coffee declines substantially."

"I'll bet that would be interesting news to latte-sipping liberals," commented Rich not so subtly in Sofia's ear.

José-Ernesto continued. "Fair trade certification is an important issue. To be eligible to sell their crop through fair trade networks, a producer must be certified. This means that his farm should comply with a set of environmental and labor standards. Some of these growers are very poor, so compliance is not perfectly enforced but the regulations say that growers must comply 'as far as possible.' The cooperative to which they belong must also meet requirements for democratic participation of members, especially in regards to how the social premium is spent by the cooperative. An umbrella institution in Germany called FLO-CERT oversees a network of inspecting organizations in coffee-producing countries that each certify growers for fair trade, administer the *sello*. The certification process costs each grower a little more than six cents per pound for the first certification and a little more than three cents per pound each year after that for recertification."

Alex redirected the conversation. "Fernando, tell us about the advantages of fair trade over free trade."

Rich interjected with a smile, "Gee, I always thought the two were the same thing." Alex turned and looked at Rich, shaking his head slowly and disapprovingly.

Sofia rephrased the question. "What do *you* see as the benefits and costs for growers of fair trade coffee, Fernando?"

"*Pues*, to me it wasn't an easy decision. There is the cost of getting the sello. And sometimes the fair trade price is much better, and sometimes it's only a little better. It is a gamble. If I get the sello, then I'm betting that coffee prices are low. If I don't get it, I am betting that the price is high."

"And what about the organic coffee channel?" Sofia glanced up, sketching some kind of complicated diagram on her notepad teeming with the different channels the coffee beans might take.

José-Ernesto answered. "Organic and fair trade often go together, but not always. About 75 to 80 percent of fair trade coffee is organic, and most organic coffee is fair trade. The benefit that the organic growers receive is not so simple because of the relationship between fair trade and organically grown coffee. If arabica fair trade coffee is certified organic, then it does receive a higher price, right now $1.61 per pound. And to have, for example, Starbucks certified coffee, a grower receives a certain number of points, and farms with increasing numbers of points can get a higher premium from them, sometimes $30 to $35 per one-hundred-pound sack. And fair trade coffee can fetch a higher price by being certified as bird-friendly, which automatically means it is shade-grown as well as organic."

"Do you grow organic coffee, Fernando?" asked Angela.

"*No.*"

"Why not?" she asked.

"*Pues*, it depends on coffee prices. If regular coffee prices are very low, then I would do better with organic coffee. But if prices are high, then I would do worse with organic."

"What matters badly with organic?" Alex asked in Spanish. Any talk of organic or fair trade not being an obvious choice under all circumstances appeared to make him edgy.

Fernando explained. "Because organic costs more to grow. You have to pay for more *jornaleros*, the agricultural day workers, because there are many more tasks with organic. Because you can't use pesticides, you have to spread compost carefully around all the plants and do about twice as much raking and weeding. Your coffee plants die more often, so you also must replant more frequently. So when regular coffee prices are high, I do better by getting higher yields on regular coffee using pesticides and chemical fertilizers."

"It is unjust not to compensate borrowers for such added costs," pronounced Alex to the others. It was clearly shocking for him to see a coffee grower involved in fair trade living in poverty.

But Angela and the others were discovering another piece to the puzzle: entering into the potentially beneficial fair trade and organic coffee channels involved some significant costs to growers. It wasn't a straightforward decision.

"There is another problem," added Fernando. The students

listened. "The cooperative tells us they can only market a certain amount of coffee through fair trade channels because the market for fair trade is only so big, only about one out of every four sacks. So I only receive the high price on the part that can be marketed as fair trade. *Es un problema.*"

"So how much of your crop do you sell to the cooperative and how much do you sell to the coyotes?" Angela asked. The students had learned about the coyotes, local buyers who appeared at the farm gate every day during harvest, offering to buy growers' coffee. The coyotes offered lower prices but paid in cash right away.

"It's hard to wait such a long time to be paid," Fernando explained. "Last year I owed a great deal of money for school fees. I needed money right away, so I sold about two-thirds of my crop to the coyotes for $120 and the rest to the co-op."

"So let me understand," said Angela to clarify, "you didn't get any of the benefits of fair trade with two-thirds of your crop, and with the remaining one-third that you sold to the cooperative, only a quarter of that could be sold as fair trade?"

"*Sí*," said Fernando. "But prices weren't too bad last year, so I got by. A few years ago when prices were so low, it was terrible, especially for people without fair trade. Some people never even bothered to harvest their coffee because just the cost of paying the jornaleros was more than what they got for their coffee. Some growers couldn't pay their debts, and everybody was leaving to immigrate illegally to the United States. It was really bad. In those days, the fair trade premium helped me and my family and other members of the cooperative to make it through okay."

Angela was surprised to discover that the benefits of fair trade coffee were so finely nuanced, and that they were so heavily dependent on coffee prices.

They thanked Fernando and Juana for their time and for the wonderful lunch, then asked if Alex and Rich could come back tomorrow to do some cost calculations on Fernando's crop. Fernando said it would be his pleasure, and he would see them tomorrow. The students began the two-mile walk back to the Hotel Chinita.

CHAPTER 8

Alex

ALEX AND RICH WALKED TOGETHER AS THEY DESCENDED THE mountain path. Angela and Sofia followed somewhat behind them. Only momentarily after their departure, Alex remarked, "Did you hear that? The problem is incredibly obvious—not enough people buying fair trade. Why can't lazy, rich coffee drinkers wake up and see how much they are exploiting the growers down here?"

"Alex, I have a question for you," Rich replied carefully. "Do you think Fernando and Juana's poverty is caused by lazy, rich coffee drinkers?"

"Of course," he replied. "And the corporate conglomerates that sell coffee to them. Wherever there are weak and vulnerable people in the world, the free market is expert at finding them and exploiting them to increase the profits and welfare of the rich. It all makes me sick."

"What do you think about the US embargo against Cuba?" Rich asked him. Alex suspected this could be some kind of trap, but could not see it, so he decided on the earnest answer: "I believe it profoundly sucks."

"Hmmm . . . okay . . . Not allowing countries like Cuba to export their products is oppressive. But when the United States signs a free trade

63

agreement with a Latin American country, that's oppressive too. Kinda leaves you wondering whether trade is a good thing or a bad thing, doesn't it? I swear, Alex, if you put the collective brains of the antiglobalization movement in a gnat's butt, it'd fly backwards."

Alex didn't quite make the connection between brains, gnats, butts, and globalization, but he persisted nevertheless. "Don't you see, Rich, trade between rich and poor countries is fundamentally unfair. It always benefits the wealthy."

"Gee, I was always under the impression that free exchange benefited both parties. Otherwise, why would they exchange? Well then, if you're right, Alex, Cuba sure must be a lot better off with that embargo than those poor Latin American countries with the trade agreements who have access to the world's biggest consumer market."

"The world's biggest consumer market is exploitative."

"I don't understand your use of the word 'exploitation.'"

"You are right. You do not understand it."

Rich grimaced. Sweat was starting to leave dark patches on his tightly fitting Hawaiian shirt, and it obviously wasn't just from the hike.

As a master's student scrapping with the doctoral candidate from Berkeley, Alex was beginning to see himself almost in a Davidic role, and he felt like he was at least effectively annoying Goliath with a few pebbles to the forehead.

Goliath responded, "Frankly, I find 'exploitation' to be an ill-defined word that is used by some folks to mean whatever they want it to mean. What I understand is 'better off' and 'worse off.' Would Fernando and Juana be worse off if they were prevented from selling their coffee on the world market? Obviously they would because they believe it to be their best option, unless of course you view them as incapable of making good decisions for themselves. Moreover, I never said that through international trade they would become rich as oil sheiks.

With or without trade, poor folks are unlikely to be better off than rich folks. I just said that trade would make them better off than otherwise. Besides... didn't the good Lord himself say that the poor would be with us always?"

Alex remembered this quote from someone in a debate he had attended once at his university. "Yes, indeed I believe so. But wasn't it to Judas?" For the first time Rich didn't seem quite sure what to say. With a flick of his shoulder-length hair, Alex turned to Rich, looking him directly in the eye. "If globalization is so wonderful, how can Fernando and Juana be remaining in destitution when they sell some of the most flavorful coffee in the world that you so fondly enjoy drinking?"

They arrived at the hotel, Rich looking sweaty and exasperated.

It was time to say good-bye until tomorrow when José-Ernesto would guide Sofia and Angela as they explored the fair trade cooperative that bought Fernando's beans. Rich and Alex would be working together to carry out cost estimations on his coffee.

CHAPTER 9

The little bundle nestled against the young woman's back began to stir. It was hungry. The young woman slowly rose up out of the hay and in one motion pulled on the knot in the colorful blankets, bringing it around in front to nurse. Somehow the infant had remained asleep through her dash to the barn, the screams of villagers, the gunfire.

Just as it began to nurse peacefully, they were jolted by the sound of the officer shouting orders through a bullhorn. The woman sat up to look. The bullhorn was aimed at a group of villagers who had locked themselves inside of the *Iglesia Pentecostes*, the local Pentecostal church. She knew the pastor of that church, Pastor Juan. She was fairly certain he was not a guerilla sympathizer. However, he may have sympathized with some of those who sympathized with the guerillas. She wondered how far removed from sympathy one would have to be in order to be safe from the army. Many of those locked inside the church were certain to be his parishioners. They were unlikely to be sympathizers either.

The army had come to the village once, to remind

the villagers about the perils of helping the guerillas. They had delivered a stern lecture in the center of the village. They had encouraged villagers to tell the civil patrols if they suspected a particular person of helping the guerillas. The guerillas could not exist without villages friendly to their movement. They were like rats. If you take away the garbage, the army had explained, the rats will stay away. People who helped the guerillas were like garbage, and the guerillas were like rats. And so to get rid of the rats, the garbage had to be eliminated. This was how the villagers understood what the army had said to them.

The young woman considered what the army had said about rats and garbage. Some guerillas, she had agreed, might be like rats, sneaking around at night, stealing food, and causing trouble. But the guerillas who had come into the village, at least the ones she had met, were not like rats. They were mostly starving and wounded from fighting the people who were threatening them.

And she and Mildred had given them help.

One of the guerillas was Alberto. He showed them scars where bullets had come in and out of his leg, just below his knee. He was proud of the scars, proud to show them to her and to Mildred.

They had stayed up late one night and talked, the three of them, when Alberto was in the village. Mildred had asked him why he fought. He said that he fought the government because the government did not care about the Mayan people. It wanted them to be slaves of the *ladinos* forever, working their coffee as underpaid *mozos*. The government did not want to provide them education, he said, because it was operated by coffee owners who wanted to keep the mozo stupid and dependent, reliant on the landowner for work. He was fighting for a new government, he said, one that would bring dignity back to the Mayan people.

They were fascinated listening to Alberto. He was brave and had bold ideas, even if they did not understand much about a new government, or even the old one. People in their village had mostly preferred to be left alone by the government. That, they found, was generally how things turned out best. When the government came to their village, it always seemed to spell trouble.

She saw at least four pickup trucks and two large wagons with canvas covers, which she assumed had brought most of the soldiers. There must be at least thirty of them, she thought, plus the members of the civil patrol from the village. She could tell even from a distance that the soldiers were not from this part of the country. They never were. Alberto had explained that the government always deployed soldiers from different parts of the country for counter-insurgency operations in an area that needed to be cleansed of guerrilla sympathizers. It made communication in indigenous language between the enlisted men and local villagers nearly impossible and played upon old rivalries between Mayan groups. Yes, Alberto had explained all of this to them. And he had told them other secrets as well.

—

Angela

June 11, 2007

After contacts with the growers had been established, Sofia and Angela began to pursue the second link in the coffee value chain: the purchase of Fernando's harvest. They hoped to find more clues that would help explain how coffee growers cultivating some of the best arabica beans—brewed in some of the most expensive cups of coffee in the world—could be living in such destitution, even as they marketed through fair trade networks.

They had learned that coffee growers in Huehuetenango had essentially two options for marketing their harvest. The first was selling their coffee to the local wholesale buyers, the coyotes, who appeared doggedly at the farm gate during harvest offering immediate cash for their crop. Aside from the quick cash, another benefit of selling to the coyotes was that they were relatively lenient on quality. Ideally, coffee cherries should be picked when they have turned fire-engine red, but the coyotes would allow a small fraction of immature greenish or yellow-orange cherries in the mix. But the prices the coyotes offered were relatively low. The other option for growers like Fernando was to market their coffee through a local cooperative, which offered a higher price and had access to fair trade markets. But the cooperatives insisted on higher quality and required the grower to transport the coffee to the cooperative.

Sofia and Angela decided to explore the next step—the coffee that was marketed through the cooperative. The cooperative was located in Huehuetenango, about an hour and a half away by bus.

Sofia and Angela met José-Ernesto and they waited patiently at the bus terminal, their bus arriving about forty-five minutes after it was due to depart. The arriving passengers dismounted one by one, followed by the driver, who got off the bus and made a beeline to the bus station cafeteria.

"Good thing our appointment time is flexible," remarked Angela.

The bus driver returned a half hour later, mounted his seat, and entered in some information in a torn leather notebook. The three were first in line as the hydraulic doors to the bus banged open. With a gracious gesture of his hand and a deferential bow, José-Ernesto motioned Sofia and Angela ahead of him to board first. They mounted the steps and took seats in a row toward the middle of the bus as the bus driver cranked up the diesel engine. Other passengers climbed aboard as the bus idled.

After the old Blue Bird bounced awkwardly down the curb and headed out of the station, Angela asked José-Ernesto, "So for Guatemala, why coffee?"

"Indeed, it is our biggest export, *sin duda*," he replied—without a doubt.

"Can you tell us a little more about it?" asked Sofia. "I know we skimmed the surface at Fernando's, but why is Guatemala's economy so dominated by coffee?"

"*Si pues*." José-Ernesto cleared his throat, shifting in his seat excitedly. Angela could see his passion for the subject.

"You see, for nearly 250 years after Europeans set foot on its soil in the early 1500s, the most important Guatemalan exports to Europe were neither food nor precious minerals. Rather they were indigo—plants—and cochineal—insects—used in the extraction of blue and red dyes, respectively. But in the latter half of the eighteenth century, the indigo encountered plagues of locusts. Moreover, countries such as Venezuela and India had increased their own supply so that market prices fell precipitously.

"So as Guatemalan exports of indigo declined, cochineal began to supersede indigo as our country's chief export during the first half of the nineteenth century. Large cactus plantations were created to host the cochineal insect, which after being boiled, dried, and pulverized in batches of millions, yielded carmine, the bright crimson dye used to tint the clothing and military uniforms of Europe. Through slight variations in the processing of cochineal, one could extract different shades of color, ranging from orange to purple. It was a highly valued commodity, and it began to dominate the economy of Guatemala, comprising between 50 and 80 percent of exports. But as synthetic dyes began to be developed in Europe, Guatemala began to diversify its export base toward a greater emphasis on alternative commodities."

Angela watched José-Ernesto as he talked and decided he was an example of someone who, if life had been kinder to rural Mayans, would have been a professor of one thing or another at the university. At the university he could have relieved this pressure valve of bursting knowledge at regular intervals in his classes. But as life would have it, he was a spirited soul trapped in the wrong life, and she wondered who else he had in this life with whom to expel this bulging warehouse of worldly erudition. She and Sofia listened attentively to him, occasionally smiling at each other and glancing at the rugged mountain scenery passing behind him through the window.

"Now in 1871, the Liberal party under Justo Rufino Barrios took control of the government on a platform of economic reform. Looking to examples of modern economies in countries such as yours—the United States, Argentina, and Europe—the focus of the Liberals was not to provide education and services to the poor in rural communities, but to modernize the Guatemalan economy. A principal focus of this effort was the intention to develop coffee as a principal Guatemalan export, and to jump-start the coffee industry they needed economic reforms in finance, land, and labor. They made easy credit available to those wishing to begin coffee cultivation, but they needed land, and the main obstacle of the Liberals was that previous Guatemalan governments had given much of it to the indigenous Mayan peoples in the form of *ejidos*, or communal property. But the Liberals regarded the ejidos and other communally owned lands as symptomatic of economic backwardness. So they' enacted a number of laws that fostered the leasing and purchase of indigenous lands by commercial agricultural interests at low prices, with the intention that they be brought into coffee production."

Angela was missing a few of the words in Spanish—he was using some words that she didn't understand, but she continued to listen. José-Ernesto lifted the sunbaked straw hat off his head, wiped his brow with his sleeve, and continued as the aged school bus chugged through the countryside. "Now as you know, coffee is an extremely labor-intensive crop during harvest, and access to capital and land still left open the question of who would work the coffee fields of Guatemala. Not surprisingly, my ancestors—the native peoples—showed little interest in the task. So to induce them into agricultural labor, managers of the plantations created a system of *habilitaciónes*, or advanced payments on wages. Under this system, workers received up-front wage advances but remained in legal debt to plantation owners and were barred from leaving the land until the habilitación was repaid through agricultural labor. Repayment of the debt in money was disallowed. You see, the habilitaciónes essentially created a system of slave labor. Many indigenous Guatemalans, who were bound to their employer through their debt from wage advances, could be threatened with imprisonment for leaving the plantation or failing to perform laborious agricultural tasks."

Angela considered that some of her ancestors were probably caught up in this too, and she frowned.

"The government of Barrios established a series of laws in 1877 that sanctioned and strengthened the habilitaciónes system. Moreover, they legalized the practice of *mandamientos,* a national system that used a military-style draft to commandeer indigenous labor for work on coffee plantations. Barrios also passed a 'Law against Vagrancy' in 1878, where those without work could be legally sequestered for agricultural labor. Through these policies and heavy investment in the country's road and train infrastructure, the Liberals of the 1870s tried to launch Guatemala into a new era of economic growth and prosperity."

"Did it work?" asked Angela.

José-Ernesto looked out at the mountains. "No. *Lamentablamente,* it did not. It helped cement a silent class system in our country that formed the antecedent of our long civil war. Sadly, this class system remains to this day, although few speak openly of it."

Angela thought about how many of her ancestors probably worked as virtual coffee slaves with little opportunity for self-improvement or education. She was beginning to see how the roots of poverty ran deep in Guatemala, and they were a product of the evolution of history, something she learned little about in her economics classes at UCLA.

The bus announced its arrival into Huehuetenango with several blasts of its magnificently loud horn. The cooperative was located on a dusty street near the outskirts of the city. The three travelers got off the bus at the main station and walked about a mile through the streets of Huehuetenango to reach the cooperative. Huehuetenango was a bustling regional capital, its dusty streets full of noisy, crowded buses and the smell of diesel. The high altitude combined with the air pollution on the streets made Angela's lungs ache. They finally arrived at the cooperative headquarters.

As soon as they walked through the front door, it was evident that the cooperative ran on a slim budget. Empty coffee boxes, an archaic copy machine, and a lone personal computer decorated the spartan office. Old coffee promotion posters with smiling peasants were affixed with yellowed scotch tape to the gray concrete walls. A man emerged from a back room. He looked like a coffee grower himself, about five feet tall and of Mayan descent, with rough coffee grower's hands that looked to be permanently tattooed with dirt.

He greeted the students cordially, and José-Ernesto introduced them to Juan Zegarra, the cooperative manager. *"Buenos dias,* Angela, *buenos dias,* Sofia."Juan extended one hand and smoothly reached into his vest pocket to hand them his card with the other.

"Mucho gusto." Angela and Sofia shook hands with him and glanced down at his card.

"Please have a seat, and excuse the mess. We seem to be in a chronic state of reorganization around here. I understand from your professor's e-mail that you're here to learn a little bit about our cooperative."

"Yes, we are on a research project sponsored by USAID on the coffee value chain," said Sofia. "We'd like you to tell us anything you can about the relationship you have with your growers and how you market their crop." Sofia had a spiral binder on her lap, and Angela was prepared to tap out notes on a laptop.

Juan explained the need for fair trade in terms of stability. "Our cooperative has been certified as a 'fair trade' cooperative by TransFair. You see, coffee price volatility has a dramatic effect on the income of growers. Over the last decade, New York arabica green coffee prices have gyrated between $1.58 and $0.61 a pound. Given the normal costs of production of one of our farmers, even a seemingly modest fall in the world price from, say, $1.40 to $1.20 could cut a grower's coffee earnings in half. One of the goals of fair trade coffee is price stability, and this is arguably more important than trying to achieve the absolute highest price in the good years."

"We were interviewing one of your members, Fernando Ixtamperic in San Pedro Necta," Sofia explained. "He says that only about a quarter of the coffee that growers send to you is marketed as fair trade."

"Yes, unfortunately the market for fair trade and organic coffee is much smaller than we wish it would be. Of course, we would like to see that fraction grow." José-Ernesto nodded in agreement.

Angela could see that Sofia had keyed onto something.

"How does that fraction of coffee you can sell at the higher fair trade price vary with coffee prices?" Sofia asked.

"Interesting that you ask that question. We have noticed that this fraction that we are able to market at the higher fair trade price falls as coffee prices decrease, and it becomes larger as prices increase."

"I believe I can tell you why," said Sofia.

"Please do."

"I believe if you look at your records, you are likely to find that as coffee prices fall, more growers want to become fair trade certified so that they can obtain the higher fair trade price, and the volume of coffee marketed through your cooperative increases."

"And since the demand for fair trade is independent of price fluctuations, this reduces the share from the cooperative that is able to be marketed under the fair trade price," interjected Angela.

"I do not have to consult my records; indeed you are correct. I know for certain that both certification and volume increase during low price phases." He reached for some papers in a file drawer anyway, and showed them the data.

Sofia turned to Angela and said in English, "This trip was worthwhile."

CHAPTER 10

Alex

As Sofia and Angela interviewed the director of the cooperative, Alex and Rich carried out an inventory of Fernando's costs of coffee production.

"Fernando, what is average cost of production?" Alex read directly off the questionnaire slowly and carefully in Spanish. He wiped his sweaty hands on his shorts. Doing formal interviews in Spanish made him a little nervous, but he knew the practice would be good for him.

"*No sé,*" confessed Fernando. "I don't keep very good records."

Rich broke down the question a little. "What are some of the costs involved in growing your coffee?"

Fernando seemed to answer that easier. "Well, fertilizers, the wages of the jornaleros I need to help maintain my plants and for the harvest, transport of my crop to the cooperative, a few taxes . . ."

Alex looked through entries Fernando kept in a small journal for wages paid to jornaleros and tried to carefully sum up all of Fernando's costs.

As he did this, Rich asked another question. "Fernando, how much do your children work on the crop?"

"When they're being lazy, or when they're not being lazy?" responded Fernando.

"How about an average amount of lazy?" Rich grinned.

"Oh, maybe a couple of hours a day, and dawn to dusk during harvest," he replied.

This struck Alex as strange. He looked up from the journal. "Why are you asking that? He doesn't pay them," probed Alex.

"Opportunity costs," replied Rich offhandedly. "Never forget 'em. That's the mistake made by a lot of bean-counter accountants. Makes you underestimate true costs."

Rich and Alex worked on estimating an average cost of production. It was harder than Alex had expected, and it involved a fair amount of educated guessing.

"What do you have from the journal?" Rich asked Alex.

"Uh, seems to use about two jornaleros each day for ten days for putting on the mulch. Roughly same for harvest. Wage—thirty *quetzales* a day—can one believe such an exploitative wage?" remarked Alex. Indignant anger boiled up in his chest. "Forty cents an hour!"

"So now Fernando's moved from *exploitee* to *exploiter*?" asked Rich.

Alex glared back at Rich but offered no rebuttal. He carried out some elementary arithmetic calculations. "With exchange rate of 7.5 to the dollar, I am supposing we have about $160 for the hired labor." Rich entered this figure into the spreadsheet on his laptop. He added the cost of the organic mulch and fertilizer that Fernando used on his crop. No receipts were available for transportation costs, and so they quizzed him about this, trying to triangulate on a consistent estimate. They added in some other costs of maintaining the acreage, pruning, repairs on a fence, and included figures for the 12 percent sales tax levied by the government and a 5 percent tax on revenues. Rich continued to work on other minor costs based on some old receipts lying in a folder, but Alex stopped and put his head in his hands. Why couldn't he stop sweating? And now he was really starting to feel nauseous.

"You alright, Lefty?" Rich asked.

"I am feeling perfectly, thank you."

It was not the truth. Alex wasn't sure what he had eaten that was causing the problem; perhaps it was the leftover chicken feet, or maybe it was the salad from last night, but whatever it was, it was beginning to initiate a gastrointestinal rebellion that was progressively involving new combatants all over his insides. Another fifteen minutes passed.

"Perhaps it is possible that I don't feel so good," Alex finally conceded. He was bent over and his knees were beginning to feel wobbly as well.

Richard turned and looked at Alex. "Whoa, y'all really are looking like a member of the Green Party. You've gotta lie down or something."

Fernando was nearby, and Rich called him over and explained the situation. They tried to convince Alex to lie down on one of the three beds in Fernando's house.

"Unfortunately, I think I must do important fieldwork in the coffee plantation first," lamented Alex, and he staggered a few yards into the coffee plants. Leaning over with his hands on his knees and his face beading with sweat, he ejected his breakfast and lunch.

"Fernando, would that still qualify as organic fertilizer?" Alex heard Rich ask Fernando in Spanish.

"Sí, no problema," Fernando reassured.

Fernando helped Alex over to the bed. Rich reached into his backpack and took out a brown leather bag.

"What is this thing?" asked Alex.

"Before graduate school, did a little paramedic training in Georgia. Know a fair amount about common tropical ailments. Always better to be prepared down here." Rich opened the first-aid kit and pulled out a thermometer. Alex placed it under his tongue, and a few minutes later Rich took it out to read it: "A hundred and three. Boy, you're baking like a Dutch oven."

"You have medicine in that bag of yours?" asked Alex. "I need drugs."

Rich looked through the bag. "Shoot, must have run out of cipro after my own bout with the stomach beast."

"How convenient is that."

"Look, Lefty, patient complaint forms are located near the south wing elevators. You stay here, and I'm going to go run and get some meds in town. Probably just food poisoning or a stomach bug, but that fever ought to worry you a bit."

Alex moaned and turned over on the hard bed.

Not long after Rich had left, one of Fernando's daughters entered the house. She was medium height with dark brown, shoulder-length hair, about eighteen years old, and surprisingly didn't appear shocked to walk into her parents' home to see a foreign man lying on her bed. Like her mother, she was dressed in the traditional Guatemalan clothing, wearing the blouse, or huipil, with its embroidered flowers, and a hand-loomed skirt, or corte, with its multihued stripes and patterns. Through half-open eyes, he was still able to notice that she was quite attractive.

Alex was still feeling terrible, and Spanish was even more difficult than usual. "I am sorry. Am I being on your bed?"

"It's mine and my sister's, but that's okay. My father told me you are sick." Her face was soft and gentle, almost cherubic, and had a natural kindness about it. "Yes, I think I ate a very, very bad salad. And some old chicken feet. *Muy, muy mal*," lamented Alex. Very, very bad.

"You ate a salad here? Even *we* don't eat the salad. You are a very brave person," she said. "Or very silly." She offered a kind but mildly teasing smile.

"What is your name?" asked Alex, hoping to change the subject from his foolish mistake.

"My name is Lourdes," she replied. "I'm one of the middle ones. Two older *hermanos* and one younger one. This is my little sister Ema." Ema peeked out from behind Lourdes's skirt to look at Alex. "Can I make you some tea?"

"Sure, although I can't guarantee at this point that we will not see it again after I drink it." Alex sincerely did not want to throw up in front of the sweet girl with the angelic face.

"Let me see how bad your temperature is." She bent down and put her hand on his forehead and left it there a few seconds. Her hands were soft. "You're very hot. Let me also get a cool washcloth for your head." She turned to her sister. "Ema, *buscame un paño por favor.*" Alex lacked the energy to protest.

Ema brought the washcloth and Lourdes left, returning a few minutes later with some tea in a worn china cup and the washcloth. She put the washcloth on Alex's head but left her hand there for a few minutes, closed her eyes, and began to whisper some words under her breath in Mam, her Mayan language. Ema stood nearby, her eyes shut tight. The words sounded mysterious to Alex.

"Are you casting a spell on me?" mumbled Alex, his eyes closed, feeling like the last battle of Armageddon was waging inside his intestines.

"No, I just said a prayer for you. My pastor teaches us that when someone is sick, we should put our hand on them and pray for them to get well."

"What if I don't believe in God?" asked Alex. "Does it work still?"

She paused and seemed to consider the question. "I suppose that's up to him," she said.

Alex studied her face one last time and then began to drift off to sleep.

Rich arrived back from town to Fernando and Juana's house about the time darkness had set in. The home was now illuminated by a single naked lightbulb dangling from frayed, improvised wiring from a beam in the center of the house. Alex was still lying on the bed, his clothes drenched with sweat, weak and green. Lourdes was sitting on a stool next to the bed, trying to feed him some soup with a spoon. Ema was by her side, wide-eyed and silent, helping to care for the interesting new foreigner who had somehow landed in their house.

"You look like something the dog's been playin' with under the porch," Rich pronounced as he looked at Alex. "But seems like you're getting the best health care available. Probably don't even need the cipro."

Alex was not completely convinced Rich was joking. He responded in Spanish for the benefit of the family around him, "Rich, give me drugs. I am very, very lousy."

Rich handed him a couple of ciprofloxacin tablets and Alex washed them down with some of Lourdes's tea.

Lourdes looked at Rich. "Thank you. You are very kind."

"Oh, I know. Always getting confused with Mother Teresa."

Rich said to Alex, "You're not going to be able to walk back to the hotel in this condition, we can't get a jeep up here, and I don't feel like strapping you to the top of a mule, so Fernando and Juana have offered to have you stay here tonight. Agreed?"

Alex looked at Fernando and Juana. Fernando said quickly, "Alex, there is no problem. We will take care of you. If you get worse, we'll summon a team of men to carry you by stretcher down to the doctor."

"I am sincerely hoping this will not happen," Alex replied.

Fernando, Juana, and Lourdes took turns making Alex feel as comfortable as possible, and as Alex rested, he watched the family drink cups of coffee around the fire lit between the three rocks on the floor of their house. The family was speaking mostly in Mam, but he could understand the gist of their conversation from the interlaced Spanish: stories about the day, the sick foreigner, the usual complaints about the price of coffee, the latest news about others in the village. Alex had never grown up with a family like this. Giggles from Lourdes, little Ema, and their mother hung like sparkly ornaments on the banter. Alex liked the sound of Lourdes laughing. In low tones the family continued their conversation around the orange glow of the fire as Alex fell asleep.

Alex awoke the next morning, far from perfect, but significantly better. Fernando was already working in the field and Juana had gone into town to buy some things for the house. Lourdes was already cooking him breakfast over the fire pit.

"*Buenos dias,*" she said cheerfully as Alex opened his eyes. "Do you want some breakfast?"

"Actually, that is sounding great," admitted Alex. "I think the battle is over and the good guys mostly have won."

Lourdes laughed. "I knew my prayer would make you better."

"Either that or maybe the cipro," said Alex.

"And don't forget my soup . . . ," countered Lourdes as she cocked her head with a smile.

"Certainly that was it," agreed Alex. He paused. He studied her face now that he was feeling better, there was more light, and he could see more clearly. It was indeed a sweet face, but now he saw the depth of it. It was the face of someone who had experienced more than life's share of hardship, but had responded by developing a greater sympathy for the sufferings of others.

"Lourdes, do you really believe that prayers work?"

"I know they do. We could have never made it through *el crises* a few years ago without prayer."

"What crisis?" asked Alex.

"*El crises de café*. About five years ago my father nearly lost everything when the price of coffee went so low. We only had money to eat two meals a day, and many people in our village were almost starving. That is rare in Guatemala. Here we are poor, but we are usually not starving. That was a very bad time, and we prayed to God to help us." She was silent for a moment, and a little pensive. "Is it really true that you don't believe in God?"

"To be honest, I'm not sure. But whether there is a God or not, I'd rather put my energy into making things work better down here."

"What things?" Lourdes was curious.

"All the things wrong with this crummy world. Lourdes, there is way too much economic injustice. Look at your family, half starving because the world price of coffee happens to get cut in half one year. Do you know what caused this, Lourdes? Do you know what caused your family to almost starve five years ago?"

Lourdes shook her head; she did not know.

"It was because some imbeciles at the World Bank decided to finance a bunch of new coffee production in Vietnam, that's why. Ten million new bags of cheap coffee on the world market caused the price to go way, way down, making your lives miserable. Did your father have any say about this? No, and neither did any of the other small coffee growers in the world who suffered because of those idiots." He used the words *imbécil* and *idiota*, not realizing the extraordinarily abrasive connotations of these words in Spanish.

"But with God's help and the help of everyone in the village, we made it through okay," insisted Lourdes.

"Yes, but with a more just world, you would not have to ask God to bail you out so often."

"Alex, no matter what, there will always be troubles. Even look at you, your sickness could have been much worse. There are so many things that we try to control, but we will never be able to. We can do the best we can, but in the end it is all in God's hands."

As Alex lay in bed, they talked easily through most of the morning about growing up in Guatemala and the Netherlands. Alex's Spanish was becoming more comfortable, and Lourdes spoke slowly and helpfully, correcting his mistakes gently. She also asked Alex to teach her a few words in Dutch.

After some time Lourdes stood up and her expression turned somber. "Alex, I need to leave now to Huehuetenango for a doctor's appointment." Then she told him, "I'm going to have a baby."

Alex paused. "You . . . will have a baby?"

"Yes, in about six months. The doctor says the twentieth of November."

Alex was a little stunned. "You are married?" he asked.

"No, Alex. I must tell you it is difficult for me to talk about this. A few months ago I was walking up the path from a meeting at our church; it was night. I was . . . attacked. *Me violó*, Alex."

"Oh no, Lourdes . . ." Alex could feel the anger welling inside him. How could anyone hurt this person?

"Yes, a man from another village. He is now in prison in Sololá."

"Your father must have wanted to kill him."

"He was very angry, Alex. Yes. As I was, of course. And I also felt ashamed. I should not have been walking alone . . ."

"There is nothing for you to be ashamed about," said Alex, but she didn't seem to hear him.

"I even had a sponsor from the United States, a husband and wife who supported me all through my school. Now it will be hard for me to continue in school. How would they feel if they knew I had taken such a foolish risk after all the opportunity they have given me?"

"Lourdes, you must not think this way at all," pleaded Alex.

"Anyway, I must go." She collected a few things from around her parents' house. "I hope you feel much better, Alex."

"Thank you, Lourdes. I do feel better." He said it not just to be appreciative; he really did feel better.

"*A-dios*, Alex." She pronounced it slowly and deliberately to emphasize the literal meaning: go with God.

By later in the day Alex had mostly recovered and made the hike back down to San Pedro Necta, reflecting on the girl he had met in the *campo* and what she had told him. He joined the others at the hotel.

That night after dinner the students sat down together in Rich's room at Hotel Chinita to calculate Fernando's profit from his harvest: Altogether, Fernando's costs had amounted to $102 for 780 pounds of coffee cherries, what would become a one-hundred-pound sack of roasted beans. On the revenue side, each of Fernando's 2.5 hectares had about 2,500 coffee plants, and the yield of each hectare was about 17.6 hundred-pound sacks of roasted coffee. With a price on one-third of his crop from the co-op at $129 (of which one-quarter was marketed as fair trade) and $120 on the two-thirds of his crop he sold to the coyotes, this gave him an average price of $123 per sack, and an income of $924 for his entire crop. Added to the income of Fernando's family was $189 dollars he received during the last year from other odd jobs. That plus some remittances sent by his relatives who immigrated to Los Angeles allowed Fernando and Juana to stay out of debt and keep food on the table. Provided there were no emergencies, the family was just able to cover its bills.

CHAPTER 11

Angela

ANGELA WAS SWEATING AS THE STUDENTS COMPLETED THE mountain hike back up to Fernando's house. They had carried out some other surveys in the area, but this session would focus on background information, the history of his family in coffee cultivation. Juana greeted them affectionately, *"Buenos dias a los muchachos de California!"* Lourdes was working next to her, rolling dough to make tortillas.

"Buenos dias, Doña Juana." They exchanged the mutual kiss on right cheeks, laughing awkwardly as Lourdes and her mother tried not to touch the students with their doughy hands. "Thanks for taking care of this particular *muchacho*," said Sofia, motioning toward Alex.

"The patient behaved excellently," responded Lourdes a little shyly, looking at Alex.

"That's amazing," replied Angela, surprised. "What did you feed him?"

"Está Don Fernando?" asked Sofia, inquiring if Fernando was home. Fernando appeared shortly from the field. They sat again around the old table. Lourdes brought them each cups of *atol*.

Fernando sat down next to Angela. "And how are you finding Guatemala, *mi hija?*"

"*Bien, gracias,* Don Fernando," Angela answered, smiling and accepting the affectionate reference. The real answer, of course, was considerably more complicated. Every moment she spent inside a Guatemalan house was like a magic mirror that revealed more of the unsettling contrast between who she was and who she would have been, between her life as it was and as it would have been. This was the conflict within her heart. The conflict within her head was searching for the reasons why the contrast had to be so severe. As Fernando studied her face momentarily, she felt that somehow he sensed some of these things. But how could he?

Right now, however, it was time to continue interviews for the case study. "Fernando," began Sofia, "tell us a little about your family. How long has your family cultivated coffee?"

He began to laugh to himself and look up in the direction of the blackened underside of the corrugated iron that was both his ceiling and his roof. "A long time, *pues.* A very, very long time . . ." But the laugh that moistened his eyes began to fade, leaving behind just the moistened eyes. Angela studied his face. A deeper melancholy seemed to lie behind the answer to this question.

He looked down for a while and then returned his gaze directly at the students. "I wish all of you could have talked with my great-aunt Ester before she passed away. She was always telling my cousins and me stories about our ancestors. I think she told us some stories a thousand times. And when she got old, her memory of the old stories stayed, but she would forget how many times she had already told them to us. So she would enjoy telling them to us over and over, just like it was the first time all over again."

"What kind of stories?" asked Angela. Fernando looked at her and smiled, and then began.

—

April 1864

Isidro Ixtamperic lived during these early years of the nineteenth-century coffee boom with his wife, five sons, and three daughters. He was five generations removed from Fernando, the great-grandfather of Fernando's grandfather, and lived in a Mam-speaking village near the small indigenous town of San Felipe. The small town was in the Department of Retalhuleu, about sixty miles south of Huehuetenango, bordering the Pacific coast. Generations of his family had lived in the region, its balmy climate and fertile soil nearly ideal for subsistence agricultural plots of maize and beans. It was also land that was nearly ideal for coffee cultivation.

Isidro did not own coffee land, but worked the land of a ladino cultivator named Póncio Mendoza. The Mendoza land he worked was based on a habilitación from an advance given when Isidro needed money three and a half years ago. He needed money to buy medicine for one of his daughters suffering from tuberculosis. The child had died, but the debt remained to the Mendoza family, and well exceeded the supposed legal limit of fifteen pesos. Although in many ways Mendoza had been willing to provide for other needs of Isidro's family, the more he provided, the more Isidro's debt seemed to grow. After a while permanent debt and labor obligation simply became a way of life. As the *patrón*, Póncio Mendoza would provide, and the *peon* Isidro Ixtamperic would be obligated to him. It was a cycle that continued as predictably as one season followed the next.

With the demand for coffee surging in the rich countries of the world, Guatemalan ladinos and European immigrants flocked to the west to establish coffee plantations. Sensing the economic opportunity in the fertile land, coffee growers pressured the government to grant them access to indigenous ejido lands surrounding native towns. The government did this through a legal arrangement called the *censo*, by which commercial cultivators could legally lease the ejido land without violating previous statutes. In reality this practice had existed for decades, expanding under the production of cochineal, but it had been limited. The burgeoning coffee market had brought greater economic and political pressure on local indigenous communities to convert increasing amounts of their communal land to censo, but this pressure had been resisted by the local village council.

As a member of the council, Isidro Ixtamperic was summoned to a meeting one night to discuss the issue. Isidro arrived at the meeting and took his place on a knotted wooden bench. He glanced around the room at the concerned faces of the other members of the council. A low fire burned in the middle of the gathering, and a haze of smoke filled the meeting room. Santos Kayb'il, head of the council, nearly always wore a concerned look, but tonight his face was particularly forlorn. "Land-grabbing by the settlers under the censo increases," he informed the council, although this fact was already known to most. "The council must do something."

"Yes, but what?" responded Francisco, one of the older council members. "The national government supports anyone who wants to take ejido land under the censo. They will back the settlers with the militia. There is nothing we can do." The members of the council regarded Francisco's statement with suspicion. He had a modest-sized coffee plot himself. Some thought that he might be looking to expand his operation.

"To do nothing is not an option." Santos Kayb'il gazed sternly at Francisco. "Coffee has already taken our best hunting lands that have been with our people since before the Europeans. The settlers now defend this land like it is their own, and the government supports them. If it continues like this, we will leave our people with nothing."

The members of the council debated the issue, with some arguing for a call to action. Another council member suggested a truce with the ladino cultivators.

"A truce?" asked Santos Kayb'il. "Another truce that is only to be broken when the Europeans demand more land?" A truce had been forged two years before when the ladinos had demanded censo land with government backing. But after the truce, they refused to pay taxes or rent to the local municipality. They had even bought and sold ejido land between themselves, using titles in the exchange. This so outraged the local indigenous community that the council brought a protest to the Ministry of Government, threatening to hack the coffee plants to pieces with their machetes. The Ministry had finally brokered a compromise between the two parties in which the ladino cultivators agreed to limit their landholdings and pay rent on these lands to the municipality. The council felt like the agreement had finally been able to achieve peace in their time. But shortly thereafter, a governor carrying out an investigation of further complaints found that the only grower in the surrounding areas who was actually paying rent on his coffee land was the local Catholic priest.

Isidro knew that Santos Kayb'il had no stomach for another truce. He couldn't defend it to his people. Isidro sensed that the time had come for him to speak up at the meeting.

"We rise up," he said in a matter-of-fact tone, his head still bowed, then raised to look around the room. "We rise up and take what God has rightfully given us, what is rightfully ours. We take back all coffee land on which rent has not been paid since the truce."

"That would be, in fact, almost all of the land," noted one council member.

Isidro began to speak. "We will rise up and destroy the coffee that is on our lands, restore the lands for hunting." His voice was growing louder and more confident as he now looked squarely at each member of the council, even Santos Kayb'il. "We will restore them for producing our own food, and not fanciful drink for the Europeans."

After Isidro yielded the floor, Santos Kayb'il surveyed the room. There were some shouts of acclamation; others nodded in agreement.

"So it will be."

It was never clear which member of the council leaked word of the plan to the provincial administrator. But two days later, fifteen militia arrived at the house of Santos Kayb'il. One grabbed the throat of his wife as she answered the door.

"*Donde está Kayb'il?*" Speaking with a strong accent from Spain, a heavy officer drew his face about three inches from her own and demanded to know where her husband was.

"*Yo no sé,*" she answered, claiming she did not know, but terrified at the ladino militia.

"Are you lying to us?" said the officer. She stood there petrified, able to say nothing. They slapped her several times and threw her to the floor. "Check the field," he ordered.

There they found Santos Kayb'il about two hundred yards behind the house, hoeing in his milpa. The officer shouted sarcastically: "We have your wife. Would you like us to take her to the prison in Retalhuleu, or would you like to come in her place?"

"With what am I charged?" he had demanded to know.

The officer replied coldly: "Insurrection."

The militia followed this pattern for other houses of council members, but the ten-year-old son of another council member ran to Isidro's home.

"Isidro, Isidro!" he yelled in Mam, running as he approached the home. "They're taking away the council members to jail! They took *papa*, they took all the council!" He was crying, breathless, and hardly able to speak, but appeared relieved that he was able to reach Isidro before the militia.

"Who?" asked Isidro.

"I don't know, ladino soldiers with rifles. I'm not sure. They have Santos Kayb'il. They're taking all of them away in wagons."

Isidro grabbed his wife and children and all of the food that he could carry in a small sheet, which was about all the food that their house contained. They fled into the forest. One of his daughters returned to town after several days to ask for food from family friends. She returned with food and word that the militia had departed and were no longer actively searching for members of the council.

In total the militia had rounded up more than sixty indigenous men from San Felipe and neighboring towns: members of the council, and friends of members of the council who had scuffled with the militia as they loaded the council members in wagons, as well as the friends of these friends who fought back as their friends were being taken away. All were shackled and hauled to the regional prison in Retalhuleu.

While Isidro's family returned home, Isidro helped spread the word throughout San Felipe and other neighboring indigenous towns: "Tomorrow night, we assemble to free the prisoners and take back the censo land as our own!"

The next night arrived, and Isidro Ixtamperic had been able to amass a group of two hundred men from San Felipe and the nearby indigenous towns of San Francisco Zapotitlán and El Palmar. Many rode on horses. Most carried torches and the same machetes that they used during labor in the fields. Some carried slings with rocks, and a few had rifles. Many had been drinking heavily. The smells of liquor, the sweat of horses, and burning pitch filled the night air. Years of indignation, suppression, and abuse were now boiling over and manifesting themselves in a fuming horde.

Isidro raised his voice over the roar of the mob, dispatching parts of the group to nearby coffee plantations. The major part of the contingent, and those on horseback, he took with himself. Many in the contingent were coffee field hands who had labored beside Isidro under the habilitación. They headed first to the coffee plantation of Póncio Mendoza.

Mendoza allowed a handful of his mozos to live in a shack in front of his property, partly as protection against such an occurrence, but that night his guards had been drinking heavily and were fast asleep. They never heard the mob as it approached the plantation, but Mendoza heard it and from an upstairs window saw the horses and their torch-bearing riders assembled at the plantation gate. He attempted to usher his wife quickly through the back door. But as she delayed a few moments to collect some jewelry for their escape, it was too late. The mob had encircled the house. They smashed in the front door, charged through the house, and found a terrified Mendoza and his wife hiding in their bedroom. They hauled them out into the yard in front of the porch.

Isidro drew up to Mendoza as the flickering light of the torches illuminated both of their faces. Isidro's expression burned with anger, while Mendoza looked horror-struck at seeing his docile mozo so enraged. Mendoza recognized some of his own workers in the crowd and pleaded with them, offering to cancel their debts, even offering them coffee land.

"*Usted no comprendes, mi patrón.* We toil for you daily to repay the habilitación with our labor, and somehow we work and work and always remain in your debt. But you never pay the censo to our community for our land. Not even one time have you paid it. No, Señor Mendoza, in reality it is *you* who owe *us.* And we have come now to collect on your debt."

As Mendoza continued to plead, they forced the couple to a nearby tree and lynched the husband and wife side by side. They returned to the house and looted their possessions, taking money and jewelry, anything they could carry. When they left, they set fire to everything, leaving the two solitary bodies hanging in the flickering orange light of the burning house.

After this the mob rode off to the regional prison twelve miles down the road in Retalhuleu. But neighbors had spread the word rapidly about the lynching of the Mendozas, and the news quickly reached the local municipality. Receiving a tip that the mob was headed for the regional prison in Retalhuleu, local officials wired a telegraph message to Guatemala City beckoning for aid. Officials in the capital then quickly telegraphed an order to a nearby military base to immediately dispatch a company of soldiers to the prison.

The central government had purposely designed this rapid-response system for such a contingency. And it was something that Isidro and his company had not anticipated. A force of several hundred government soldiers was quickly marshaled and awaited the mob at the prison gate. When they arrived at the prison, the soldiers easily quelled the drunken mob, detaining the leaders. Isidro Ixtamperic was identified and arrested as the ringleader, and shortly after, he was sentenced to death by firing squad on the compound of the Retalhuleu prison on one count of arson and two counts of murder.

But his name remained a legend among the Mam for decades.

CHAPTER 12

Alex

IT WAS LATE AFTERNOON BY THE TIME FERNANDO FINISHED the story. It dawned on Alex that he had been so wrapped up in it that he hardly moved, and his right leg had fallen asleep. He looked over at Angela, who had seemed to latch onto every word of Fernando's narrative. Alex got up to stretch, feeling the pain of the pins and needles as the blood circulation returned.

"Lourdes, *mi hija,* would you fetch me some eggs at the *tienda?*" asked Juana.

"*Si, Mama.*"

Alex explained to Fernando and Juana that he was a bit hungry and would like to get a snack at the tienda, and would they mind if he accompanied their daughter? Regrettably at this particularly inopportune moment, it seemed the idea did not translate well. Fernando gave Alex a quizzical look as the room burst out in giggles.

Alex looked over at Sofia for help. "Sofia, tell me what did I just say?"

Sofia looked at him. "Unfortunately, it was something very close to 'Do you mind if I am hungry for your daughter?'"

"*Estoy extremadamente embarazado,*" he confessed to the room. The giggles were now replaced by a thunderous laughter.

"Alex?" said Sofia, looking genuinely sorry for him.

"Yes?"

"You just announced that you are exceedingly pregnant."

Little Ema's laugh was the loudest and most contagious. Alex looked helplessly at the petite nine-year-old girl who couldn't help laughing uncontrollably at the foreign man who did and said so many silly things. Lourdes was the one to rescue Alex, dragging him by the arm out the door in the direction of the tienda, shaking her head, still laughing herself and wiping the tears from her eyes.

The tienda was about half a mile away. It was a tiny store owned by a family that operated it out of the side of their house, selling food, soda, and bottled water. They purchased their items, and Lourdes asked him, "Do you want to walk down to the *arroyo*? It is quite beautiful; I would like to show it to you." It was a little creek not far away.

They sat down on a fallen tree, watching and listening to the water trickle over the round, polished rocks in the arroyo. Ferns adorned the banks of the creek, and a gentle moss covered the logs and boulders that surrounded the water, creating a lush carpet of green everywhere around them that smelled of fresh forest. An orange sunset provided a canvas for the shadowed outline of some willows that hung over the water. They sat in silence for a while, enjoying the sensory delights of the arroyo.

Finally Alex asked, "How do you feel about the baby?"

"God gives life, Alex. Sometimes even through sin. But he has a bigger plan. Even my family has had to learn this."

"Your family must be eager to see justice done to this man."

"I had to forgive him, Alex."

"You what?"

"After it happened, I went to his cell. It was hard for me at first to look at him, I must confess to you. But I forgave him. I have myself been forgiven; it was the right thing to do."

"And?" Alex asked.

"He cried."

"But you choose to have this baby. Why?"

"There is a purpose in every life, Alex. The baby will be loved by all of us. In the end with my family there is always grace and love."

Alex thought for a moment. "Your family is different than mine, Lourdes."

"How?" she asked.

"If such a thing should happen to my sister, my father or mother would of course offer to pay for an abortion. But if she for some reason chose to keep the baby, they would not have supported her as much as your family. She would probably live alone somewhere with the baby. Somewhere in Amsterdam, somewhere in an apartment," he guessed.

"That apartment sounds like a lonely place," said Lourdes.

Alex reflected for a moment. "I believe my family was a lonely place."

Lourdes glanced down at Alex's arm. "But I'm not sure you would like being in my family. They do not like tattoos," she smiled.

"Oh, that. I got the sea serpent with some friends after a party. Let's say I was not in a very discriminating frame of mind. Do you like it?"

"No," she said, still smiling at him just the same.

Here it was again, the mysterious separation of transgression from tenderness.

Alex laughed, helped her up off the log, and they headed back to the house.

CHAPTER 13

ANGELA NOTICED HOW THE RAIN IN GUATEMALA DIDN'T fall randomly throughout the day and night like it did in California. The months that North Americans call summertime—June, July, and August—are what Guatemalans call winter. She learned that it was not because the weather is colder during this time, for the temperature remains virtually the same year-round, but because this is when it rains. Ninety percent of Guatemala's rainfall occurs from April to October. She became used to the regular pattern, the rain starting its pitter-pat like clockwork at about two every afternoon, and gradually increasing in its intensity until about four. About four thirty, the sun typically made a brief reappearance and then set quickly around six o'clock in its vertical arc perpendicular to the horizon. Combined with the extensive comida that everyone unhurriedly ingested with their family around one o'clock, it created a substantially reduced workday for the average person. But for students with a limited number of weeks to complete their fieldwork, it made for soggy afternoons and wet clipboards.

Most of their time each day was spent walking the steep paths between the *fincas* of coffee growers, taking surveys of coffee production costs, household data, and coffee yields. Despite the rain, Angela enjoyed this time in the outdoors, free from the burdens of her problem sets and papers and the assorted anxieties created by the constantly impending deadlines of graduate school. The coffee growers were generally cooperative and found the students to be a novelty. Many appeared to take a curious interest in the students' interest in them. And outfitted with her Gortex parka and heavy leather hiking boots that she had wisely purchased for the trip, the warm rain didn't bother her much.

After a month of surveying, interviewing, and compiling coffee production statistics, the students had collected coffee data from over a hundred members of the cooperative. One grower belonging to the cooperative, Guillermo Ixicuat, had been randomly chosen for a case study, and lived about fifteen miles outside of the town. The last ten miles of the trek were impassible by jeep or even by horse or mule, except with a very experienced rider, and so had to be taken on foot via a narrow walking path through the high jungle. The four set out before dawn that day under the steady guidance of José Ernesto.

Alex noted the size of Rich's pack, which was quite hefty, especially since they planned to return that night. "Rich, do you plan to leave us and continue hiking all of the way to Mexico with that backpack?"

"Yes, didn't you guys know? Rich is carrying out his own simulated experiment on illegal migration by foot from Guatemala to the Tijuana border," said Sofia.

"Hey, Rich, what have you got in that gi-normous *mochilla* of yours?" asked Angela, piling it on.

"Stuff," Rich replied, his mind apparently on something else despite the teasing.

"Like what kind of stuffs?" probed Alex curiously.

"Like stuffs we might *need*." He added a little extra twang to the last couple of words to indicate the tinge of annoyance. "Funny how same people accusing me of hauling the county hospital around are usually the ones later needing meds for their tummies or moleskin for their blisters."

"Keep an eye out for snakes," José-Ernesto said as they left their four-wheel-drive vehicle and walked along the narrow path.

"Snakes?" asked Sofia. She turned to Angela. "I like almost everything about fieldwork, except . . . . that," she said. Angela looked at her face. It was clear she wasn't joking.

José-Ernesto led the group with a machete, hacking bushes, vines, and small branches away from the trail as they made their way up the side, through the wet brush, and over the pass of a large mountain. Angela wasn't sure if José-Ernesto had made the comment about the snakes because there really were snakes to be concerned about or just to liven up the hike a little.

"Couldn't we have randomly chosen some growers a little closer to San Pedro?" Angela asked Rich.

"Well, if we would have done that, it wouldn't have really been a random sample, would it?" replied Rich. "Being lazy and cutting corners. Great way to introduce bias in your study. You think living way out here in the bushwhacks ain't correlated with impact?" Angela got the point, and there was a pause in the conversation for a while.

"Are there really snakes here?" she asked outside the earshot of Sofia, and in English so José-Ernesto wouldn't be offended. To be honest, she was a little concerned too.

"Are you kidding, Junior Trekker? You got your different coral snakes that are all more than plenty venomous, your coffee snake—bright red as a fire truck but luckily not nearly as poisonous as it looks—just freaks the heck out of you when you come across it by surprise. Then you got your Guatemalan palm pit viper that likes to bite barefoot people between their toes and sink its venom right there in that little tender spot. And that's forgetting to mention the *barba amarilla*, or yellow beard, that'll drop a full-grown man stone hard cold to the ground with a single strike to the leg. Probably what we've got slithering around up here is your common Godman's montane pit viper, which the Mayans call the *Sheta*. Not quite as venomous as the yellow beard, but let's just say you wouldn't want it curling up with you in your sleeping bag."

Angela was surprised Rich possessed such a wide-ranging knowledge of Guatemalan snakes, and now a very large part of her wished she hadn't brought it up. But it gave her more confidence that José-Ernesto knew what he was doing.

Less than an hour later, Alex and Sofia were engaged in a conversation, walking slightly ahead of José-Ernesto on a relatively spacious part of the trail. Alex was first in the line of hikers with Sofia following right behind. Suddenly everyone in the back of the group heard a yell from Alex up front. Then Sofia screamed and yelled something Angela couldn't understand in Spanish. Angela knew immediately what it was.

Sofia sprang back away quickly from the snake and immediately looked like she was about to pass out. Angela saw the brown snake with black spots that Alex had casually stepped over in his shorts. It now was raising its head to strike him on his bare leg. The viper missed Alex, extending its lean body across the trail after the attempt. José-Ernesto quickly ran to the front, expertly trapping the Godman's montane pit viper directly behind the head with the V-shaped notch at the bottom of his walking stick. Pinning the snake to the ground with the stick in his left hand, he reached blindly behind his back for his machete with his right hand. The back end of the snake flicked and thrashed about from behind the notch. José-Ernesto raised up the machete and slashed off the viper's head, kicking it into the woods with his boot.

José-Ernesto grinned. "*Sí, Angela, existen colebras en Guatemala,*" he said. There *are* snakes in Guatemala. "And my English is little better than you thinks." He finished off the second sentence in English proudly as he flung the snake's headless body off the trail with his walking stick.

Rich laughed. "Lefty, it's too bad there wasn't an Olympic high bar right there when that snake was slithering between your ankles. After that jump, you'd have been on the center of that medal podium with the Dutch national anthem playing!"

He said this chuckling to himself as he and Angela passed by the area on the trail where Alex and Sofia had encountered the snake. Glancing down just to the right of the trail, he spotted a writhing mass of Godman's pit vipers next to a rotten log, many of them not more than a foot long, but with a few larger ones that looked like they meant business. Angela saw them too, but Rich was closer and it seemed to have more effect on him. "Aaaahhh!" he yelled. "There's a whole freakin' nest of them!—Run!" They sprinted, Rich with the metal canteen and drinking cups flailing and clanking from their straps on his backpack, nearly passing the rest of the group as they scrambled down the trail.

All of them stood breathless after the sprint. Sofia sat down on a tree stump, looking pale. She fumbled in her backpack for an inhaler she kept for her asthma. The combination of the snakes and the running had been too much and clearly caused a flare-up. Angela walked over, sat down, and put her arm around her.

"Thank you, Angela," she said.

Alex was also gasping for air. Even so, he was nearly doubled over laughing, a tear running down his cheek. Finally, he said, "Rich, you . . . would have won the gold medal too . . . but instead of high jump, for the 100 meter sprint! You really got that extra tire cycling very, very fast."

"Well, let's just say incentives matter, and leave it at that," he replied. "You okay, Sof?"

Sofia nodded without much expression.

After several breaks for water, but none for food, they reached the house just after noon. The house was a dilapidated adobe with two small rooms, surrounded by milpa fields, where beans were sown among the maize. A couple of clucking chickens chased each other in the yard. The predominant smells were of a pile of weeds smoldering to the side of the house, the mild stench of chicken droppings, and, on the positive side, the aroma of fresh tortillas being cooked on an open grill. About two or three hectares of coffee lay behind the beans and maize, planted on the side of a mountain, the coffee stopping only when it became far too inclined to cultivate.

"Don Guillermo!" José-Ernesto paused and listened for an answer. "Don Guillermo!" He called for him and strode up to the front door. In place of Don Guillermo, it was Don Guillermo's wife who greeted them. "Ah, Doña Beatriz, *bueños dias!*" She seemed taken aback by the approaching group. Angela got the feeling it was unusual for Doña Beatriz to receive spontaneous foreign guests at her home. She looked around and the loneliness of rural isolation weighed on Angela; it brought forth feelings of sympathy in her for Doña Beatriz and others who lived in dilapidated hovels located miles from even the tiniest village.

"Doña Beatriz, these are students from the United States who have come to study the coffee growing of our cooperative members. Would they be able to talk with you and Don Guillermo?" asked José-Ernesto.

Doña Beatriz apparently did not speak much Spanish, so José-Ernesto switched into Quiché. Even so, they heard her say, *"No está."* He wasn't there.

"He's not here?" asked Rich. "Well, when will señor return?" He was obviously a little frustrated after walking ten miles through brush and snakes to find that the intended source of their interview wasn't around. Doña Beatriz rattled off something in Quiché to José-Ernesto.

"She says she doesn't know when he'll be back," José-Ernesto said to the group in Spanish.

"Well, how come?" asked Rich.

"Because her husband is in Houston," José-Ernesto responded.

"In Houston?" asked Angela incredulously.

"Yes. Since four months ago."

"Why Houston?" asked Rich. "Have an errand to run at the strip mall?" José-Ernesto roughly translated the question back to Doña Beatriz, and she responded at some length.

"She says he just couldn't make coffee growing work anymore, and their family was starting to starve." Angela felt deflated, not only for the long hike that now seemed to be for nothing, but also for the thought of a coffee grower, a fair trade coffee grower no less, literally being starved off his land. She looked again at his coffee plants across the field of milpa. Most of them were scraggly, unpruned, and untended.

Beatriz began to talk to the group now in broken Spanish. "He just couldn't keep it up this year, the coffee. Too much work. Not enough *plata*." She used the Spanish slang for money, rubbing her thumb against her index finger. "In old times, prices they were good. Now we suffer too much. Nobody remains here to help harvest the crop. The workers, they are also in Houston. Live in the same place, many together. They say it is better there, and my husband, he says one day we will live there too, and our children will grow up to speak English. Don Guillermo sends me money by Western Union. I pick it up in the town every month."

Sofia was curious about this. "How many of the men who have coffee around here are in Houston now?"

"All—all in Houston," she responded.

"All of them? What do they do?" probed Sofia.

"They do everything, everything that the *Norte Americanos* don't want to do because they are too rich. They build their houses, they paint their houses, they dig their gardens. The women I know there have jobs caring for little children. Guillermo works washing cups and dishes in a café."

"So Don Guillermo has moved down the value chain in the coffee business," Rich noted in English to the others.

"I'm sorry I cannot help you answer questions about my husband's coffee. I turn our acreage over to a neighbor. He pays me a little plata so he can take whatever the plants produce. He works little, however, on our plot. Would you like some tortillas for lunch? I'm sorry, my youngest son is sick, and I have not had proper time for meals. Any of you are a doctor?" she asked in a faint hope.

Rich answered, "Well, a couple of us are studying to be doctors of a kind, but unfortunately not the kind that would be ideal to you right now. But I have some background. Mind if I take a look at him?"

Angela looked around at the children playing around them. None of them looked particularly healthy. One boy near them, who looked like he had a bad cold, was chasing his little sister around them with a stick.

"Boy looks like he's hosting a banana slug race under his nose," commented Rich to Angela, who responded with a wince. She joined Alex and Sofia as they walked toward the house to watch the improvised examination.

The sicker boy looked to be about four years old. He had dark circles under his dull, lifeless eyes. His skin was pale and he had blisters on the inside of his lower lip, and crusted blood was under his nose and in his underpants.

Angela watched Rich as he examined the boy; she had never seen an economist interact with a suffering child. And what seemed to move Rich were statistics. Statistics, she had heard him tell Alex, "are the plural of anecdotes," and when properly handled, come very close to the real truth. Anecdotes and individual stories can mislead—"too often just outliers—that's why they're interesting." But perhaps there was something different in Rich's face as he looked down at the boy, this one boy, this anecdote.

Rich extracted from his backpack the formidable medical kit that he had used in his former life as a young paramedic, and took out a thermometer, a small blood pressure monitor, and a miniature stethoscope. He gently reached down and took the boy's temperature and some other vital signs. He called over to Sofia, but Angela and Alex followed.

"Sof, come here a sec." Sofia walked over closer to him. He talked in a low voice to her in English. "This boy's got a belly full of worms."

"Are you sure?" she asked.

"Positive. Got all the signs. Wretched beasts are slithering around his intestines and eatin' up all his vitamins."

"Do you have anything in your kit that could help him?" Sofia asked.

"Well, just happen to have some albendazole with me. That ought to take care of the little freeloaders. He's a trifle young, but I'm going to give him a whole tablet, and that ought to do it. Better in my opinion than underdoing it."

Rich explained the problem in Spanish to Beatriz. "Señora, I think I know what is making your boy sick. It's *lombrices*."

"Lombrices?" She was shocked. "No!"

"*Sí*, señora, but I have a pill that will make him better. Do you want me to give it to him? It's good medicine. He might get a little tummy ache, but there is little risk."

"Of course. What will happen, Doctor?" Beatriz inquired.

"Well, it's going to be hard for me to describe this in a delicate manner, but in a day or two, he's going to anally expel a whole bunch of worms that's going to look like a big plate of spaghetti . . ."

"Rich!" Sofia slapped him on the arm.

"I think I'm going to be sick," said Angela under her breath.

Thankfully for most of the group in the house, Beatriz didn't know about spaghetti, so Sofia explained to her slowly in Spanish what were to be the likely effects of the medicine without the culinary details. José-Ernesto retranslated into Quiché so that everything was clear.

"Now, you've got to make sure this youngster is wearing shoes every time he goes outside, or the worms will come back," admonished Rich. "Worms usually get inside little kids through the bottom of their feet from fecal matter in the soil, and this isn't going to do a bit of good in the long term if this boy is shoeless. Now you take some of that Western Union money and run right down to the little shoe store in San Pedro and get this boy some shoes, *me comprende?*"

She nodded. *"Gracias, Doctor."*

"Well, I ain't a doctor, but unfortunately I'm the best you've got right now," he said.

"Sí, Doctor, gracias."

Rich looked down at the boy and leaned down and whispered something in his ear. The boy looked back at Rich and nodded; the beginnings of a smile appeared on his face.

Angela asked Rich as they walked away from the bed, "What did you tell him?"

"That his mama promised she would buy him a new pair of shoes, but to keep bugging her relentlessly until she did. Boy seemed to like that idea."

Doña Beatriz brought them over to the part of the house that served as a kitchen and fried up a dozen tortillas, on each of which she placed a generous ladle of beans. The students were famished by this point and appreciated the lunch, yet aware that they might have intestinal battles of their own to wage once it was over.

During lunch Sofia asked Beatriz more about her husband's

decision to migrate to the United States. Beatriz responded, "The money he sends, it is good. He earns eleven dollars in one hour cleaning up tables in the café. That is what he earns in maybe two days here working the coffee."

"It must be difficult for you to have your husband away in the United States," said Angela.

"Well, I'll be honest. Financially, we are much better with him away sending us the money. But I miss him greatly. This is not a place for a woman to be living alone with her children. Guillermo is a good man, and is very frugal. He does not spend the money he earns on gambling. He lives with three other men from our area in a small apartment in Houston and sends me much of his wages so I can buy things we need. But . . . I understand the temptations of men. This is what is my worry sometimes."

"That he might be unfaithful to you?" asked Angela sympathetically.

"Sí. That is the thing that worries me the most. Some temptations are too much to bear even for a very good man, if he is very far away for a long time."

José-Ernesto interjected, "Many rural families thrive financially on the remittances from illegal immigration to the States, but there are many other insidious results from it. For example, networks of narco-traffickers to and from the United States from Central America have evolved through the immigrations that began in the 1980s with the civil wars. It has led to organized crime seizing influence over much of our government and police. The poverty of our countries sets the stage for entry into this lucrative criminal activity. It's the irony of the immensity and power of the United States and its proximity to us. It is a great source of both opportunity and problems."

Doña Beatriz continued, "Yes, we need the money, but my four children are growing up without a father. It is sad and causes many problems. The children without fathers here often get into trouble when they become older."

After lingering awhile after lunch, the students bade good-bye to Doña Beatriz and headed back down the trail to town. "Thank you, Doctor Rich, for helping my little boy. *Gracias a Dios por su visita*." She thanked him warmly as they left and handed him a sack of extra tortillas.

"Migration is depleting this countryside of men," Sofia said as they marched back down the trail.

"Caused mainly by poverty?" asked Angela.

"Yes, by the huge difference in wages, but this is just the surface of it."

Angela wasn't content to understand only the surface of it. "What lies underneath the surface?" she asked.

They conversed as they ambled down the trail. "A professor of mine explained it to us once this way: Capital and labor roam the economic landscape in search of one other. Labor always wants to move to places where capital is abundant, and capital is always seeking out places where labor is abundant. The two are constantly chasing each other around the globe. New capital makes workers more productive, and higher worker productivity leads to higher wages. Higher wages lure in workers from other places, and there you have migration."

"And the opposite side of migration is multinationals coming down to poor countries to chase down cheap labor and exploit it," added Alex. Angela just shook her head.

They had finished walking up a steep hill. They were all sweating heavily. Sofia's asthma was acting up again and she stopped to unzip her backpack and pull out her inhaler. She closed her lips around it, spritzed it a couple of times into her mouth, and inhaled a deep breath. She exhaled slowly while taking in the resplendent vista of the gorge from the trail, and resumed the discussion.

"Actually, the vast majority of it doesn't go to poor countries. Although many people in poor countries probably wish it did," she said as she tossed the inhaler back into the pocket of her backpack and rezipped it. "Capital doesn't necessarily want to go where wages are lowest. Otherwise all of the foreign investment would be in places like Haiti and Bangladesh. Most of it goes to rich countries where productivity is highest."

"Except for the dirty jobs," said Alex.

"Perhaps," she replied.

There was silence for a while as they continued on the trail back to San Pedro Necta, mostly walking downhill now, which was a blessing for the return. Angela's feet were starting to ache. Clouds had formed and it was cooling down as it usually did in the early afternoon, but that also meant it would rain soon. The path led them along the side of an enormous mountain with a gorge dropping two thousand feet below. The view was spectacular and they could see several of the volcanoes of western Guatemala in the distance. Rich was talking with José-Ernesto about something as they walked together in the front while the other three walked behind.

As they reached about the halfway point, the clouds began to open up. Angela looked at her watch. Two o'clock, right on schedule. The students put on their parkas and pulled over their hoods. It was a warm rain, and the sound of a billion small droplets crashing to the ground echoed across the mountains, interspersed with the cry of soaring birds in the canyon retreating to their nests. As they looked across the landscape from their mountain vista, layers of mist and clouds produced a contrast of subsequently lighter and lighter mountains and volcanoes as the view faded into the distance toward the Pacific coast, moving from green to dark green, then to gray and finally to off-white. The air smelled sweet and clean, scented with particles of dust from the forest floor kicked up by the first droplets of rain.

For the last five miles they hiked through mud, and the conversation stilled. This was partly because the students were tired, now having hiked nearly twenty miles for the day, and partly because the noise of the rain muffled the words of a person speaking in front. Yet in the quiet slogging, a peaceable contentment reigned over the group.

—

A few days after their mountain hike, Angela and Rich visited another one of the coffee growers on their list, Maximo Pérez, who they learned also happened to be one of the local growers who owned a pulping machine. Many of the cooperatives, intermediaries, and other buyers preferred to purchase coffee from growers in parchment form, with the cherry removed but the beans still encased in the delicate parchment skins.

Angela and Rich greeted him as his wife summoned him from the house.

Maximo was a bulging middle-aged man, of both Spanish and Mayan descent, whose diligent wife was clearly not neglecting her job of providing him with a regular supply of delicious meals. Unlike many of the other growers who lived in adobe houses, his was made of concrete block. Maximo possessed one of the larger coffee operations in San Pedro Necta. There was a Toyota pickup in the front yard and a small satellite dish on one corner of his tile roof. By now Angela understood: these were telltale signs of membership in the Guatemalan rural middle class.

His plantation and machines were located not far from Fernando's, and so it was Maximo's pulping machine that Fernando used with his own harvest. Angela saw that he had forearms like ham hocks. As she moved forward to shake hands, she was overpowered by Maximo's brawny grip and the scent of his aggressive aftershave and hair gel.

After going through the standard list of questions, they asked him how the machine worked. Maximo was like many Guatemalan men, who could be shy when first approached with a question, but once engaged with a comfortable subject, often yielded an enchanting fountain of information.

"Well," he began, "I first must convey to you what I deeply believe is the right way and the wrong way to process the coffee cherry."

"Let's start with the wrong way," Rich broke in with a grin.

"Yes, the wrong way . . ." It seemed as if Maximo had prepared to discuss the right way first. He cleared his throat and began, "The wrong way—in my opinion, of course—is what is called the dry method. This is when a farmer takes the cherries and sorts them by hand or with a screen. Then he spreads them out in the open air, sometimes on trestles and sometimes just on the ground, for anywhere from ten to thirty days. By then, if the grower is lucky and it doesn't rain, the beans have lost almost 90 percent of their moisture, and they are ready to be shelled."

"So why is the dry method the wrong way?" asked Angela.

"Well, it works all right when you know you won't get any rain. And it works all right when you know exactly when to shell the dry cherries, but this leaves your quality to chance. If you let them dry too much, you get cracked beans. And for buyers, a cracked bean is a bad bean. If you don't let them dry enough, or if it rains too much, you can get mildew, fungus, or other bad things. *Esto no me gusta.*" He obviously didn't like the dry method.

"Is that partly because you own one of the local pulping machines that use the wet method?" asked Rich. Angela cringed inside a little at Rich's unremitting predisposition for directness.

"I am not biased because I own a pulping machine, Señor Rich. I own a pulping machine because I am biased!"

"Touché," responded Rich, smiling at him as he took down notes.

But he obviously had taken Rich's accusation of bias to heart and felt that he needed to justify his stance more fully. "With the wet method you need a lot of water. No water, and you are stuck with the dry method. But if you have water, you immerse the cherries in a tank. And here is the beautiful part: the good cherries sink to the bottom, but the bad, unripe ones float to the top. This makes the sorting easy. Then the pulping machine pops the seeds through a screen, separating them from the husks and the pulp. The pulp actually makes excellent fertilizer too. It takes less than two days, and you end up with higher quality beans in less time. This is why I prefer it."

"But isn't it more expensive than the dry method?" asked Rich.

"Yes," he maintained, "*pero vale la pena.*" It was worth the trouble. "The only people who use the dry method around here are very poor people, or people who don't know what they're doing, *en mi opinion,* of course."

"What do you charge the other growers for pulping?" asked Rich.

"Ten or twelve *quetzelitos* per sack," Maximo replied. It was about a dollar-fifty. "There are others who will do it for this price if I tried to charge much more."

Angela could see that this was clearly not a major profit center along the value chain. They would have to look elsewhere to see where all Fernando's profit was going.

"*Gracias,* Don Maximo." Angela and Rich each exchanged a final bone-crushing handshake with Maximo, and they walked down the road to interview their next grower.

CHAPTER 14

From her new vantage point in the barn, the young woman could make out the officer with a heavy mustache at the opposite end of the village. He wore the uniform of an army lieutenant. His voice was like the growl of a rabid dog as he snarled orders through a megaphone to the villagers who had sought refuge in the church. It was not her church, but it was the church of many of her friends in the village, the church of the *evangelicos*. Maybe those seeking refuge in the church thought that the soldiers would have orders not to kill people in such a church. The president was an evangelico. Would the president allow the army to kill members of his own church? Of this, the young woman was not sure.

She decided to return to her place behind the feeding trough. If the soldiers looked in the barn, perhaps they wouldn't see that there was space behind it to hide. Perhaps they would be in a hurry and search other places. She prayed that this might be the case.

As she nursed her baby in the hay, the thoughts of the young woman returned to Alberto. She and Mildred had asked Alberto many questions as he was recovering from his wounds, and he had told them much about his experience as a guerilla fighter. Why did he tell them these things? Perhaps he wanted them to sympathize with the guerillas? She didn't know. With a warning that they should never tell anyone, Alberto told them how they would live in the forest, where they would get supplies, how they would obtain food. He even told them where they hid, and how they came to know where the government would look for them. There were informants in the government, he explained, those who sympathized with the plight of the people. The young woman didn't understand much about how the government worked, but Alberto had told them how these people in the government had been very useful to the insurgency.

One time, he explained, they received word from one of these informants, a man named Felipe Perez. Señor Perez had told them about a military exercise that would be conducted by government troops. He even told them when and where it would happen. Alberto told them how his platoon carefully prepared to engage the enemy the night after the exercise when all the troops would be tired. They brought extra ammunition into the battle so they would not run out. They practiced exactly how they would fight, and how they would kill as many of the enemy as possible. They had surprised the government troops that night, firing shells into their tents while they slept after the day of hard exercises. Usually the guerrillas would flee from the government troops. This time they watched the government troops flee from them, into the jungle. And into the jungle they chased them, shooting many in the back as some ran helplessly in their underwear. It was a great night for the insurgency, he told them excitedly, a proud night. Alberto shared many secret stories like this with them.

Sometimes Alberto would linger with her after Mildred would say good night. It wasn't often that a peasant woman who made her living tending coffee felt worthy of attention from such a brave fighter. They would sit by the place they had prepared for him to sleep in the shack behind their house. It was the shack where they kept food and hay for their animals. They would sit and Alberto would talk and she would listen. She listened to his stories late into the night and shared some of them with Mildred the next day. Some, but not all.

Mildred was her best friend, and she knew that Mildred only had one fault. It was difficult for Mildred to keep exciting thoughts inside her, especially when she knew something important that others didn't. And the young woman learned while Mildred was washing clothes at the river with some of the other women, she could not resist the urge to tell them some of the exciting stories they had been told by Alberto. The young woman felt nervous when she learned that Mildred had told the others some of Alberto's secret stories. But Mildred assured her that the women understood they mustn't tell a soul; it was to be kept in confidence, and she had received assurances.

The young woman also understood the temptation

to share Alberto's secret stories. In fact, she had told one or two women herself, of course only very trustworthy women. But telling these secret stories made her feel good. Only an important woman would be privy to such information. Yes, Alberto had told them much about the guerrillas. Perhaps he had told them too much.

—

Alex

Fernando and Juana had invited the students to eat breakfast with them on a Saturday. Alex was looking forward to the promised meal: papaya from the coast, fresh eggs, *frijoles*, handmade tortillas, and some of Juana's best goat cheese. They arrived at the door, and Ema, who was preparing the breakfast with her mother, greeted them with an enthusiastic wave.

They sat in the main room and talked for a while as Alex shared the story with Ema and Lourdes about their hike to try to visit Guillermo Ixicuat, about the snakes and how loud Sofia had screamed and how high he and Rich had jumped. This made the sisters laugh, and it reminded Alex how much he liked to hear Lourdes laugh.

Juana had joined the conversation and one of her small grandchildren slowly emerged from behind Juana's skirt, seemingly entranced by something about Alex. As they continued to talk, the boy walked over and touched him on one of his arms resting on the wooden armrest of his chair. Focused on the conversation, nobody except Alex noticed at first as the boy examined it closely and then began stroking it slowly and curiously, back and forth. Alex sat there patiently with his arm on the wooden armrest, slightly self-conscious, but more amused by the little boy's fascination. Suddenly the boy's interest in Alex's arm caught the attention of the group, and they began to laugh.

"He's stroking that thing like it's his new pet hamster," said Rich.

"*Es el pelo de su brazo*," laughed Juana. It was the hair on his arms.

"He must not have seen hairy arms before," said Sofia.

The boy was also fascinated with the tattoo of a sea serpent on Alex's right wrist.

"You can touch it," said Alex. "It won't bite." Now the focus of unwanted attention, the little boy shyly retreated back to Ema, his young aunt.

Alex noticed that Lourdes was beginning to show just a little bit, and he went over to her and offered to help her cut the papaya.

"In Guatemala men do not help women in the kitchen. It is considered unmanly," she informed him.

"I think werewolf arms here has built up some credit in the manhood department," shouted Rich from across the room as he looked for a place to stretch out. "Just keep the hair out of the papayas . . . *por favor.*"

"You know, I think I could become comfortable with this," said Lourdes. "Do the European women expect that you will help them in the kitchen?"

Alex considered the question. "Well, I have never been married, of course, but I think if husbands never help with cooking and chores, the women where I come from get mad and call them lazy. In fact, I think I remember my mother calling my father that a number of times when I was little, before they got divorced."

"They got divorced because your father didn't work enough in the kitchen? That would not happen here." Lourdes looked puzzled. "Is that common among Europeans?" she asked.

"Well, I think it was more than issues about kitchen work. Unfortunately, my father began to find other women more interesting to him than my mother, one woman in particular. And yes, it is unfortunately a little bit common," said Alex.

"I'm sorry for you and your family. Here the men are sometimes unfaithful, but the women never divorce them," Lourdes noted to him.

"If the men know that they will never divorce them, is that making it more likely they are to cheat?" asked Alex.

"Not if they are faithful Christians," responded Lourdes. "Men who are faithful Christians respect women and do not have relations before they are married to them. And they do not cheat afterwards."

"I suppose that is true, but we all do make mistakes," observed Alex.

"Yes, but that is a very *big* mistake."

"Isn't your religion sufficiently large to have enough..." He fumbled for the word in Spanish. "... *gracia?* ... to forgive when someone makes even a very big mistake?"

Immediately after he said this, he remembered, and he felt foolish. Moreover, a new and unsettling revelation swept over Alex. It was the first time in his life that he had ever personally encountered what he might have quaintly called "virtue" or "purity" and not been almost immediately repulsed by it. Indeed, everything about this girl and her family, whether relating to forgiveness, temperance, sexual restraint, or even concern for strange foreigners who ended up sick in their house— seemed to be part of a seamless garment woven around love and respect.

"I am sorry, Lourdes. Now I ask *you* to forgive *me*."

"*No te preocupes,* Alex." She smiled again. "Would you like to come to my church with me tomorrow?"

"Lourdes, I'm not sure about that. We have—"

She laughed and shook her finger at him. "I know you do not work on Sunday!"

He was trapped and acquiesced, "Of course . . . I would be . . . extremely delighted."

Lourdes turned toward Angela. "Would you like to come with us?"

"*No gracias,* Lourdes. Sunday morning is *para mi primer sueño.*" It was when she got her beauty sleep. Lourdes laughed.

They settled down to a delicious breakfast, crowding around the small wooden table with some spare wood benches from behind the house.

"Doña Juana, I must say," Rich said with both cheeks full of scrambled eggs, "these are the freshest eggs I've tasted south of the Mexican border." A small portion of the delicious eggs had attached themselves to the beard stubble northwest of his mouth. Alex made a subtle wiping motion to him from across the table, and he quickly addressed the issue with one of the simple paper napkins Juana had placed next to each plate on the table.

"Absolutely agreed," said Sofia, "and because I grew up south of the Mexican border, for me that covers a lot of eggs." The Ixtamperic family laughed, happy to provide something new to people from abroad, who seemingly had already done and experienced everything before.

Fernando announced at the end of the meal, "Today is pruning day." He looked around at the students. "Would you like to learn how to prune coffee plants?" They all were interested.

Fernando took them to his plot. A warm midmorning sun activated the natural humidity of the coffee field, yet the temperature was not stifling. It was a good temperature for work. He began his presentation. "The first thing to understand about arabica coffee plants is that the coffee should grow off a single stem system. That means you want one main stem going up from the trunk base with the secondary branches moving off from this main stem. These branches and the ones that shoot off from them are the ones that you want to produce the coffee."

He showed them an example from a plant right next to them. "You see how many years ago I cut off a competing stem?" He pointed to a tiny stump on the main trunk. "This stem would have produced a lot of coffee, but reduced what the whole plant together would yield for us. With coffee plants, much of it is about competition for light. You maximize yield when you get every branch enough light."

He took some weathered pruning shears out of an old leather pouch attached to his belt and pruned as he lectured. "Now when I start pruning, I cut off all the dead branches that don't do anything except take away light and nutrients from the plant." He demonstrated as the students watched. "Then I cut off all the branches that are drooping to the ground."

He walked over to a shady area. "In the shady areas, sometimes vines grow up the trunk, and we have to remove all of this kind of thing. It hurts the yield." He demonstrated by yanking off a strand of ivy that had begun to wind its way around one of the trunks. "See this," he said, holding up the ivy to the students. *"Malo."* He tossed the sprig into a burn pile.

"Now off the main stem, you don't want the secondary branches that bear the cherries to be too close to each other. Notice, they should be at least thirty or forty centimeters from each other, so I cut off the little shoots that compete with these big, beautiful, cherry-producing branches. What you want is one main stem with a good number of coffee-producing secondary branches. But not too many. *Me compreden?"* The students nodded.

Rich walked over a few feet and pointed to an odd-looking plant that had all its branches chopped off on one side. "What happened to this poor specimen?" Rich inquired. "The thing looks like it's been sideswiped by a runaway buzz saw."

"Sí," said Fernando, chuckling along with Rich at the bizarre-looking plant. "This is side-pruning, a technique I learned from an official in the agricultural service. *Pues,* to get more from an older

plant, you cut off all the branches from the east side of the plant like this, see?" He pointed to the bare side of the plant. "Then you allow a shoot like this to grow up from the trunk along the eastern side of the main stem. When it reaches maturity and begins to bear cherries, you prune off the old main stem. This makes a coffee plant bear plentifully for many years."

Sofia assessed the situation. "Well, let's get at it!" she proclaimed. The others nodded.

"The students want to help?" asked Fernando, standing up, surprised.

"Sure, you shouldn't have to do this all yourself," said Angela. "We'll be your mozos. You'll never find labor as cheap as this." Fernando laughed and feigned a new insight.

"*Ahora comprendo.* Now I understand. Gringos travel south, crossing the *frontera* to find agricultural jobs in remote areas that pay nothing. Happens all the time here. Okay, only if you let Juana fix you lunch." They spent the morning pruning coffee plants and later enjoyed a delicious lunch of chicken, tortillas, and frijoles.

After lunch Rich and Alex fell asleep on a couple of mats in the main room.

CHAPTER 15

Angela

SOFIA AND ANGELA WERE ENGAGED IN CONVERSATION WITH Fernando, seated at chairs around the spartan dining table. Angela glanced over and noticed Rich and Alex still asleep, Rich snoring face-up with his mouth wide open. She motioned to the two with a cock of her head. "So much for your hardworking mozos."

"They have earned their sleep," replied Fernando.

Angela looked back at Alex. He was so much less infuriating when he was asleep. She studied his European features that now perhaps seemed less petulant than before.

Juana brought coffee to Angela and Sofia. They sipped their hot cups as Juana tended to the crackling fire. Outside it began to rain. Angela looked at the colorized picture hanging in its simple frame on the wall. It was a black-and-white photograph of a proud Mayan couple, perhaps taken in the fifties, maybe even the forties. The man wore the traditional male dress garments for the Maya of the Huehuetenango region—the vividly patterned shirt with embroidered collar, brown-and-white checkered skirt covering striped pants with a sash around the waist, topped off with a straw bowler hat. He stared proudly into the camera, arm around his wife, whose head was encircled by a cinta with brocaded designs, large tassels hanging from the left side. It was no wonder they wanted to colorize the picture. Black and white couldn't capture the Mayan culture.

Angela was curious.

"Fernando, who are the people in the picture?" she asked.

"My grandparents."

"Were they coffee growers?"

"*Sí.* For many years."

"What were they like?"

Fernando smiled. "I will tell you about them."

―

March 1935

Several of Isidro Ixtamperic's grandchildren and great-grandchildren were resident coffee laborers, or *colonos*, for the Ehrlichmann family of Mazatenango, a prosperous household of German immigrant coffee growers. Under the Liberal regime in Guatemala, there existed three official categories of coffee workers: *mozos habilitados*, those who did not live on the plantation but had received wage advances and were therefore bound to a landowner until the debt was paid off; *mozos no habilitados*, who worked for a wage and were free both from debt and to go wherever they pleased but were subject to a *mandamiento*, or labor draft; and *colonos*, who lived voluntarily on the coffee plantation but often had rental or labor contracts that bound them to a particular plantation owner for a specified amount of time, after which the contract could be renewed.

Compared to other plantation owners, Otto Ehrlichmann treated his workers relatively well, especially his colonos, some of whom had resided on his land for decades. His father had done much the same, providing his workers additional payments that allowed them to share some of the bounty from the coffee boom of the mid-1890s, while shielding them from the worst effects of the price crash of 1898 that destroyed the lives of many indigenous laborer families. Otto had learned well from his example, and even during the disastrous British blockade of exports to Germany during World War I, the Ehrlichmann family, as well as its colonos, somehow managed to pull through together, in no small part due to Otto's ability to forge new channels into the North American market. When the war was over in 1919, the plantation, now enjoying a more diversified portfolio of buyers for its product, seemed to thrive more than ever.

This was not to say that there were not social divisions between the Ehrlichmanns and their colonos, for there were indeed. If not accompanied by the usual contempt for the indigenous Mayans, the divisions were nevertheless clear. Basilio Ixtamperic was the great-grandson of Isidro and the grandfather of Fernando. Of all of Otto Ehrlichmann's workers, Basilio seemed to understand the most about coffee cultivation, and even more, how to train, manage, and motivate the mozos. Unlike most plantation owners, Otto had made sure that the children of his colonos obtained several years of formal schooling, and Basilio had gone even a little further, completing the eighth grade. For an indigenous Guatemalan in 1928, this was a substantial achievement. His natural good looks, strong frame, and the confidence that accompanied his literacy and fluency in Spanish and German caused him to stand out as a leader among his peers and to his patròn.

The years of 1924–28 were some of the best for coffee in Guatemala. Strong exports and high coffee prices, supported by Brazil's withholding of a substantial amount of its production off the market, allowed the coffee industry in Central America to thrive. The additional resources flowing into Guatemala not only brought benefits to plantation owners, but also resulted in improvements for coffee laborers. The government built more rural schools, and because coffee labor was scarcer than ever relative to desired production, plantation owners sweetened contractual arrangements to lure workers.

Basilio was a beneficiary of these times along with Ester, his younger sister, who in many respects was his female counterpart. Only fifteen, her beauty, education, and charm were already attracting the attention of a number of young men, and not only within the indigenous community, a fact to which she was still mostly oblivious. When she wasn't at work helping her mother with cleaning and taking care of her younger siblings, more than anything she enjoyed teasing the young mozos who worked on the plantation. They didn't seem to object much, but when any of them would try to charm her, she was an expert at keeping potential suitors at arm's length. At this point in her life, she preferred fun over romance.

One of those attracted to Ester was Friedrich, the eighteen-year-old son of Otto. Like his father, Friedrich was fluent in Spanish, and unlike many of the indigenous girls, so was Ester.

Because of Friedrich's fair complexion, he wore a dark brown leather hat with a wide brim while at work in the fields. He liked the hat, not only because he thought it made him look older and more handsome, but also because it protected him in the sun and kept his face from acquiring the permanently reddish tint that characterized the faces of so many of the other fair-skinned Germans in Guatemala. Every so often Ester and the other girls on the coffee plantation would try to coax him to take the hat off, an effort that never succeeded due to Friedrich's self-consciousness over his thin, white-blond hair, looking even thinner when pressed down to his scalp by the sweat under the brim of the hat.

One day while he was relaxing and having a drink of water between chores, Ester sneaked up behind him, grabbed the hat off his head, and ran. "Hey!" yelled Friedrich, caught off guard. He got up to chase her, but Ester was surprisingly fast. She also had a head start. Friedrich tried to catch her as she turned the corner and headed behind the stable. After several minutes of chasing and eluding, Friedrich managed to playfully grab Ester on the run by one of her arms.

"No lo tengo!" I don't have it! She was laughing hysterically, almost completely out of breath, and only partially able to free herself from Freidrich's grasp. Ester's laugh was usually contagious, and by now all of the mozos who had been watching the scene were now also laughing, as well as Otto Ehrlichmann. Through a merciless bout of tickling, Friedrich finally got her to confess, Ester now hysterical to the point of tears. "I don't have it . . . *Bonzo lo tiene!*" Friedrich turned to the barn, where Bonzo, Otto's faithful *buro*, was now proudly sporting Friedrich's leather hat, which was neatly tied in a bow under his neck, gazing placidly out of his stall at the commotion while he chewed his hay.

"I will get you!" exclaimed Friedrich in vain, trying to sound half-way serious but unable to keep from laughing himself as Ester escaped his grasp again. She ran back to the protection of her girlfriends, the whole group laughing, including Otto.

Every coffee crop has a window of only a few days when the crop must be harvested. This window begins when the majority of the coffee cherries begin to turn from yellow-orange to bright red. Picking the cherries inside this window avoids the bitter taste of unripened cherries as well as the sour taste of coffee produced from cherries that have begun to ferment on the plant. The key to a successful coffee crop in western Guatemala is marshaling the appropriate number of laborers for the harvest to begin on the right day.

November 2, 1929, was such a day on the Ehrlichmann plantation, and with the help of Basilio, Otto had enlisted a full complement of over one hundred mozos to work the harvest. Otto and Basilio walked through the plants in the late morning, monitoring the workers as they quickly picked the cherries, filling the straw baskets with the red, ripe fruit. Suddenly a deep explosion thundered across the highlands, which frightened many of the mozos so badly that they dropped their baskets and began to run.

Otto turned to Basilio. He had never heard such a noise before. "What in heaven's name was that?" he asked him, as startled as anyone.

Baslio gazed into the mountains behind Otto's head, standing openmouthed as he witnessed a dark cloud rapidly projecting into the sky above the gigantic *Volcan Santa Maria*, which loomed over the area to the northwest. Otto turned around immediately and saw the cloud of ash projecting high up into the sky. He stood, stunned and speechless, his voice almost paralyzed. It was a surreal, cataclysmic event.

"Mein Gott . . . ," he whispered to himself in German.

The coffee laborers stood stupefied as the ash cloud extended across the sky in the general direction of the plantation, the volcano continuing to belch a hellish storm of smoke and ash. Spreading in every direction, but particularly toward the south, it now began to cover the sun so that even before noon it seemed like twilight.

Ester had been nearby, picking with the other workers. "Basilio, what is happening?" she yelled to him, alarmed. It seemed like the end of the world.

"It's the Santa Maria—it's erupting!" he shouted.

The Santa Maria volcano, looming at over twelve thousand feet, had exploded nearly three decades before in 1902, covering the nearby region with six feet of ash, completely destroying fields, cattle, houses, and people. It was this 1902 eruption of the Santa Maria that had caused the formation of the Santiaguito volcanic dome complex lying adjacent to the Santa Maria to the south. The dome had begun to swell noticeably since 1922, pressure continuing to mount underneath its black, volcanic surface. It had finally blown its top.

Deep rumbling noises continued to be heard from the distance as the cloud enveloped ever greater portions of the sky. It was thicker now, causing the day to grow increasingly dark. Midday twilight was rapidly turning to early-afternoon dusk. Now ash began to rain down out of the sky, and some of the smoke was descending from the cloud. The shiny red coffee cherries on Otto's plants were becoming a dull gray, coated with small particles of ash. The smoke was causing some of the workers to cough and panic. Some of them had inhaled pieces of ash and were choking and coughing uncontrollably. Otto ordered everyone to cover their faces with handkerchiefs.

"Basilio, we must find some way to get the workers and their families farther away from the volcano. Let's try to get them on wagons and head to the coast," directed Otto above the noise of the fray. "I think Gerhard Meier has extra wagons. He lives northwest of here, so it means you'll be heading toward the volcano for some miles, but I think it's our only hope."

Basilio tied a red bandana over his mouth, mounted Erlichmann's stallion, and drove it at full speed in the direction of the Meier plantation. Ester remained with the Ehrlichmanns trying to help calm some of the workers and their children, who themselves were now being coated with soot and ash. She hustled them inside houses on the plantation and comforted some of the crying children. Ester had them cover the windows with wet cloth to keep out the ash.

The dirt road from the plantation led northward, toward the volcano, for several miles. As Basilio drove the horse on, the smoke and ash became more intense, stinging his eyes and making it hard for him to breathe. He shook the ash out of his bandana and replaced it over his mouth. It was also getting hotter. Basilio could now glimpse orange rivers in the distance from the torrid pyroclastic flow that surged from the volcano. He stopped for directions on the road when he encountered a mountain dweller who had seen raging rivers of molten lava sweeping through an indigenous village less than three miles away from the base of the Santiaguito dome. Hundreds of people had perished in an instant.

Basilio headed west off the main road, finally locating the Meier plantation. His hair, eyebrows, and eyelashes were now filled with ash. His breathing made a wheezing sound. Gerhard Meier was in the final stages of evacuation, but had extra wagons. He was also planning to flee to the coast and was heading in the general direction of the Ehrlichmann plantation anyway. The horses were frightened and resisted being bridled. But Gerhard and Basilio hitched them to the wagons as quickly as they could, and drove the horses with the wagons toward the Ehrlichmanns.

With tears of relief, Ester saw Basilio approaching on the road through the clouds of smoke and ash, leading the team of horses and wagons with Meier and his family. When they arrived, Otto and Basilio immediately loaded women and children of the worker families onto the wagons. They also loaded a few days' supply of food and water and other provisions.

All of a sudden Otto shouted in a distressed voice above the crowd, "Where's Irma?" His six-year-old daughter wasn't on any of the wagons. He had been distracted with preparations for the evacuation. "Friedrich, find your sister!" Friedrich sprinted back to the area around the house, his footprints kicking up ash clouds several feet high as he ran. Although it was midday, it was now almost as dark as night. The darkness combined with the densely falling ash made it difficult to see.

As the first wagons began to leave, Ester yelled, "I'll check in the coffee field!" She started running through the rows of coffee plants, even searching under them to see if Irma might have taken refuge underneath from the falling ash. Every time she brushed away a group of branches to check, it created a cloud of ash that enveloped her face, making her choke.

Five minutes went by, and then ten. The Erlichmanns were beginning to panic, shouting for Irma. Otto's wife wept as she searched in vain around the barn and stables. Finally, Ester gave a loud cry, "I found her! She is here!" Irma was indeed hiding under a coffee plant toward the back of the plantation where she had been playing with some of her friends when the chaos had started.

Irma ran to her parents who hugged her, and they quickly tossed her up onto the last wagon taken by Friedrich, Basilio, and Ester. The remaining mozos jumped on horses, two or even three on the back of one horse. Striking the confused horses repeatedly with switches, they sprinted away toward the Pacific.

The coffee harvest that year was badly damaged by the volcanic eruption, the yield reduced by about half. In the weeks after the eruption, nearly a foot of ash had continued to cover the ground, frustrating their attempt to salvage the remainder of the harvest and making living and working conditions almost unbearable.

Basilio then approached Otto with an idea. He had heard from some of the older mozos that after the eruption of 1902, a few farmers had turned the ash in their coffee plantations deep under the soil. The coffee yield the following year had been enormous. Although this would be a significant investment of time and money, Otto consulted with some of the older growers and agreed. They brought in dozens of new workers to go over the entire coffee plantation, turning as much of the ash as possible under the dirt and mixing it with the soil, especially in the areas closest to the base of the plants.

The subsequent years were difficult ones for coffee growers

everywhere, for the Great Depression in the United States and Europe cut coffee prices in half. But the coffee yields on the Ehrlichmann plantation were nearly 30 percent greater than their historical average due to the nutrient fortification of the soil. The effect lasted well until the mid-1930s. Only then did the yields begin to regress to normal levels.

In the years after the eruption, Otto would put his arm around Baslio after picking and mutter something like, "Well, Basilio, we can thank your Santa Maria for this harvest again, can't we?" It was a playful double entendre, a reference to Basilio's Catholic faith which was different than his own Lutheran upbringing, but also an affectionate recollection of how he had helped save the plantation from the eruption not only with his bravery, but with his resourcefulness too.

Otto's affection didn't extend quite as far, however, to the emerging relationship between his son and Basilio's sister. Over those same years, the relationship between Friedrich and Ester grew until one day, when Friedrich was twenty-five and Ester was twenty-two, he was reminiscing on the wooden porch with his father. They sat in old rocking chairs as they gazed at the tall pink clouds that hovered over the Pacific. A cool evening breeze relieved the sweltering workday.

Otto recalled the life of the family back in Europe and the voyage to Guatemala. Together they recalled the many trials of the coffee plantation, the volcano. After a time they were silent except for the quiet squeaking of the old chairs rocking on the loose floorboards. A soft gust of wind rustled the leaves of the coffee plants near the house.

Friedrich broke the silence. "Father, I want to marry Ester."

A different type of silence, a thicker and tenser silence, followed the proclamation. Friedrich felt the pain in his stomach at his father's disinclination. "You won't let me because she is Mayan." Otto didn't know how to respond, and so the silence continued. "Father, I have loved her from the first moment I was able to be in love, from a time when she was so young it would have been wrong of me to say that I loved her. I have never loved anyone else. You know this." Otto nodded, put his head in his hands, and rubbed his eyes.

"Why won't you let me marry her?"

Otto finally looked up at him, his expression pained. "Friedrich, you are German."

"Am I, Father? You are German. I am a Central American with parents from Germany. This is my home. I do not even know Germany. Isn't it all right to marry someone from my home? I love her. You care for her and her family too. Where would you be without her brother? She even saved my sister, your daughter, do you remember? Will you at least consider giving your consent?"

Otto wanted to convince Friedrich that his best interests lay elsewhere, or that he owed it to his family to marry a European bride, yet he knew this would be fruitless.

"Yes, I will think. I will consider."

Because of the large number of German families cultivating coffee in Guatemala, the dictatorial government of President Jorge Ubico had enjoyed close economic relations with Germany. But the regime had gradually moved toward stronger relations with the United States. The new relationship was not only political, it was also economic: the United States had substantially increased its imports of Guatemalan coffee under the Inter-American Coffee Agreement of 1940.

But as Hitler's armies began to march over Europe at the dawn of World War II, the United States became concerned with the German population in Guatemala. Reports of Nazi activity in some German social and business organizations in the country had reached the United States government. It was unclear whether this merely reflected a new German patriotism or a desire to expand the influence of the Third Reich to their new land in the western hemisphere. But the Americans were in no mood to take chances. They had come to view the three thousand Germans living in Guatemala as a menacing outpost of Nazism in their own hemisphere. If the United States should enter the war on the side of the Allies, Guatemala, with its strong economic connections to Germany as well as its claims against the British in Belize, might enter the war on the side of the Axis, creating a southern front on the United States that could divert British and American troops from defending Europe. It needed Guatemala to eliminate a threat to American national security.

Guatemala had its own reasons to look northward to the United States. As coffee exports to Europe were virtually shut down after the onset of the war, it became essential to find new markets for Guatemalan coffee. Responsive to American interests and in keeping with the "good neighbor" policy now in place between the United States and its southern Latin neighbors, Ubico ordered that all German social societies, schools, and sports clubs in the country be shut down as well as many German firms and plantations. Any German coffee exporters identified on a United States "black list" were forced to turn over the export of their coffee crops to the state. Then, six months after the Americans entered the war, an order came from Washington: All German citizens in Guatemala were to be deported to the United States, where they would be held as prisoners of war until a suitable exchange could be made and they would be sent back to Germany.

The news hit the Erlichmann family suddenly on June 12, 1942: All German families were to board trains immediately bound for the port of Veracruz on the east coast of the country, where American ships would pick them up for immediate deportation to New Orleans. There they would be transported to internment camps in the United States. Coffee plantations would be ceded to the Guatemalan government, to be held indefinitely.

Although Friedrich loved Ester, he also admired and respected his father, and strongly desired his father's blessing on their marriage. And while Otto had not urged them to break off their relationship, he had not yet openly assented to the idea of their marriage. Moreover, the turmoil that had surrounded the family in recent months had taken everyone's attention off such matters. And all of a sudden, it was time for Friedrich and his family to leave.

A small group of Guatemalan soldiers approached the house to escort the family to the train station. They were allowed to take only the possessions they could carry. Friedrich and Ester embraced, kissed, and tried to say good-bye. Numb with disbelief at what was transpiring, they seemed almost unable to bear the moment. Friedrich looked at her directly and promised, "Ester, I am Guatemalan, and one day I will come home for you, and we will marry and live together in our country. You must believe me."

Hardly able to respond from overwhelming feelings of anger and confusion, she managed to say, "Yes, I believe you, Friedrich."

And then he was gone.

Communication was poor during the war, and the first letter that Ester received arrived nearly eight months later. The news was not good. Otto had died of a heart attack in the American camp while waiting to be returned to Europe. Friedrich's mother and Irma had been sent to Germany in exchange for some British prisoners taken by the Germans. Friedrich had decided to stay in the United States under an agreement with the American government that any Germans who swore opposition to the Nazi regime and wished to stay in the US could remain in the camps until the war's end.

Years passed, and although Ester received a letter every four or five months from Friedrich, her parents—and even Basilio—counseled her to move on. She was twenty-eight now, virtually qualifying her for spinster status in Mayan culture. There were a number of sincere young men in the village who had expressed interest to her father. Even Basilio urged her to consider. But every time a letter arrived from the United States, she grew more recalcitrant to the pleadings of her family.

The war with Germany finally ended, and then the war with Japan. It had been nearly a year since she had received any communication. One day in November 1945, Ester arose early to begin picking for the harvest. She dressed, cooked some tortillas and beans for breakfast, and prepared to make her way outside to the field. Basilio summoned her from outside. She walked slowly out to the pasture and saw her brother.

Basilio was holding their bridled buro with a leather hat perched on his head. "Ester, someone has arrived who wants to see you."

She saw him as he walked out from behind the stable, took the hat off the buro, and put it on his own head. Both his body and his hair were even a little thinner than when he had left, but he was alive, he was home, and he was well. She saw tears well up in him as he smiled and laid eyes on her for the first time in three and a half years. They walked slowly toward each other, looked in each other's eyes for some moments with ravenous joy, and then embraced. He held her head against his shoulder and caressed her soft, dark brown hair as her sobs were muffled in his ragged shirt. Uncle Friedrich, brother-in-law of Fernando's grandfather, had come home.

CHAPTER 16

Alex

July 29, 2007

LOURDES CAME DOWN FROM THE VILLAGE TO FETCH ALEX to go to church. Sofia was also awake and went with them. They approached a large concrete building at the edge of the center of town that had the words *Iglesia Pentecostes* painted in purple under the eave. Even standing outside the church the sound vibrations from the amplified music were starting to make their feet tickle. "Have you ever been to a Pentecostal church before, Alex?" asked Sofia in English. He shook his head.

"Well . . . you're in for a new experience."

As they strolled inside, the band was pounding out the rhythmic pulse of the first song of the morning. The beat from the drummer, a Mayan teenager dressed in a tie and nice clothes, grew in intensity and volume as instruments were slowly added in sequence: bass, acoustic guitar, electric guitar, tambourine, and some other indigenous percussion instruments that Alex had never seen before. The catchy backbeat drove on awhile as the last people filtered in, and continued in the background as a young pastor strode up onstage.

"Todos listos a amar al Señor ésta mañana?" he shouted to the congregation. Were they ready to love the Lord this morning? There was a loud roar from the congregation as they entered, but apparently not nearly loud enough. The background rhythm picked up in intensity.

"I said, ARE YOU READY TO MEET THE LOVE OF GOD THIS MORNING?" He bellowed it so loud and in such close proximity to the microphone that the amplifier severely distorted his voice. This time an acceptably boisterous and collective shout emerged from the church, so voluminous that it caught Alex off guard. The few times he had been to a church, it was full of quiet old ladies and an aging priest, sleepwalking through a set of harmless but banal rituals. To say the least, this was an altogether different atmosphere. Furthermore, nearly everyone in the crowd seemed to be under thirty, another aspect he found surprising.

The band ratcheted up both volume and beat another notch. The bass player, drummer, and other percussion instruments played with the synchronicity of pistons in a four-stroke engine. A young Mayan woman in a colorful, gypsy-like dress strutted onstage playing a tambourine to the complex beat, perfectly syncopated to the pulse being laid down by the band, and went into a frenzied dance while chanting in an unintelligible language. Was this a Mayan dialect or was she speaking in tongues? Alex really had no idea. Regardless, the band was really cooking now. Some parishioners, many of the women wearing the Sunday best of their colorful indigenous clothing, began to dance around the aisles and others just stayed in one place subtly swaying in rhythmic gyration to the tandem pulse of the bass and percussion.

Lourdes looked over and smiled at Alex, and raised her eyebrows in a smile that suggested, "Well, here we are in my world. Does it suit you?" While Alex wasn't exactly comfortable, he was engaged enough in the general atmosphere of things to genuinely smile back. He looked over and saw Sofia clapping with the rest of the congregation and danc-ing around a little bit in front of her seat. She seemed to feel at home, so to hell with self-consciousness, he might as well too. Alex began to clap and even sway with little baby steps. Some words finally appeared on an overhead projector at the front of the room and the people started to sing enthusiastically as the jumping and dancing continued. The band cranked up song after song, each more fervent than the last.

During the animated time of worship, several people went up to receive prayer, for what Alex couldn't tell. A couple of them fell back-ward after receiving prayer, apparently fainting. They were caught by some ushers standing behind them who seemed to be prepared for it. The people were gently pulled away from the altar toward the side of the church. The ushers' hands supported their shoulders as their feet dragged along the floor, blissful expressions illuminating their faces as the band continued to play. After more than an hour, sweat poured down the faces of the worshippers; now it was time to sit down for the sermon.

The sermon was a little long, a little loud, and more than a little confusing to Alex for both linguistic and theological reasons, but he tried to understand as much as he could. After church, they had lunch with some of Lourdes's friends at a comedor near the Hotel Chinita. Alex enjoyed Lourdes's friends. They were friendly to him and asked him lots of questions about Europe. Outside of the church, they seemed completely normal.

After saying good-bye to Lourdes, Sofia and Alex walked back to the hotel. "Well, are you glad you went?" she inquired with a smile.

He glanced at Sofia with an awkward look on his face. "Yes . . . you know, believe it or don't, I am glad to go."

CHAPTER 17

Angela

AFTER A NUMBER OF WEEKS OF HARD WORK IN THE FIELD, Sofia asked the group, "How would you guys like to spend the weekend in Panajachel?"

Angela eagerly anticipated the trip. It was a place she had read about in the travel guides, located on the rim of spectacular Lake Atitlán, one of the most beautiful lakes in the western hemisphere, surrounded by breathtaking volcanoes.

They made their plans together for travel, and the next Friday they were headed back down the Pan-American Highway toward the lake, about four hours away. Angela was put in charge of ground travel and made sure that they upgraded their journey this time from the usual chicken bus to a Pullman, which departed from the city of Huehuetenango, taking them straight to the lake.

They hopped up into the bus, which had individual seats made of comfortable suede, contrasting with the green vinyl bench seats of the chicken bus. It had a restroom of sorts in the back. Assuming their passengers needed to be visually entertained throughout the journey, it came with a television monitor mounted above the first row of seats, visible from the front half of the bus. Apparently judging that hair-raising vehicle passes on the winding mountain roads didn't suffi-ciently spike the adrenaline of the passengers, the video entertainment for this trip was a series of grainy, yet uncommonly violent, kung-fu movies poorly overdubbed in Spanish. The movies were densely packed with a truly extraordinary number of fights per scene. Angela tried to have a conversation with Sofia, but the volume being at least two to three times what would be comfortable for the normal human ear, precluded the possibility of any normal conversation. The groan from each body blow and nunchuck strike reverberated throughout the bus. Angela noticed, however, that many of the Guatemalans, even the older Mayan women, seemed captivated by the film series.

Rich yelled up at the bus driver to turn down the volume, *"Señor, puede bajar el volumen, por favor!"* Angela laughed at Rich. The driver's attention was difficult to attract above the chaos of the movie. Moreover, his concentration was singularly focused on tailgating and aggressively overtaking every vehicle that lay in his way, especially the lower-caste chicken buses with inferior horsepower. But after a few of Rich's shouts, the bus driver, without acknowledgment or emotion, reached his arm over and adjusted a nearby knob, setting the volume at a compromise that was perhaps only 75 percent louder than normal.

As the bus turned south off the Pan-American Highway and began its winding descent into the Lake Atitlán basin, Angela gazed for the first time at one of the most breathtaking landscapes in Central America. Enormous volcanoes ascended from the shores of the large, pristine Lake Atitlán, over nine thousand feet into the clouds. The sheer natural beauty of it produced a pleasant new feeling inside Angela; she felt almost proud to be related in some small way to the breathtaking natural beauty unfolding before her.

Small Mayan towns adorned the flat aspects of the encompass-ing mountain range, hazy clouds of smoke rising above them from hundreds of small household fires. Angela could see several large ferries crossing the lake in different directions, taking local residents and tourists from one lake town to another. It was the easiest method of transportation, for there was no easy access through these steep mountains by road. Although she had been to Lake Tahoe in California, even Tahoe in its deep blue enormity was no visual match for Atitlán.

They wound down toward the lake through the regional capital of Sololá, finally arriving in Panajachel. For the bohemian connoisseur of indigenous American art and handmade tourist paraphernalia, Panajachel was a mecca. Shops hawking everything from backpacks to purses, from pajamas to hacky sacks—all constructed from handwoven Guatemalan textiles—lined Calle Santander, the main street of the town. Angela was bewildered by the variety of textures and colors of indigenous Guatemalan handicraft. It again made her proud, that people in her native country were so adept with art. She laughed with Alex, who looked like he'd gone to heaven as he purchased a pair of pajama bottoms made from patches of pink and purple indigenous textile.

There were lots of North American and European tourists, almost all seemingly in their twenties. The only exceptions were a few older ones who, she learned, had fled to Panajachel during the late sixties to avoid the draft during the Vietnam War. Entranced by the easygoing lifestyle of the place, they never returned home.

The four checked into an inexpensive guest house just off of Calle Santander. The rooms were a little musty, and the beds were even harder than at the Hotel Chinita, but it worked for a weekend.

It was dinnertime, and Angela was famished. She and the others slowly ambled down the main street toward the water looking for a suitable restaurant, taking in the sights and smells, trying to pull Alex away from the bin full of multicolored hacky sacks. They settled on the

Sunset Café, located right on the lake with a perfect view more than ten miles across the water of the Volcán San Pedro, one of the enormous peaks that lined the lake.

The place had drawn its usual Friday night crowd, and they had to wait for a table. The students mingled with the others in the queue. Angela watched as Alex struck up a conversation with an American wearing Levis with holes in the knees and a collared shirt with Mayan patterns. He and Alex appeared to be engaged in an animated conversation about social justice issues.

Alex brought him over and he introduced himself to the rest of the group. "How ya doing—Gary Kautsky from the State University of New York."

The first thing that Angela noticed about Gary was that he was an extraordinarily hairy human being. Along with his shoulder-length hair, an unbroken carpet flowed from underneath his nostrils down to a voluminous mustache and beard that covered his lips, which in turn fully connected with the chest hair protruding from his open collar. He looked to be in his early thirties and wore narrow wire-rimmed glasses and spoke with an East Coast accent. He reminded Angela of a late sixties John Lennon strutting fully bearded across Abbey Road.

When he introduced himself to Angela, she could sense his eyes lingering on her birthmark. *Get past it, buddy,* she thought to herself.

Rich interrupted and offered his hand. "What do you study, Harry . . . I mean, Gary?" Angela suppressed a giggle as Sofia elbowed Rich hard in the ribs without breaking her smile and eye contact with Gary.

"Yes . . . well . . . sociology. Doing my dissertation on fair trade networks and alternative movements to, you know, the normal exploitative commodity channels. Alex says you're doing something similar in economics?"

"For the time being, yes, I suppose we are," Rich offered.

"I'm Sofia. Pleased to meet you, Gary."

Angela noticed how the focus of Gary's attention now seemed to rest on Sofia. She wore a tank top that night and her long brown hair now fell softly over bronzed shoulders.

"Are you also an economist?" he inquired. Angela surmised that Gary was probably hoping for something closer to sociology.

"Yes, I'm at Berkeley in the same program as Rich. Most of my work is in development."

"Wait . . . are you Sofia Cavallera?" he asked.

Sofia nodded. "Er . . . yes."

"I read your paper, the one that applies semiparametric estimation to understanding causal effects of development program impact. It was suggested reading at an international social sciences conference I went to. Math was a bit over my head, but the paper has some interesting ideas."

"Thank you," Sofia replied.

All conversation was drowned out temporarily by a pickup truck rolling by with a loudspeaker announcing a church service later that evening.

"These evangelicos crawling all over Guatemala drive me nuts," Gary observed.

"Why's that?" Sofia asked. Angela recalled that Sofia had grown up as a pastor's daughter, but had shared her disenchantment with some of the preachers on American television, where, as Sofia had put it, "the ratio of spiritual encouragement to hair gel was a little low." Even so, she told how she had been introduced to a place in Berkeley called the Spirit Garage, where she had met some of her good friends who joined together on Sunday nights to sing songs, pray, and take communion. It was a little mysterious to Angela; her own family was mildly Catholic but not particularly religious.

"They're too loud, too zealous, and their music is irritating," Gary blistered.

Sofia raised her eyebrows in mock surprise. "Wow, my dad is a pastor. I should warn him about that."

Before an obviously flustered Gary could respond, the restaurant hostess interrupted, summoning the students for their table. "Gary, you will join us for dinner?" Alex suggested.

"Be happy to . . . if that's okay with everybody." He looked around the group.

"Absolutely, come join us," invited Sofia with a forgiving smile.

They were given a table directly overlooking the lake. The sun was setting behind a tall bank of puffy cumulous clouds to the west that rose from behind the mountains and extended thousands of feet into the sky. It created a mélange of orange, rose, and pink that formed a backdrop to the volcanoes draped in dark brown shadow in the foreground. The sunset projected onto the lake, creating reflective orange ripples that danced hypnotically on top of the deep blue. The lake was quiet except for a few fishermen working alone in small boats, casting nets in the twilight.

Gary lit a cigarette and exhaled a cloud of exhaust. "Mind if I smoke?" he asked the group. It was a little late to object. The nicotine haze lingered under the thatch roof, slowly dissipating through the small cracks. "Pretty crazy, this coffee business, isn't it? Such a classic case of a postcolonial system that's been perpetuated to serve the interests of the corporations in the core countries at the expense of the periphery."

This vocabulary was somewhat new to Angela. "What's this core-periphery thing?" she asked him. Must be something she had missed at UCLA. Maybe this would help explain the mystery of how growers like Fernando who grew such high-quality coffee could be so poor.

"Well, the world works like this." He took a quick drag on his cigarette and blew the smoke upward again with his lower lip and glanced quickly over at Sofia. She was listening, and he straightened up slightly in his seat.

"Internationally speaking, there is a core and a periphery, and a semiperiphery if you want to get technical about it. The core countries are the powerful countries, the ones with all the resources and all the money. By virtue of their power, they write the rules that govern the international economy, naturally to benefit themselves. The periphery, on the other hand, this consists of the poor countries, like Guatemala. The periphery lacks capital, lacks education, lacks most things in fact, which causes them to be exploited by the core. The core countries use the countries in the periphery for their natural resources, agricultural commodities, and low-wage manual labor, while maintaining a grip on technological superiority, advanced forms of capital, and so forth. Military superiority helps lock in power. The semiperiphery is made up of countries like Brazil, Costa Rica, and Mexico, which have some characteristics of the core, but are also subject to its domination. But it's this peripheral position to the core countries that is the root cause of poverty in poor countries." There was a short silence.

"Why, that's a very interesting theory, Gary," Rich broke in after the pause, flicking a tortilla chip into his mouth and crunching it loudly.

"Yes, it's called World Systems Theory," continued Gary. "Do you know it?"

"Oh yes."

"I take it you're not a proponent." Gary suddenly looked agitated.

"You're right, I'm not," said Rich. "Gary, my new friend, where do we even start with this? I mean where does, say, China fit into this theory about the world? Shoot, there's no country that makes as much stuff for the 'core,' as you call it, than China. And here you're talking about somewhere around half a billion people being pulled out of poverty by being part of your 'periphery.' Now they hold over a trillion dollars of US debt in their hands. Does that make China a core team member now?"

Gary thought for a moment and took another reflective drag on his cigarette, the burnt end lighting up to a bright orange glow. He expelled the smoke. "China is a country that has been exploited by the West for centuries. Part of the people's movement that led to socialism in China was a reaction to their status on the periphery. A very natural reaction."

Rich responded quickly. "Yes, but while it stewed in its own Marxist juices for three decades, it remained poor. Only when it reintegrated with the world economy and became a big exporter to the 'core,' did it start becoming rich. It doesn't fit with your theory. Your theory says that integration into the world economy causes poor countries to remain poor. The greatest movement out of poverty in the history of the world controverts bankrupt ideas like World Systems Theory, which are essentially just recycled Marxist gibberish."

"Hmmph." Gary stood up. "Anyone want a drink?" His offer was to the group, but his eyes were directed only at Sofia.

Sofia smiled. "No thanks, Gary, I'm good." As Gary headed to the bar, Angela caught Sofia's eye and winked at her. Sofia shook her head as she smiled back and subtly rolled her eyeballs. Angela had watched countless episodes of guys hitting on girls before, but this particular one was special to behold. She could tell that Gary saw Sofia as a prize that could only be won by the mind of an incisive scholar. In her mind she likened the conversation that had arisen to an intellectual bullfight where Gary was the matador and Rich was the bull. To win his prize, Gary had to slay the bull.

Alex kept the discussion going while Gary got his drink at the bar.

Bruce Wydick

"Rich, China has reintegrated on its own terms. China is a very proud, independent country, and difficult to compare to, say, Latin America." They discussed China for a while.

Gary returned as Sofia was commenting, "There is certainly some truth to this. For example, in the 1990s the International Monetary Fund wanted China to liberalize its capital markets with the other emerging Asian economies. To its benefit, China held its ground and as a result was able to withstand the Asian economic crisis, while the countries that followed the bad IMF advice, like Thailand, Malaysia, and Indonesia, fell into huge recessions." Angela could read Gary's mind: critical view of the IMF, another plus.

"Sof, sure . . . right, but this is beside the point," said Rich, only slightly annoyed. "The main issue is whether, as 'World Systems Theory' says, integration with the world economy causes poor countries to remain poor. I've got nothing against leftist theories about the world, but what really steams up my goggles is when people keep promoting their favorite economic theories without empirical evidence to back them up, just assuming they're true because it's what they want to believe, supporting them with a few spicy anecdotes here and there. It's storytelling, not solid science."

Gary was sitting at the table again, John Lennon peering through his gold wire glasses at the group, captivated by the long, shiny brown hair flowing delicately across the bronzed shoulders of the social scientist sitting across the table. He lit another cigarette, waved out the match, and began again. "Since colonial times the poor countries of the world have played servant to the European and European-settled nations. The patterns of trade that emerged in the twentieth century followed the patterns that had been established by colonialism. It was clear that the nature of engagement between the periphery and the core had to change."

Alex interjected, "You're talking about import-substitution-led industrialization."

Gary nodded favorably, like a teaching assistant at a research university affirming the response of a younger student-disciple. "Yes, exactly, Alex. Countries like India, Mexico, Brazil, well, most of Latin America actually and a lot of the rest of the developing world, protected themselves against the imports from the core and developed their own manufacturing industries. India called it the Third Way, between the communism of the East and the capitalism of the West."

Rich butted in. "And so, Gary, tell us how that all worked out."

"Well, it led to the industrialization of much of the periphery," he responded, "and a lot of economies being at least somewhat liberated from their peripheral, subservient role to the core." The matador bowed toward the crowd after a difficult pass by the bull.

Rich retorted sharply, "Yes, and a world full of bankrupt economies. Definitely a case of the grass being greener above the septic tank. You see, a lot of these wonderful industries Gary is talking about couldn't get going unless they had help from the political system, and boy, they got it. So much so, that these industries couldn't exist without dipping their hands in the government kitty around election time. They were like heroin addicts, quiverin' little hands reaching for the needle of government cash to shoot into their veins. Politicians lived off the monopoly profits of the state enterprises, and the state enterprises were protected by the benevolence of the politicians they bought off. And guess what? By the 1970s and early 1980s, the governments couldn't support them anymore, so you know what they did? Because no politician could get elected without shaking out the goody bag to these industry captains who now had control over a good part of the economy, they printed money and gave it to them that way. Guess what they got in return? Hyperinflation. These people; if they had only slightly less brains, you'd have to plant 'em in dirt and water 'em twice a week . . ."

Sofia commented, "Yes, that definitely gave the World Bank and the IMF something to do after they finished cleaning up Western Europe after World War II. Their new mission became rescuing the bankrupt economies of the developing world."

Alex looked around the table and couldn't resist—"Ah yes, the World Bank, the IMF, and the WTO. The Axis of Evil." He grinned menacingly, glancing over at Rich for a reaction.

"Yeah, right . . . the Axis of Evil," Rich repeated satirically in a dramatic, diabolical voice.

Sofia broke in, "The truth is, though, Gary, that with few exceptions, the import-substitution strategy was mostly a bust, especially in India and Latin America. Regardless of what you think about the World Bank, Rich is correct: the best evidence shows that as countries have opened up to world markets, economic growth is somewhere between one and a half to two points higher." The sharp horn of the bull had just inflicted a significant wound on the matador.

Angela decided it was time to enter the fray, even in a small way. "It's hard to point to many cases where countries have thrived by turning inward, at least in the long run—doesn't seem like socialism provides good incentives for long-term prosperity."

Rich jumped in again. "Does the pope wear a funny hat? Yes, Angela, socialism does not provide very good incentives for long-term prosperity." Rich could have been more affirming; she was only trying to help.

Gary looked again at the Argentinian economist with the long dark hair. At this point he seemed to merely be fighting for her respect by finding pertinent anecdotal exceptions to Rich's generalizations.

Gary contended, "Okay, if globalization helps the poor, then shouldn't it benefit people in all parts of the world? Sure, there are always going to be a few capitalists who get rich in the globalization game, bringing up the average income in a country while the poor are left behind, but with globalization inequality has increased."

Rich interrupted him. "Now, Gary, let's not move the target to the other side of the barn. Your claim was that developing countries get poorer when they trade with the rich countries, while the evidence indicates the opposite. Now you seem to admit that this may be true, but that it's *inequality* that's getting worse. Gary, in your world if you have two people in poverty, and one becomes wealthier, is that a bad thing?"

"Not if that increased wealth is used for socially beneficial purposes," said Gary.

"Are you kidding?" Rich exclaimed. The bull was very much alive and continuing to charge the cape aggressively. "So we take it from the guy who's taken the risks and worked hard to improve his family's life, and give it to the guy who didn't? You'd have to be dumber than the back end of a chicken to ever try to accomplish anything under that set of rules."

Sofia intervened. "Look, these are obviously difficult issues. International economics and poverty traps are a lot more complicated than people want to think, but this is exactly what makes me uncomfortable about ideas like World Systems Theory as well as blanket statements about the free market taking care of everything. First of all, people in poverty traps aren't poor because they don't work hard; they're poor because their economy is stuck in a low-level trap. Second, having an economy open to trade may spur economic growth, but it is obviously insufficient alone to eliminate poverty. Look around us." Angela watched Gary as he became mesmerized by Sofia's articulacy and her smooth features dancing in the candlelight.

Sofia continued, "But as for the inequality in developing countries getting worse with globalization, international trade gets blamed for a lot of inequality, but there are a lot of other factors that increase inequality, like the introduction of new technologies that decrease the demand for unskilled workers and increase the demand for skilled ones, even in rich countries. This is a much bigger contributor to inequality than international trade."

Gary seemed to be relieved to have discovered a patch of common ground with Sofia on the inequality issue. "Yes, the inequality globalization creates in rich countries is just one more reason to oppose free trade. One of the great social movements of our time has been through the alliance of American blue-collar workers whose jobs are threatened by globalization and those who stand against offshore manufacturing and Third World sweatshops."

"With no mixed motives, whatsoever, of course," quipped Rich. "Forcing firms to offer industrialized country wages to people in poor countries is a surefire way to keep those workers in developing countries wading around in their rice fields filled with poisonous snakes and away from their manufacturing jobs . . . American unions . . . such big hearts for social justice."

Rich continued, "Gary, you're right. The main two groups of people protesting those jobs you call 'sweatshop' work are brainless leftists who probably need to find a job themselves, and overpaid union workers who are internationally noncompetitive. It sure ain't the people in developing countries working in the factories. There are lines around the block to get those jobs. I've seen them all over the world. And they don't need guys like you to watch their backs by taking their jobs away. What poor countries need is capital investment, not boycotts. And I'm going to say something even more shocking to you, Gary. My concern with Africa is not that there are too many of what you call sweatshops there, but too *few*."

Angela watched Gary sit blankly at the table, too stunned by this overwhelming barrage of apostasy for an immediate response. The bull was snorting and rearing up on its hind legs, directing its horns at the matador for the kill. But Sofia gazed at Rich pensively for a moment across the candle on the table.

"Rich, you're just a little too . . . *homo-economicus* for me." She smiled wryly at him.

"Sof, you're breakin' my heart. Does that mean we shall never wed?" Rich teased her affectionately.

"Yes, unfortunately so, I'm afraid." The matador was still alive.

"I agree with you that globalization is mainly a good thing, but there are a lot of other noneconomic factors involved that I think should make economists more sensitive than they typically are about job losses."

"Like what?"

"Like the importance of *identity*, for example," Sofia replied. "A steel worker, say, derives his happiness not just from income, but from his identity as a steel worker, being part of a group of steel workers. It's the focal point for his relationships and how he regards himself."

Gary saw an opportunity and jumped in. "I couldn't agree with you more about identity, Sofia. Any sociologist would tell you that identity trumps income." Angela watched him glance a little nervously at the bull. "Why do you want to publish research articles anyway, Rich? It can't be for the money because there isn't any money in it. It's about identity, isn't it? Conforming to a vision of what you think you should do and be." He had managed to deliver the aggressive bull a flesh wound with his rapier.

The dinner arrived, and the students eagerly dug into their food. The Sunset Café specialized in Mexican cuisine, and a cast-iron skillet sizzling with chicken, beef, and an assortment of vegetables was delivered to the table along with warm sacks of tortillas.

Gary crumpled his cigarette in an ashtray when his burrito arrived. He took a bite and continued, washing down a mouthful of cheese and beans with his drink. "Really what I'm talking about is the simple issue of exploitation. Even if some people get rich from globalization, it's all too often corporations increasing their profits on the sweat of low-income workers in poor countries. How can you justify a system that allows American consumers to save a few dollars on a pair of jeans that have been sewn up by a woman slaving for fifty cents an hour? It's unethical, and I can't see how anyone can defend such a system in good conscience."

Just then a Quiché woman approached their table, selling a potpourri of handmade Guatemalan products, which she carried on her head wrapped together in a blanket. She approached the group and unpacked the blanket at the end of the table, displaying small leather purses, bracelets, and even a Rastafarian skullcap made of Guatemalan cloth with a set of dreadlocks hanging from the back. Alex tried on the skullcap, displaying it for the group.

The woman approached Gary. "*Quiere, señor?*"

"*No gracias,*" Gary answered. He turned to the group. "I'll bet the women who made those things earned even *less* than fifty cents an hour. Won't be part of that."

All of a sudden Sofia interjected, "Gary, that's sort of it, isn't it?"

"What?" he asked. The matador had either just achieved something brilliant or delivered himself a mortal, self-inflicted wound with his weapon.

"Well," Sofia explained, "what I mean is this: Before globalization, the poor mostly suffered in silence. They plowed their fields with their animals. They had their children. They died young. And nobody outside of their village knew about it, or felt responsible for it."

"What's your point, Sof?" Rich was interested. Indeed, all of them were interested.

"I think some of the rancor over globalization, in a way, is a cognitive issue. What I mean is, before globalization, that peasant family suffered alone; they owned their own poverty. But now suppose globalization offers a member of that family a chance to earn a slightly higher wage making something for rich people in industrialized countries. Obviously, if he takes the job, the former peasant believes he is better off, otherwise he wouldn't have preferred the new work over the old work, and the consumer in the rich country is better off because he pays a lower price for his good, since it now costs less to produce."

Sofia continued, "But now with globalization, the person in the rich country is indirectly paying the wage of the person in the poor country. He is involved. In a sense he now owns the poor man's poverty. Now whatever he makes each day comes from the rich man's wallet. No different for peasants who grow coffee for people in rich countries to drink.

"Are the poor man and the rich man better off because of globalization? Yes, they're both a little better off but, at least for now, the poor man is still very poor. And while not quite as poor as he used to be, the gap between the rich man and the poor man is still glaring, and a source of guilt for the rich man. 'What have I done,' he says, 'that I have caused this man to be so poor?' And of course he must be causing the poor man's poverty since it is he who is paying him."

The group pondered this thought for a few moments.

Then Gary looked at Sofia. In the pregnant pause Angela could see the question leaving Gary's mouth well before it did. Like herself, Gary had to know. And somehow in the last few minutes the question itself had appeared to become more important than slaying the bull. "So if the rich man isn't *causing* the poor man's poverty, then what *is*?" he asked.

"I don't think we know the answer to that question yet," she said. It was time for Sofia to eat her fajita. "But trying to answer it is why I love economics."

Chapter 18

Angela

ANGELA AND SOFIA SAT IN ONE OF THE TATTERED SEATS OF A chicken bus as it lumbered through the rugged western highlands, dropping elevation at nearly every turn, finally merging back on the Pan-American Highway. After weeks of helping Rich and Alex with interviews and gathering coffee production data in San Pedro Necta, one fact had become obvious: almost none of the profit made from some of the best arabica hard bean in the world was accruing to the cultivators of this premium coffee. They had interviewed hundreds of them. Most of these families lived huddled together in a single-room mud hut. Their children were malnourished and taken out of school to work, their families broken up through the economic necessity of migration. Nearly all of them lived in poverty or on the edge of it. Where were the coffee profits going?

While Rich and Alex continued to collect data from the growers, Angela and Sofia followed the coffee to the next link in the value chain: the headquarters of the fair trade cooperative Café Justicia in Guatemala City. There they would look for clues that might help them to understand where all the coffee profit was going.

They had learned from José-Ernesto that Café Justicia was one of the larger exporters of fair trade–certified coffee in Guatemala, collecting the coffee from its member cooperatives and selling it all over the globe. The office in the capital marketed the crop that its members harvested.

The bus arrived in Zone 5 of Guatemala City, a roughly hewn, run-down area, even by Guatemala City standards. Aged concrete buildings with faded paint lined the streets, their facades stained with years of exposure to fumes from diesel-belching buses. Few of the pedestrians on the streets wore the traditional Guatemalan clothing except for a few *campesino* women who apparently had come into the city to beg with their infant children. Compared with the rural charm of San Pedro Necta, they found the general atmosphere of the city to be dirty, crowded, and stressful.

Angela and Sofia walked several blocks from the bus station with their backpacks, following the crumbling sidewalks to the co-op headquarters. On top of its scruffy location, the office was not as nice as they expected for such a large operation. A burly security guard cradling a shotgun greeted them at the door and let them in. A young, professional-looking ladina woman at the reception desk regarded the backpacking students with a curious smile. After they explained their business, she invited them to have a seat in the waiting area and a cup of coffee from a pot that was brewing on a nearby table.

Sofia looked down into the sugar bowl. "Angela, have I shown you the special sugar additive we use in Latin America to fully enhance coffee flavor? Here, look . . ." Sofia mischievously opened the lid to the sugar bowl. Looking down, Angela saw that its contents resembled an ant farm with a rather breathtaking population density. Angela repressed a small scream, and they opted to take their coffee black.

Worn furniture was scattered throughout the waiting area. Plastic seats of different colors adorned the room. Burlap coffee sacks bearing the names of different Guatemalan harvest sites covered the walls. As Angela peered into the main area of the office, the lone sign of twenty-first-century commerce she noticed was a huge flat-panel computer screen covered with coffee price quotes.

They had an appointment with Gustavo Morales, the marketing manager for the cooperative. About twenty minutes after their scheduled appointment time, Gustavo came out to the waiting area. He turned for a moment to talk to a secretary, and above his shirt collar the ripples in the back of his husky neck resembled a pack of hot dogs. He was a portly ladino, middle-aged and buzz-cut bald, wearing a tight-fitting suit with a loose tie. As he approached to greet them, Angela noticed that he left his top shirt button open under the necktie to relieve some of the pressure.

"Don Gustavo, thank you for agreeing to meet with us." Sofia shook hands with Gustavo, followed by Angela, which gave her hand the feeling of being enveloped by a giant beanbag. Angela quickly glanced at his silver wedding ring, which was easily as big as the ring on a keychain but still appeared to be cutting off circulation.

He looked at Angela. *"Guatemalteca?"* he asked.

"Originalmente. Sí." Angela smiled. She was becoming more comfortable saying it. He ushered them toward his office. The cacophony of a dozen phones ringing at once filled their ears. The people on the other end of these phones, he explained, were either sellers or buyers negotiating coffee deals.

Initially Gustavo seemed harried. After sitting down in his leather seat, he began their visit with a quick but obvious glance at his watch. Angela thought that perhaps he was tired of doing interviews with curious students who kept him from answering his phones, and who weren't buying or selling coffee. Even so, they began to pepper him with questions about his link in the value chain, and the international market for fair trade coffee. He interrupted them several times to answer his phones.

"Don Gustavo, I don't mean to be blunt," said Angela, smiling, *"pero que haces todo el dia?"* But what do you do all day? Gustavo's demeanor began to thaw and he seemed to understand the point. They were students who had learned theory after theory about the nature of markets, but genuinely wanted to understand how it all actually worked.

His face was a smiling potato. "Ladies, I studied business economics at *Universidad Rafael Landivar* in Guatemala City many years ago. I know how to speak your language. Now that you know this, I must tell you," he announced almost in a whisper, "I am a real-world incarnation of *la mano invisible.*"

"What do you mean?" asked Angela.

He was happy to fill out his thought. "I am Adam Smith's invisible hand here in Guatemala. Or at least a little finger of it." He held up the portly index finger on his right hand in front of his eye and wiggled it back and forth for them for visual emphasis. "You know that graph people study in economics, where that supply curve intersects with the demand curve at what we call *P*?"

They nodded. "Yes, the first thing every new student in economics learns is that *P* is the price where supply meets demand in a free market. It's the price that clears the market, where there is neither excess supply nor excess demand," replied Angela.

"Pues..." He paused for dramatic effect. "I am *P*."

Angela and Sofia looked at each other, and Sofia decided to run with it. "So, what does it look like to be la mano invisible?"

Gustavo kept it going. "It doesn't look like anything, of course. As the invisible hand, I am invisible." They laughed at his joke.

"In many ways, actually, it is true. I sit here in my office, hidden from everyone, matching supply with demand. I am both the doula who nurtures my coffee beans to the market and the midwife who consummates the birth of an international coffee transaction. I, along with hundreds, maybe thousands of other people like me, establish the international price of coffee in every second of every hour of every day of every year. There is not a single coffee-growing peasant across the world who is not affected by the international price of coffee set by myself and my colleagues."

Gustavo paused momentarily for reflection. "But to put it in more mundane terms . . . I spend nearly all of my day on the phone." The two women laughed at Gustavo's self-deprecating charm.

Not being able to help himself after this mild letdown, he started up again, pointing to one of the half dozen computer monitors in his office. "You see that screen over there? That screen gives me forecasts for weather in Brazil, Colombia, Vietnam, Ethiopia, and other important coffee places around the world. Every time I see that good weather is forecast in Brazil, I sell *como loco* at the highest price I can right that minute, because you know what? In only a few minutes, maybe less, the world coffee price is going to drop. I have to protect my growers."

He continued, "And every day I pray for bad weather in Brazil. Every day I say, dear God, let there be drought in Brazil, or hurricanes, floods, pestilence, mudslides, lightning storms, Exodus-like insect attacks—anything—because you both know very well that when supply goes down, price goes up, and this brings better returns to the growers in my association. I also wish for these calamities in Vietnam, Colombia—everywhere they grow lots of coffee," he laughed. "Except of course Guatemala."

"Well, Gustavo, we have now pinpointed who to blame for global climate change," said Sofia. "We'll be sure to notify the authorities as soon as we return home."

Gustavo smiled. *"Quieren saber la verdad?"* Did they want to know the truth?

They certainly did want to know the truth, especially Angela.

He moved his head closer to theirs, feigning like he was going to share his deepest secret with them. "The truth is that my prayers are *good* prayers—for all the growers."

"What do you mean?" asked Angela. "How can praying for storms and pestilence and lightning and horrible things across the globe be good for coffee growers?" There was a short silence that Sofia broke.

"Because it's a Prisoners' Dilemma," she said, revealing the secret before Gustavo did.

"What?" asked Angela. Gustavo grinned and slowly nodded in agreement with Sofia.

"Remember the game you were taught in undergraduate economics, or political science, or psychology? I think they teach it everywhere now," said Sofia.

Angela remembered. "Yes, the Prisoners' Dilemma. Two suspects are apprehended after a big theft, but the police don't have any direct evidence to convict them. So they take them down to the station and put them in separate interrogation rooms. Each is told separately that if he alone confesses to the crime, he'll get to go free, but the one left who doesn't confess will get, like, ten years in jail. If they can both keep silent, they can only be charged with trespassing and get a few months in jail, but if they both confess, they get five years. However, each prisoner realizes that no matter what the other one does, it's better for him to confess. So in the end they both wind up confessing and get five years in jail when they could have had only a few months." She paused. "So what does this have to do with coffee?"

It was Gustavo who answered. He looked at them solemnly, revealing the mystery in low tones. "The bad weather keeps the prisoners silent."

Angela saw it now. "Yes—it's the irony of bad coffee weather for producers. Given the lack of sensitivity of consumers to coffee prices, coffee growers would be better off collectively if they would all reduce their supply. But whether the other coffee producers reduce their supply or they don't, each affects the world price so insignificantly that he wants to market as much coffee as he can. Because they all think this way, there is oversupply, and everyone loses. Individual rationality leads to collective irrationality—just like John Nash demonstrated."

Sofia finished up for Angela. "And if there is poor coffee weather around the world, as long as it isn't concentrated too much in one place, all the producers are better off than if there had been perfect weather and a worldwide bumper crop. It's like nature's dark side doing the job of enforcing a cartel for coffee growers."

"And the prisoners are better off," summarized Gustavo.

"Yes . . . the prisoners . . . are better off," muttered Angela to herself.

"But what keeps the prisoners from helping themselves?" asked Angela.

"This I will tell you, if the two of you agree to have lunch with me."

—

Angela guessed that lunch was probably one of Gustavo's favorite times of the day. As they walked to the restaurant, he told them, "Ladies, did you know that I grew up poor, the son of a maid? But being poor is no excuse for being poor. Do you understand?"

They nodded, seeming to go at least halfway with the statement.

"Being poor is a state of mind. My mother and I were poor, but we never really believed that we would stay that way. We had aspirations," he said as they walked together. "You can never overestimate the importance of aspirations in how people escape from poverty. And look at me now, a coffee-marketing executive discussing international economics with two bright graduate students from the United States.

And the day gets even better—later this afternoon I have a meeting with the international coffee buyer from Dunkin' Donuts."

Angela and Sofia laughed. "Well, at least we understand now where we rank in the larger hierarchy," said Sofia.

"I want to get back to the prisoners," said Angela.

"To understand why the prisoners—and by this I mean coffee growers—live in poverty, I must tell you something of the history of coffee in our hemisphere. You see, in the 1940s the prisoners realized they were killing each other with overproduction of coffee. They understood the dynamics of their dilemma, and how individual rationality among coffee growers was leading to collective irrationality in overproduction and rock-bottom coffee prices. They knew that they had to do something to reduce the supply of coffee on the market, or the growers around the world would ruin each other with overproduction. So the Inter-American Coffee Agreement established quotas for each coffee exporting country. Some people say the United States allowed the quota system to keep Latin America from going communist. That may be so, and I think there is some truth to this point."

"So why are things still so lousy for the growers?" asked Angela.

"The problem is that the higher the prices from the quota restrictions, the greater the incentive to plant more coffee. So the high prices led to greater prosperity among growers, but also to a lot more coffee planting around the world. Then all of a sudden in the late 1950s, prices fell through the floor."

"But why can't growers just abide by the agreement?" asked Angela.

"Well, the coffee price crash in the late 1950s led to another attempt to limit supply—the International Coffee Agreement of 1962, in which coffee-producing countries through the new International Coffee Organization essentially established a coffee cartel with quotas, not only for export countries, but for import countries as well. The agreement was renegotiated every six or seven years, 1968, 1976, and 1983. Even though there was some price volatility during that time, arabica coffee prices never dropped below $1.20 a pound. It worked pretty well in that sense, but it unraveled in the late 1980s during the Reagan presidency."

"Why was that?" Angela asked.

"Well, as we know, your Reagan was no fan of market interventions, and he stocked his negotiating team for the ICA with a bunch of University of Chicago economists—not a bunch of folks naturally sympathetic to cartel behavior and price manipulation. The United States ended up dropping out of the agreement, and prices began their long march downward pretty much all through the 1990s. Then came some good weather—which remember is bad—and the crisis in 2001. Things got really bad, so bad that the United States even decided to rejoin the ICA in 2005 under a Republican administration. That's bad, let me tell you."

Sofia responded, "So for you, calamitous coffee weather in Brazil and other coffee-growing places is a substitute for the good old days of the supply-side reductions of the ICA?"

"Sí," Gustavo replied, grinning, but he began to wax philosophical again. "What man fails to do, let God mercifully do instead."

Angela chimed in. "This reminds me of a picture I saw in a magazine one time of some Florida orange growers riding bulldozers over a mountain of their own oranges. This was not a crude way of making marmalade. They were actually destroying part of their crop to keep the price of orange juice high. So you're saying coffee should do something like this to reduce world supply?"

"To a degree, nothing could be better for growers. In its place, however, has emerged the fair trade movement. Fair trade guarantees a price of $1.31 per pound to growers. In addition to this there is the ten-cent premium that goes to special development projects in the communities of the growers—schools, roads, water systems, and so forth—and a further fifteen-cent premium if it's organic."

Angela was curious. "What's so special about $1.31?"

"Well, it's gone up a little bit over the years and will probably continue to. But this is a price level that many believe allows growers in most countries to cover their costs and provide at least in a minimal way for their families, food, clothes, schooling for children. But small coffee-growing peasants aren't getting rich off $1.31 a pound, trust me."

"Don't worry, we know," said Angela.

"I read some book awhile back about the origins of the fair trade movement," said Sofia. "Originated back in the 1860s, a book called *Max Havilar, or The Coffee Auctions of the Dutch Trading Company*. Focused on all the abuses of the Dutch coffee traders in Indonesia. The hero of the book, this fellow Max Havilar, was a bureaucrat who became a defender of the native people of Java working in the coffee fields under the Dutch colonial system. Seems that the book has been to the fair trade movement what *Das Kapital* was to Marxism."

Gustavo added, "Yes, but the movement didn't mature until 1997 when the Fairtrade Labeling Organizations brought certification to the whole fair trade industry. The FLO network includes TransFair, which oversees, certifies, and promotes fair trade products in the United States."

"So fair trade has gone mainstream to some extent then," summarized Angela.

Gustavo rocked his head back and forth ambivalently. "You have to realize that certified fair trade still makes up a very small percentage of world coffee sales, still only a few percent. It's mainly in Latin America and not nearly as big as it could be."

He summed up his opinion on the movement. "The problem with

fair trade is that it depends too much on the goodwill of consumers. Notice I can barely sell a quarter of my crop under fair trade. A lot of coffee grown for fair trade has to go through the standard channels. A couple of big weather disasters in places like Brazil or Vietnam is frankly far more effective. The impact of fair trade is much less."

The lunch came, roasted chicken with black beans and tortillas. It smelled delicious. Gustavo carved out a large bite of chicken and continued, explaining more about Café Justicia. "Our co-op is certified by TransFair—we are a fair trade cooperative and provide our members with a range of services. We process the cherries for some members, give them access to credit, technical training, warehousing, and we market their coffee harvest. The co-op processes the coffee cherries using pulping machines that squeeze the little beans out of the red coffee cherries. Then coffee beans are held in large fermentation tanks owned by the co-op for several days, washed over and over with a lot of water. Then the beans are dried to create 'parchment coffee' until just before it's sold to an exporter. After we make an agreement with a buyer, the little parchment layer, just a thin beige skin, gets hulled from the bean by machine, and it becomes classified as 'green coffee.' This is the coffee commodity for which price quotes are given constantly online and at the New York Board of Trade, and for which prices appear on my computer screens. All deals that we and other exporters make with buyers are for green coffee."

"Who buys your coffee?" Sofia asked.

"Nearly all of our bags of green coffee are loaded and sent by freighter to the United States and Europe. Some of our coffee will be imported by industrial coffee roasters who then sell their roasted coffee to retail firms. The rest gets sold to—whom we try to affectionately call"—he grinned—"the *Chicos Grandes*, the big boys, large roaster retailers who roast their own coffee and market it through all their famous consumer brand names.

"You have to realize that the coffee world isn't dominated by coffee growers. Most of them are just little campesinos like those you've been interviewing in San Pedro Necta. Neither is it dominated by cooperatives like us. The real players with market power are corporations like Procter & Gamble, the huge conglomerate who sells Folgers coffee, and Kraft who sells under brand names like Maxwell House and Yuban. Then to round out the Chicos Grandes you add the Swiss firm Nestlé, the largest food company in the world, who sells Nescafé and Taster's Choice, and the German conglomerate Tchibo, as well as Massimo Zanetti of Italy, who acquired the Sara Lee brands in your country—MJB, Hills Brothers, Chase & Sanborn, and Choc Full o'Nuts. We sell our coffee to all of the Chicos Grandes, some industrial roasters, and even to Starbucks."

"And only about 25 percent of your crop is marketed as fair trade?" asked Angela.

"Yes. The market for fair trade is just not big enough for me to do any more."

As the conversation wound down, they shook hands, thanked Gustavo for the lunch, and walked back to the bus station.

"What did we learn?" asked Angela as they walked.

"Too many sellers and too few buyers," commented Sofia. "The millions of growers have too much of an incentive to overproduce and lack the institutions to regulate supply. Poverty keeps the children of coffee growers uneducated, which keeps them in the business of growing more and more coffee because that's all they know how to do. Greater supply means that prices stay low."

"A vicious cycle of the Prisoners' Dilemma."

"Yes, I think that prisoners is a very good way to put it," said Sofia. And they hopped back on the bus.

CHAPTER 19

It was just over a year ago now that Alberto had come to the village, thought the young woman. They had given him tortillas and beans and she had let him sleep in the shack behind her family's house where they kept food and hay for their animals. They had filled the shack with wool blankets over the hay so he would be comfortable, and he had been grateful for the help that she and Mildred had given him.

But one night after Mildred had left, the young woman stayed. She and Alberto talked long into the night. She lay down and they rested in the comfortable blankets over the hay as they talked. It was there that he told the young woman that at night he would dream of her beautiful face.

The young woman had never been told such things by someone as handsome as Alberto. And as the moon shone through a gap in the wall of the shack on Alberto's face, he drew his head close and whispered to her that he wanted her. Tomorrow he would walk back to his platoon and to battle, he explained. But soon he would come back for her and Father Dias would marry them. He promised this to the young woman. She was awed by Alberto, for he was brave and important. As his lips touched hers, she felt a fire of powerful emotion rise up inside her. And as his hand moved slowly and softly above her knee, she acquiesced to him.

And the next morning he left.

It was only a month later when a member of Alberto's platoon arrived one night in the village bearing news. Alberto had died in an ambush by government troops, the messenger explained. It happened at night when they least expected. He was a hero, standing shirtless in his underwear outside his tent, firing his pistol into a nest of machine-gun fire. As he held off the attacking government troops, many in his platoon had escaped. If one of their company should die for the revolution in battle, he explained, a chosen member of close kin would be notified by a surviving member of the platoon. Alberto had chosen the young woman to be informed.

And it was less than a month after this that she realized she was carrying Alberto's baby. She considered the situation and understood this would be a shame upon her, on the child, and on her family. Father Dias would be disappointed.

But there was one solution that would prevent all shame.

A boy named Domingo had been courting her for months, even proposing marriage to her. Now she would accept, and Alberto's baby would be his baby. And although she did not love Domingo in the way that some women loved their husbands—at least when they first married them—Domingo would be an honorable husband.

He would provide for her and she would be faithful to him. In this way she would remove the shame that her family and this baby never deserved to experience.

Domingo was elated at the young woman's change of heart; they were married within weeks. When she told Mildred of her secret, Mildred vowed to keep it to herself. She hoped that Mildred was not disappointed or jealous. But even Mildred had agreed that to marry Domingo was best under the circumstances. And she and Domingo and their baby had been a contented family—until today.

Distracted by a distant motion outside, the young woman peered outside through a crack between the boards. A woman from the village was pacing toward the barn.

It was Eva, the wife of Adolfo, one of the leaders of the civil patrol, in whose barn she hid. Had Mildred told Eva of her hiding place? She knew that Mildred would do this perhaps only under a great threat, perhaps only a threat of death. Because the young woman was now standing, she was vulnerable and could be seen. She looked down at the hay. If she moved quickly to hide herself in the hay, she would make too much noise and might be seen at a short distance through the cracks in the barn. Instead she tried to stand as still as possible, hoping to blend with the shadows. As she pressed herself into one of the corners of the barn, the baby began to stir. No, the baby must not awake. In movements that were as subtle as possible, she tried to soothe it with the most imperceptible degree of motion. Even so, the baby unclutched from her nipple and began to murmur little noises. She quickly switched to her other breast, so that the child might continue nursing. The baby must not cry.

But for a single moment, it did.

A wave of panic rushed through the young woman as she saw Eva raise her face up to the barn in response to the noise. As the young woman stood motionless, she watched the silhouette of the middle-aged Eva silently move past the slats of the wall of the barn, pacing steadily toward the entrance. At that point there seemed no choice but to seek refuge behind a nearby hay bale. Perhaps Eva's own footsteps through the weeds would muffle the sounds of her own movement. She prayed that they would, and she prayed that Eva had some other reason to come to her barn. Had Eva been at the river washing with Mildred when she had told the women some of Alberto's secret stories? They washed in the same location, so it was possible.

She lay behind the hay bale, the infant nursing at her side. Sweat was pouring off her forehead. In the moment she could hear only two noises, that of her own heartbeat and the footsteps, slowing as they approached the back door. She shut her eyes, nearly unable to bear the sound of the barn latch sliding open. For a brief moment she opened her eyes and saw a short pitchfork lying a few feet from her, and the terror of the moment stirred a horrible thought in the young woman's mind. She would have to kill Eva. She was younger and stronger; if she did it quickly she could hide her body in the barn and it would not be discovered until later. Perhaps the soldiers would be blamed. She had never remotely considered killing another human being before; Father Dias had always told them all killing was a sin. But it was not something she needed to be told. Yet her mind recalled Eva's deliberate pace through the center of the village to the barn, unthreatened. This was not the action of one fleeing. It was that of one who had been granted freedom in exchange for helping those who would kill. And if she were killed, her baby might be killed. This thought was too much to bear. Her hand slowly reached over to the pitchfork and she drew it to her side next to the baby.

The footsteps continued slowly and quietly across the floor of the barn toward her, rustling through the hay. Then there was an agonizing silence. And more silence. Perhaps Eva had gone. Then a wrinkled face appeared suddenly over the hay bale. The closeness and appearance of the face shocked her and she flinched, terrified. Eva looked down, face devoid of surprise; only a cold, blank expression met the young woman lying in the hay. Eva's finger was flush across her cracked gray lips. "Shhhhhhh," the older woman whispered slowly. "You stay. Your secret is safe with me."

In a momentary decision that she knew would affect everything, the young woman's fingers loosened on the pitchfork. And just as quickly, Eva was gone.

—

Angela

Sofia asked Angela if she would like to stop to visit a friend from her department on the way back to San Pedro Necta who was also doing fieldwork. It was about an hour north, off of the Pan-American.

"Who is your friend?" asked Angela.

"Her name is Jennifer and she is working on a microfinance project near Chichicastenango. Want to go?"

"Sure. I've always heard a ton about microfinance, but never seen it in action. What do you think about it?"

"Well, the number of growers involved with fair trade coffee is dwarfed compared with the number of borrowers in the world with a microfinance loan."

"Does it work?" asked Angela.

"Well, that's something that people like Jennifer have been trying to find out. We know that people keep borrowing and repaying, so borrowers must find the loans beneficial at some level. But it's not as easy as one might think to answer the impact question."

They took the chicken bus for three hours from Guatemala City and got off with their backpacks at Los Encuentros, another diesel-caked intersection along the Pan-American where people change buses. Then they got on another bus headed north on a twisty, one-and-a-half-lane road toward Chichicastenango. On the way Angela relayed something she had learned from her mother back home.

"Sofia, I got an e-mail from my mom yesterday."

"Oh yeah? What's new in LA?"

"Said that she wrote the adoption agency in the capital to see if she could find out exactly where I'm from down here."

"And?"

"They're not positive, but they think it was either Huehue or Quiché province. Think any of the coffee growers look like my cousins?"

"Pretty much all of them, actually."

Angela laughed. In some ways it was true. But she couldn't get the thought out of her mind. It dawned on her that for the first time in her life she was in a place where nearly everybody looked like her.

A ways into the journey, Sofia called Jennifer on her cell phone about twenty minutes before she thought the bus would arrive, so she was waiting for them when the bus pulled into the center of Chichi.

"*Hola, amiga!*" A short, spunky woman with freckles and short, light brown hair wrapped Sofia in a bear hug the moment she stepped off the bus. Sofia introduced her to Angela, and she gave Angela an enthusiastic handshake. Jennifer was about as American *gringa* as they come, pure Wonder Bread from the Midwest. It was clear that she also had a Midwestern sense of welcome and hospitality, and was a power-packed little ball of energy. "Angela, you can call me Jen," she effused. "Would you guys like to hang out here in Chichi a bit before we head up to my place? It's market day today."

They strode onto the main square of Chichicastenango. It was a Thursday and the market was in full swing. Adjacent to the market was the impressive Iglesia Santo Tomás, a large white cathedral facing the main square. On the steps of the cathedral, Mayan priests were carrying out some sort of ritual in which they waved canisters of burning incense. Angela had never seen anything quite like it. A greenish-gray haze of incense filled the air all around the church steps.

Jen told them a little about the cathedral. "The Santo Tomás isn't exactly your mother's Catholic church. It's a mixture of Catholicism and Mayan religion. The eighteen steps that lead up to the front doors represent the number of months in the Mayan calendar. A lot of the saints in the church are more or less Mayan deities given apostolic names. You might say it's syncretism in its purest form." She laughed heartily at her own joke with a funny laugh that sounded like a little child being tickled.

Angela surveyed the market, which clearly catered to an eclectic crowd. There were the usual household wares offered to the Chichi locals, but there was also a plethora of articles for sale aimed at the North American and European tourists who were scattered among the crowds. Beautiful handmade Guatemalan textiles and indigenous art adorned nearly every wooden kiosk. One vendor who sold cortes, the colorful Guatemalan skirts, seemed to attract a mixed crowd of local women, who were buying them to wear, and tourists who were likely to use them as a table decoration back home. They mingled among the market crowd for about half an hour.

"Ever been to Chichi before?" Jen asked Angela.

"This is my first time back to Guatemala. I was adopted."

"Welcome back then. Want to reconnect with your Mayan ancestors a little? Come with me. I'll show you guys something very cool."

"How cool?" asked Sofia, who was getting a little hungry. Angela remembered that she liked to eat lunch on time.

"*Very.*" Her eyes narrowed into an impish smile.

Angela and Sofia glanced at each other for a moment, a quick cost-benefit analysis in the context of imperfect information. "Okay, lead the way," said Angela, and Sofia acquiesced.

Jen led them away from the plaza south down the *Avenida Acro Gucumatz*. They turned right on a narrow rural lane for a few hundred meters until they came to a path that jogged off the main road to their left. The path led through the forest.

"This way," she motioned.

"Where are you taking us?" asked Sofia, not seemingly worried, but curious.

"You'll see," came Jen's mischievous reply. The wooded area around the dirt trail became thicker as they walked past a few homes. It led directly to the base of a small mountain and then began to wind upward, switching back and forth as it led them toward the top. Although only about a mile from the center of town, they were in fairly dense forest now. A dark canopy of branches and vines hung over their heads. Nevertheless, the path was well traveled. More than a few people had made this trek in the recent past. Angela noticed bits of candles tossed to the side of the path, and a few other bits and pieces of strange artifacts. It was humid. The women began perspiring as the climb became steeper, and their hair stuck to the sides of their faces.

Soon the concave slope of the small mountain began to level off, and they reached the summit. They stopped for a rest. Sofia was breathing hard after the climb. She unzipped her backpack and took out her inhaler from the side pocket, pumping in several quick bursts. "This better be good," she said as she flipped it back into her pack.

They found themselves on a forested plateau. Angela heard a faint, enigmatic chanting sound through the trees, but could see nothing. They reloaded their backpacks and resumed their hike along the trail. The chanting continued. It grew louder. Now through a grove of trees, Angela could see smoke coming from a small campfire. A half dozen people were gathered around the fire, all indigenous Mayans in traditional dress. They were led, it appeared, by a man who to Angela seemed like he must be some kind of priest. The fire burned next to a primitive stone shrine that was covered with lit candles and the wax of decades, if not centuries, of candles before these. The forest was filled with the redolent aroma of incense mingled with the smoke from the ground fire. The stone face of a god with protruding nose and lips, looking like a small version of an Easter Island statue, stared stoically ahead at the front of the shrine.

"It's the shrine of *Pascual Abaj*," Jen whispered to them. They kept at a distance behind the ceremony, crouching behind a fallen log in the grove of trees.

"Pascual who?" whispered Angela back as Sofia leaned in.

"Pascual Abaj. It means 'sacrifice stone.' This is a shrine to the Mayan earth god Huyup Tak'ah. That's his face on the shrine."

Through the branches of the forest they watched the priest take two eggs and hold them up in the air as he closed his eyes. After a two-minute incantation to Huyup Tak'ah, he took the eggs and smashed them together over the fire, allowing the yokes to dribble into the flames. The stench of burning eggs filled the air. He then picked up a bottle of rum sitting on a nearby rock and poured splashes of rum over the burning eggs. Colored flames shot up above the fire pit as the alcohol ignited. There were more prayers. Another woman handed the priest some flowers. The priest tossed the flowers one by one into the fire. More rum was decanted over the orange flame, which again flared momentarily into blue-green. At that moment Angela noticed a nervous-looking chicken cramped in a very small cage near one of the women.

"What's that chicken doing there?" Angela asked Jen.

Jen was curious as well. "I don't know, but based on what happened to the eggs and flowers, I don't think it looks good for the chicken," she whispered. They waited. More chanting.

After several minutes the woman reached down and handed the caged chicken to the priest. He drew the chicken from the cage and held it in the air.

"Uh-oh," whispered Sofia. "Time to close your eyes."

"Oh my G—" said Angela, looking at Sofia, who responded in kind with a squeamish look on her face. The priest reached for a long butcher's knife sitting on one of the rocks. Holding the chicken upside down with one hand, he carefully drew up the knife and, in one horizontal motion, slashed off its head. The head fell into the fire. The priest held the headless chicken upside down by its legs over the fire, chanting a Mayan incantation. Its wings continued to flap slowly for a few moments as the headless chicken bled out into the flames.

"Ick," Angela remarked to the others.

"Told you that you wouldn't be disappointed," whispered Jen.

"How'd you know he'd be up here?" asked Angela.

"He's up here all the time, kind of like a priest working his confession booth. People come up to him here with their petitions and he seems to know the appropriate sacrifice for everybody's problem."

"That chicken must have stood in for a big issue," guessed Angela. "Well, at least it wasn't a goat, or a cow . . ."

"Or a virgin," added Sofia. They all laughed under their breath Angela wondered for the first time if her ancestors ever sacrificed any virgins. "You know, in Latin America we've made some notable progress over the last five centuries."

As Angela joined in the quiet laughter behind the log, out of the corner of her eye she perceived the subtlest of movements on the ground next to her. A paralyzing electric current surged through her limbs as she witnessed the long body of a venomous barba amarilla emerge from under the log and slowly slither between Jen's boots. Crouching on the other side of her, Sofia immediately saw it after sensing Angela's recoil, while Jen's happy expression remained unchanged as she continued to focus unawares on the activity at the ritual site.

Angela was impressed that Sofia did not faint immediately. Indeed, as her own mouth seemed incapable of forming words in any language, Sofia spoke to Jen in a tense but calm voice.

"Jen, I believe it is very important that you keep looking ahead and hold very still," whispered Sofia. The snake continued its slow and inauspicious exit from under the log through the blue-jeaned arch of Jen's crouched legs. "Perhaps it's better if we don't talk now." They all continued to crouch, still and silent, Jen's eyebrows now raised and teeth clenched after a torturous glance between her knees revealed the source of the anxiety. Angela watched as the tail of the barba amarilla unhurriedly made its way past her boots, behind them, and into the woods. They closed their eyes in relief and slowly stood up as the snake slithered across some leaves and down the hill.

They moved as quickly as they could away from the fallen log and back on the path. "*Gracias,* Sofia," said Jen. "That was one for the ages, ladies."

"How did you not *lose it*?" Angela asked Sofia.

Sofia took a deep breath and shrugged. "I'm not quite sure. Well, lunch, anyone?"

The three women left the shrine and headed down the mountain.

—

After lunch they walked back toward the central square and Jen asked, "Would you like to visit a few microfinance clients?"

"How do we get there?" asked Sofia.

"Well, you could take a taxi, or we could ride together on this." She pounded the seat of a rather large motorcycle they had just approached that was parked on the street.

"This is yours?" Sofia asked.

"Yep."

"*Three* of us?" Sofia asked incredulously.

"Sure. Person on the back gets the helmet!"

They aligned themselves on the seat with Jen pushed so far forward that she was sitting on the gas tank. It was fortunate that she and Angela were both fairly small. They laughed at being jammed together in such a tiny sitting space.

"Hang on!" Jen revved the accelerator and the bike rocketed down a cobblestone street. The feet of Sofia and Angela fought for a spot on the lone rear footrest.

A cool breeze blew through Angela's hair as they rumbled out of town toward the mountains. Jen adeptly churned her way through the gearbox with her left foot as they passed small rural houses, grazing cows, and countless fields of coffee. Angela was in the back. Sofia's long, dark mane was flapping in Angela's face, making both of them laugh. Angela remedied the situation by flipping down the visor on the helmet.

Jen moved her head to the side and yelled back to them over the noise of the motorcycle, "It's interesting that you are working with coffee growers, because so am I. At least half of the borrowers taking microfinance loans in my study grow coffee."

"Do they take the loans for coffee production?" yelled Angela.

"The loans are supposed to be for investment in rural microenterprises, but I suppose some of it could get diverted into their coffee," she yelled back. "Money is fungible, after all. Purpose of the program I'm evaluating is to finance alternatives to agricultural production in general, and alternatives to coffee in particular. There's no money in coffee these days."

After a fifteen-minute ride, Angela felt the motorcycle engine begin to coast, and they pulled into the front yard of an adobe house surrounded by fields of maize and coffee. The three women, one at a time, somehow managed to untangle all of their limbs from the bike, laughing at their predicament. Regaining their composure, they approached the front of the house.

"Señor Bixcul? . . . Señor Bixcul?" called Jen, hands clasped around her mouth for projection.

A voice emerged from a small adobe workshop next to the house, and the voice was soon matched by a person. Señor Bixcul strolled out to greet Jen. He shook hands with her and her two friends as they all were introduced. His hands were dry and rough, but the handshake was warm and firm. Angela figured that he was probably about sixty years old, but the age was perhaps dwarfed by the mileage. Despite it all, Señor Bixcul had an amiable smile that, even with a few missing teeth, shone through his dark, wrinkled skin. He invited them into his workshop.

"He's a coffee grower, but also makes corte, the Guatemalan cloth that women use for skirts," Jen informed them. The skirts were famous for their multicolored stripes and intricate designs, subtle Mayan patterns and pictures of people and different kinds of animals. He explained to them the process he used to dye and mark the designs on his thread. There were hundreds of yards of thread of different colors drying in the sun on racks outside his shop. Each distinctive marking on the thread, he explained, would produce different types of designs on the cloth. Señor Bixcul had applied for a $400 loan to help him purchase a new *telar* so that his son could work with him, and a large bag of colored thread.

"How much extra income per month does the microloan earn for you?" asked Angela in Spanish, wanting to understand whether it was having any kind of positive effect.

"*Quizas tres-cientos quetzales al mes,*" Señor Bixcul replied. It was about $40 more per month.

"Not bad," said Angela.

"No, it's not bad at all," agreed Sofia. "But it's not surprising, either. Capital is usually more productive in the hands of someone who has very little of it than in the hands of someone who already has a lot. The credit market without interventions like microfinance is not only biased against the poor—it's inefficient."

"How are things in the business otherwise, Señor Bixcul?" asked Jen.

"*Bien.*"

Angela could not resist. "Señor Bixcul, how do you really use your loan money?"

"*Pues*, there is something I must confess to you," said the old man.

"*Completamente confidencial*," replied Jen. She turned to the other women and spoke in English. "He understands that we are not his loan officers—just researchers, so he'll be more open with us."

"I do not use all of my loan for the weaving business."

A violation of his lending contract, Jen explained, but interesting. "What do you use it for?" asked Angela.

"My son does not work on the loom all day. In the afternoon he goes to school. I use much of the loan to pay his *colegiatura*." He used it partly for the school fees.

They thanked him for his sincerity and spent a little more time talking with Señor Bixcul, then said good-bye. Their last image was of him shaking his head from side to side, watching the three women trying to fit on the motorcycle. His wide grin showed off all of his missing teeth. Before Angela had time to feel self-conscious, Jen's wrist yanked back on the accelerator and the overburdened motorcycle lumbered down the road.

They stayed at Jen's house that night. It was a small cottage she leased during her fieldwork, not too far outside of Chichicastenango. As Jen cooked at the stove, she fielded questions from Angela about microfinance.

"What effect do you think this microfinance has on the coffee growers?" asked Angela.

"Well, a lot of coffee growers here operate a small business on the side that helps them to diversify some of the risks associated with the volatility in their yields as well as the volatility in coffee prices. This gives them some income in times other than the harvest season, and if coffee prices are down, it provides something for them to fall back on," said Jen. "A few borrowers reach high enough levels of enterprise capitalization that they leave coffee production altogether."

"Interesting," said Sofia, reflecting on the day, "that after his weaving business, Señor Bixcul views his son's education as a better investment than coffee production. Notice when he cheated, he cheated toward education, not coffee." She continued reflectively. "Aside from economic diversification, perhaps microfinance may have another important role to play in the welfare of the world's coffee growers."

"What's that?" asked Jen.

"To wean them off growing coffee."

The two other women looked at Sofia.

"What I mean is, we just interviewed a fair trade marketing executive in the capital, who literally clings to his rosary beads as he begs for negative worldwide supply shocks. He said that the best thing that could happen to all coffee growers would be for there to be fewer of them and less coffee."

Sofia paused and then continued. "You say that giving coffee growers microfinance loans leads some of them to abandon coffee growing in favor of doing something else. Today we talked with a man who secretly uses his loans to finance more education for his kid. Well, given the sensitivity of coffee prices to supply, even this fair trade marketing executive admits that a significant reduction in the worldwide production of coffee would probably do more for more coffee growers than fair trade ever could. Higher world coffee prices would benefit *every* coffee grower, not just the growers who are privy to the special fair trade marketing channels. Perhaps the best development programs for coffee growers might not involve coffee at all."

"To solve the dilemma of the prisoners," said Angela.

"Exactly," said Sofia.

The women continued the conversation into the night until they fell asleep on mats laid out next to the low-burning fire in the fireplace.

The next morning Angela and Sofia boarded a bus heading back to Huehuetenango.

In another week it would be time for Angela and Alex to return home.

Chapter 20

Alex

ALEX HAD NEVER BEEN ONE FOR GOOD-BYES. IT WAS A FEEL-
ing he had developed from his childhood. After his parents' divorce
he split time between them, staying at his mother's house during the
weekdays and his father's apartment on the weekends. Twice a week,
there was the inevitable good-bye to one of his parents, which he
quickly came to dread, and then despise. And as the years wore on, the
routine of the biweekly good-bye failed to anesthetize the pain of it. It
had made him cynical about traditional institutions, including family,
and maybe especially family. In all of these traditional arrangements
someone was always getting ripped off, getting hurt, feeling pain.
There were always motives of which to be suspicious.

Now it was time to say good-bye to Lourdes and her family, one of
the few families he had met where there was love and warmth between
family members, despite their modest means. And just as he was still
trying to understand all of this, time had run out. They hiked up the
long road from the Hotel Chinita to their house. Juana was expecting
them for lunch.

When they were still fifty yards from the house, she greeted them
from the kitchen window where she was working, as always. *"Buenos*

tardes muchachos de California!" she broadcasted from her spot at the window to the entire neighborhood, waving enthusiastically. Ema ran out to greet them and extended her hand for Angela's and pulled it to her cheek. They walked together with the others toward the house.

"Donde está Don Fernando?" they inquired.

"Oh, I cannot tell you how sorry he was not to be here to say good-bye. A neighbor's son had to be taken to the hospital in the capital, *apendicitis* I think it was. He had much he had left to say." She turned to Angela. "Especially to you, *mi hija.*"

Once again she had prepared them the traditional *almuerzo tipico*: tortillas and beans, some fresh avocado, a square of goat cheese, plantains, and one of the chickens that had been rummaging around the yard yesterday morning.

Over lunch they talked about plans for the coffee crop that year, about Angela's and Alex's work back in San Francisco, and about plans for the baby. After lunch Juana brought out coffee for everyone, and they chatted a little more until the conversation naturally died down and came to a satisfying rest.

Alex talked in front of the house with Lourdes, the conversation heavy with the weight of a looming good-bye. But the survey of the coffee growers was complete. Rich would be returning south to his tropical fruit project. Sofia would remain a few more weeks to work on her own branch of the coffee research before heading back to Berkeley.

"Who will help you with the baby?" Alex asked Lourdes, concerned.

"My mother will help me, and also my father, and of course the Lord. He will help me too," she replied. He remained concerned. "Alex, don't you know that he even turns mistakes and sins into good things later? It is a promise in *la Biblia*. I have read it."

"If you say this is so, Lourdes, I do not doubt you." She smiled and his arms reached out to hers above her elbows, and he held her and looked into her eyes. And now as Alex looked into her eyes closely, she looked less certain of herself. Ever so slowly their faces drew closer together, but as he went to kiss her on the lips, she turned her head just slightly so that the kiss landed softly on her right cheek as she shut her eyes, resulting in what could be interpreted as the most traditional and culturally appropriate of gestures. Was it because she thought someone was watching, or of her own accord? Of this Alex would wonder.

After some time the others joined them in the front, where everyone shook hands and embraced with much quicker *besos* to the right cheek. The students slowly walked away from the house, waving as they turned left on the dirt road. Alex turned back one last time. Lourdes smiled, and quickly brushed away a tear with the palm of her left hand as she waved good-bye with her right.

The next morning Sofia and Rich walked Alex and Angela to the bus and bade them a warm good-bye. And as quickly as they had come, they were gone.

CHAPTER 21

Angela

September 4, 2007

JAVA JOE'S, ONE OF THE LEADING COFFEE IMPORTERS AND roasters in the San Francisco Bay Area, was also one of Gustavo's favorite buyers. He had given Angela and Sofia their contact information. The Oakland company served a large niche of a large market: the coffee shops and retailers around the Bay Area and Northern California. They imported green coffee originating from both conventional and fair trade sources. One of their preferred coffees: arabica hard bean, cultivated between 5,000 and 6,500 feet above sea level in Huehuetenango, Guatemala.

Not long after their return to San Francisco, Angela and Alex set up an appointment with public relations manager Ellen Bintz to visit the roastery.

Upon their arrival, Ellen greeted them cordially and gave them a brochure about the firm that had lots of colorful coffee bean pictures. She was interested but a little puzzled about the research project.

"You're doing what now?" She looked at them with an overproduced smile.

Angela glanced at Alex and then she stepped in. "It's a project we're working on for our master's theses that's part of a larger research project with some of our professors. We're, uh . . . following coffee beans all the way from growers—in our case, peasant growers in Guatemala—down the chain all the way to the coffee shop. We're trying to figure out where the profit is going."

"You are the next link in the chain," Alex interjected bluntly. He had told Angela that he suspected that too much of the profit was ending up with the roasters, and he was turned off by the contrast between the abject poverty he had recently seen and experienced throughout Guatemala and the shiny new facility with the plush espresso bar they were visiting now. His disposition was as gray as a day in Amsterdam.

"Well, we're honored to be so." Ellen obviously didn't get the public relations job for nothing. Unfazed by Alex's demeanor, she responded, "That sounds like a very ambitious project."

"Well, yes, I suppose it is," said Angela. "But we are working off a grant from the US Agency for International Development that is trying to determine the impact of fair trade coffee on how coffee profits are distributed along the value chain. I think they're hoping to redistribute some of the profit back to the growers. No offense to your company, of course."

"No, of course, none taken," said Ellen, still smiling unctuously. She led them to a large warehouse that was adjacent to the office. Burlap coffee sacks were piled up on pallets twenty feet high in the warehouse in several rows, each at least thirty yards long. A white-collar employee wearing a loose tie and a pocket protector stood with a clipboard talking intently to a blue-collar man in a hard hat, who was the operator of the forklift parked next to the enormous wall of coffee.

Ellen walked the students over to the white-collared man and waited patiently for him to finish his conversation. He obviously didn't want it interrupted by a pesky woman from the public relations office, and so he continued his directive to the man in the hard hat without acknowledging her. It was something about the order in which he wanted the pallets stacked.

After the extensive limit of Ellen's patience was reached, she was forced to politely interrupt. "Jerry, these are two students working on a coffee project." Jerry turned a mildly annoyed gaze in her direction, and Hard Hat ambled back to his forklift. "Angela and Alex, this is Jerry, our import manager."

"Pleased to meet you, Jerry," said Angela, and Alex smiled. The three shook hands.

Jerry warmed up a little. "Welcome to our roastery, guys."

"From where is all of this coffee?" asked Alex.

"Well, all over the place, frankly. Comes in from everywhere to the port just down the street, gets unloaded, and we truck it over to the warehouse and drop it over there," said Jerry. He took them over to the coffee, where they could read the burlap sacks that colorfully revealed the coffee's origin. "Right here we have our Sumatra, in this stack our Bolivian," he said as he slapped a bag of coffee. "Over to the left, some Kenyan . . ." Alex could see the ornate logo printed on the sack. "Over here we got a little Ethiopian . . . found him hiding between the pallets . . . stowaway." Jerry thought this was a hoot and guffawed at his joke.

Angela wondered how a guy like this survived in an ethnically diverse place like Oakland. "Any Guatemalan? . . . Er . . . coffee, that is?" she asked.

"Yep. Right this way." He led them two aisles over and about thirty feet down to several pallets stacked with Guatemalan coffee. "Got your Huehuetenango hard bean arabica from western Guatemala."

"We were just down there," said Alex.

"In Huehue?" asked Jerry.

Alex nodded. They explained the project.

"Some of the best coffee in the world if you get the right planta-tion. Grows at about 6,000 to 8,000 feet. Fruity, juicy aroma in green form. Sweet, but acidic. Almost like mangoes or lemons. Makes a great French Roast."

"Why the plastic bags?" asked Angela offhandedly.

"New trend in storage and shipping for high-end coffee. Vacuumed plastic bags make the coffee taste less like a burlap sack when you drink it," said Jerry. "Subtle, but it's there. Don't care about the cheap stuff, but if I'm paying a twenty-dollar premium for some specialty coffee, I don't want it tasting baggy."

"That could make sense," agreed Alex, nodding with eyebrows raised.

Jerry continued. "Also, you get this thing called 'container rain.' Get dew that condenses on the ceiling of the containers from tem-perature changes outside and the moisture in the coffee. Stuff drips down into the product. If you got a container on top of the stack in the sun, coffee practically starts brewing all by itself on the cargo ship on the way over. Turns a shipping container into an oversized coffee pot. Makes a big mess. Ruins the coffee. Can't happen with vacuum bags."

"Furthermore, one time some moron in a chemical suit from the United States Department of Agriculture fumigated my entire con-tainer of coffee with insecticide. Made some specialty Indonesian arabica taste like a can of Raid. A burlap sack is no barrier against that kind of stupidity. If I could find that guy again, I'd ring his freakin' . . ."

Before Jerry could fully define the manner in which he would physically punish the USDA official, Ellen thanked him and ushered the students toward a back hallway that led to a large room. It was the roastery. A half dozen coffee roasters looked like large steel drums.

"Angela and Alex, this is Gunter Erhardt, our head roaster." Gunter wore a laboratory coat and was hunched over a control panel. With his back to them, he quickly lifted a flat palm with fingers touching neatly together toward the group, motioning them to hold off as he finished calibrating one of the temperature dials on his equipment. After a few disconcerting moments, everything seemed to be adjusted. Gunter turned toward the group and, dispensing with formalities, got down to business.

"Let me give you a short background on ze woasting process," he began, pronouncing the word with a guttural *h* like "wwhrhrhoasting." Alex and Angela glanced at one another. Gunter looked like a mad scientist in a B movie. To complement his look, he had a magnificently strong German accent, was of unidentifiable age, wore thick spectacles with black rims, and had wild, uncombed hair that was a mixture of gray and its unidentifiable original color. He wore a white lab coat with a cloth name badge that read "Erhardt." Angela hadn't noticed other employees wearing this kind of formal identification.

"Woasting," he began, "is essential to creating drinkable coffee because heat is required to convert the carbohydrates and fats in the bean into aromatic flavor that is craved by the discriminating American coffee consumer." He paused awkwardly for a moment, though Angela wasn't quite sure why. "When the beans come to us in the green form, we run them through the hopper to screen out particles, debris, and little rocks that are mixed with the raw green coffee product. After undesirable matter is filtered from the consumer product, we begin the woasting process."

He paused again, expressionless, inspecting the reactions of the two students closely through his thick spectacles. Although she was genuinely interested in what Gunter was saying, Angela bit her lip to suppress a giggle. He began again. "During the process, beans are heated in drums stationed to my right and your left . . ." As Gunter continued with the lecture in an expressionless monotone, Ellen motioned her hand toward the ovens in an elegant, rolling gesture like a female assistant on a game show, apparently to add a little levity to the presentation. ". . . to temperatures up to 500 degrees Fahrenheit by the flamer of the natural gas," he said with a straight face. Nearly losing her composure at this moment, Angela's last resort was to raise her hand with a comment.

Gunter called on her. "The roasters sort of look like clothes dryers," she observed.

"Yes, in fact zis is not a joke, but rather an ashtute observation!" he declared in a loud voice that was alarmingly close to a yell. "The coffee roaster operates under the same physical principles as the spinning clothes dryer, keeping the beans in motion during the process to prevent the beans from burning up." He made one of his awkward pauses again and then continued, "First, the roasting drums are preheated and then the beans are heated for anywhere between a few minutes and one-half hour. At 350 degrees, the 'first crack' happens at about seven to nine minutes."

"What do you mean, this 'first crack'?" asked Alex.

"It is when the coffee bean makes the little pooping sound from an exothermic reaction as moisture escapes from the interior of the bean."

Angela whispered to Ellen, "Did he mean *popping* sound?"

"Yes, I believe so," she whispered back.

Gunter ignored the whispering taking place in front of him. "At this point caramelization of the sugars inside the bean commences, which gives the beans aromatic flavor. If we remove heat at this stage, the beans would have New England roast, the level most preferred by—if I may dare to say so—the *least* discriminating consumers. More roasting yields a Full-City or American roast. Roasting even a few more minutes produces Italian roast and, still a little longer, the French roast with bolder, smokier flavors."

"Once my father has described this difference to me," said Alex. "He said it is like one making a choice between Grace Kelly and Sophia Loren."

Gunter stared at Alex with a blank face and considered this thought, perhaps not altogether certain of the depth of the allegorical meaning. "Yes . . . quite an interesting . . . eh . . . metaphor."

"So how do you make decaf?" asked Angela.

"To create the decaffeinated coffee, we remove the caffeine by soaking beans in methylene chloride. Unfortunately, the methylene chloride bonds with and takes away some of the flavor too, an outcome that is currently technically unavoidable."

"What about instant coffee?" inquired Alex.

Gunter was clearly repulsed by the very idea of instant coffee, but seemingly did his best to repress all negative emotion as he responded to the question. "To make the instant coffee, roasted coffee beans, often the cheap, low-quality robusta beans, are ground into small particles that are mixed with very hot water, creating a coffee concentrate. After freeze drying, what remains are the instant coffee crystals coffee consumers scoop into their cup. For the record, we do *not* make the instant coffee here."

The final question regarding instant coffee appeared to be all Gunter could bear for the day, and he seemed eager to get back to his dials. Ellen showed them how the roasted beans were stored in large bins and then sent through one of two large machines, from which they exited in one-pound or five-pound vacuum-packed bags. This was the final product that was shipped to retailers and cafés throughout California and the West Coast.

She then led them out of the roasting room and answered a few final questions.

"What price do you charge coffeehouses for your beans?" asked Angela.

"We charge $5.25 per pound for fair trade and $4.15 per pound for the standard coffee," said Ellen. Alex was about to make what Angela anticipated was a highly inappropriate remark and she interrupted.

"Thanks for the tour," she said, heading to the exit door with Alex before he could share the fullness of his thoughts with the tour guide.

"Good luck with that project of yours," said Ellen, waving.

"Did you listen to that one?" said Alex, disgusted as they headed down the sidewalk to Angela's car. "For the pound of beans that these guys sell for $5.25, they pay we know only $1.48—what Gustavo and everyone like him can get on the free market. So we find that markup over costs for growers like Fernando is a little over 20 percent, markup at the fair trade cooperative level is 15 percent, but the markup at industrial roaster level is over 250 percent!"

"I know. That's a lot. But it must be the competitive price," Angela argued.

"It may be a competitive price, but it still means rip-offs."

"But they wouldn't be able to charge that much if they were making extraordinary profits. The market wouldn't allow it," Angela contended.

"What do you mean, 'it wouldn't allow it'? It *is* allowing it."

"That's exactly what I mean. The roasters must be just covering their costs after they pay for machinery, electricity, the rent or mortgage on their facility in this area, salaries to their employees that are enough to get them to work for their firm, health care costs, and everything else. Look, this is a competitive market. If one roaster were making an extraordinary profit by charging high prices, another one would undercut their price. This would continue until any abnormally high profits among the roasters were driven out of the system." Angela felt confident about this. How could profits remain high in a competitive market? Free entry would make them disappear in the long run.

"Perhaps they are colluding?" Alex suggested.

"You can't base your analysis on conspiracy theories. You're essentially suggesting a cartel exists between hundreds, maybe thousands of coffee roasters. I know there are the Chicos Grandes that Gustavo talked about. They may have some degree of market power in retail sectors that they dominate. But we're not talking about Choc Full o'Nuts; we're talking about Java Joe's, a reasonably sized roaster in our area, but one that faces serious competition for its product all around the western US. I just don't believe a secret cartel like that can exist."

"Angela, have you read the report by Oxfam several years ago during the coffee crisis, accusing the roasters of market manipulation and grower exploitation? This is not something people are now making up. During the 1970s under the International Coffee Agreement, producers received about 20 percent of total income in the world coming from coffee, and the consuming countries got 'only' a little over 50 percent. But listen to it: after the collapse of the ICA in 1989, the share of income to the producers of coffee fell to about 13 percent, and the income from coffee in the consuming countries increased to more than 75 percent." Alex had apparently been reading up on this.

Alex continued, "And you know? When world price of coffee dove by nearly half during the coffee crisis, retail prices of coffee only decreased a few percent. If markets are as competitive as you say, how can this happen? It doesn't make sense. It is obvious that there is something smelling like fish going on."

Angela thought about this for a while. "It may be that costs are simply higher in the developed countries, and these costs that occur from the roasting phase forward make up the majority of the costs of delivering coffee to the consumer. May come from differences in the cost of people's time between those who live in rich and poor countries, also from other added costs like workers' compensation and health insurance. Are you arguing that the workers should be paid less in the processing facilities in Europe and the United States? Should the companies drop their health insurance so people can buy cheaper coffee?"

"But why should differences in these costs have grown so much over the last twenty years?"

"Just supply and demand. The increasing margins of the coffee roasters also have to do with market forces operating at the levels of the consumer and the producer. We know the ICA held up prices artificially, encouraging surplus coffee production all around the world. Then you have the growing costs of labor in the rich countries, where the beans are processed, and a steady increase in the demand for coffee since the early 1990s. All of this adds up not to some kind of price-fixing conspiracy by roasters, but to worsening conditions for growers, and more value added at the roaster and retailer levels. And a lot of these increasing margins must be going toward higher labor costs in the form of wages and benefits."

Alex changed the subject. "What is that pamphlet in your hand?" he asked.

"It's a list of all the cafés in the Bay Area that serve Java Joe's. I picked it up on a table in the waiting room. Check these out: the Java Lounge, Kind Grind, Jumpin' Java, the Blue Danube Coffee House. And some of these are near campus in the Richmond district in the city." Angela paused.

"Alex, right here we have it—the last link in the chain."

CHAPTER 22

The young woman watched anxiously while the baby slept peacefully at her side on the colorful blanket in the hay. How could such innocence exist in a world of such reckless and pitiless hatred?

Across the village she observed that the lieutenant was growing angrier with the people in the church. It seemed they would not come out, and he was threatening them. Through the crack in the barn wall, she saw a military vehicle drive up and stop in front of the lieutenant. Another soldier carrying two large water containers jumped out of the truck. He talked with the lieutenant, and the lieutenant made some hand gestures toward the church. The soldier then began to sprinkle the water around the outside wall of the church. He also sprinkled some of the water on a cloth and tied the cloth around a stick someone had fetched from the forest. It then became clear to the young woman that what was in the containers was not water. If Pastor Juan and his followers would not come out of the church, then the lieutenant would burn the church down.

Please come out of the church, Pastor Juan, she prayed. She heard singing in the church, and the singing increased when he lit the gasoline with his torch. She recognized the song; it was *"Alabaré a mi Señor,"* a song she had sung in her own church. Father Dias always liked that song.

Some of the church building was made out of concrete, but much of it was made out of wood, and it did not take long for the fire to consume the walls. Some of the singing turned to screams. *Please come out,* she prayed. Had the lieutenant's men locked the door? Please open the door, lieutenant, please open the church door! Don't you know that Pastor Juan has six children? Don't you know that Pastor Juan and Father Dias worked together to build a new school in the village? The singing continued as the young woman began to pray and weep. The singing continued, even as the screams grew louder and more desperate. The lieutenant stood outside with his men, expressionless, while some of his men mocked the singers. They danced outside of the church and raised their hands, pretending to be evangelicos. The smoke began to billow more fiercely from the church. Flames emerged from the roof. She prayed and wept as she saw the heavy wood beams of the burning roof collapse on the singers inside, and the singing stopped.

—

Angela

October 16, 2007

The four students had stayed up a good part of the night at the Hotel Chinita at the end of their stay in Guatemala discussing and designing the final phase of the research that Angela and Alex would carry out. It would be implemented when the master's students returned to San Francisco and had two parts, one to be carried out by Alex and the other by Angela.

Alex's job was to find out just how much more consumers were willing to pay for fair trade over standard coffee—good ol' *free* trade, as Rich called it. Angela thought the economic experiment that they had designed was quite creative. They would find a café that sold both fair trade and standard free trade coffee for the same price. Alex would stand in the doorway, handing out coupons to those entering the café. Each coupon was good for only that day, and good for one of two discounts. He would start with a coupon that offered a certain discount off any cup of the standard, *free* trade coffee or a smaller discount off any cup of *fair* trade coffee. Because the coupon could be used for only one discount or the other, the customer was forced to choose between these two options. If he or she decided to redeem the coupon for the fair trade option, they would know that a particular consumer valued a cup of fair trade coffee by at least the difference between the two discount options. If a customer chose the latter, it meant that he or she valued a cup of fair trade coffee at something less than the discount difference. They would try different price differentials and see what discount differential would result in equal redemption rates between the two options. That discount differential would reveal what the median consumer was willing to pay for the benefit of drinking coffee that was fair trade.

Angela's part of the research was to see how much the actual market price of café coffee differed between fair trade and *free* trade coffee. If consumers were willing to pay more for fair trade, ostensibly to help out coffee producers, would café owners take advantage of this by charging higher prices for fair trade coffee? She would survey a large group of cafés around the San Francisco Bay Area to ascertain price differences between *free* trade and *fair* trade. The difference in retail prices, beyond any additional cost to retailers of the fair trade coffee, would measure the extent to which retailers profited by coffee drinkers' willingness to pay more for fair trade.

Together Angela and Alex visited one of the cafés on Angela's list, the People's Java, in the Sunset District in San Francisco. They walked across Golden Gate Park, wandered around for a while and got temporarily lost, but then found the café. Stepping inside, they saw that the café was decked out in wild graphics and leftist slogans in a tawdry décor that Angela had seen in several cafés in the city. Immediately, Angela's attention was captured by a mural on the wall of an overweight nude woman with a tattoo and a huge mouth shouting in a cartoon bubble down to a caricature of the pope: "Keep Your Rosaries Off My Ovaries!"

Alex addressed a chunky female barista behind the counter. "Might I find the manager available?" asked Alex.

"Yeah. You might find the manager. Why?" Her face remained expressionless. She looked strikingly like the picture of the woman in the mural. Angela was secretly wondering if it might be a self-portrait.

"We would like to talk to the manager about a research project we're doing. Is he or she available?"

"I'm the manager."

"Er . . . great . . . well, pleasure to meet you," stammered Angela. "We're two graduate students working on a research project funded by the United States Agency for International Development . . ."

"Aren't they a bunch of fascists?" she interrupted, attempting a joke, looking sideways toward a small group of customers. A couple of regulars sitting at a table with their drinks thought this was hilarious and snickered along with her.

After the laughter died down, she reengaged Alex with her

intimidating stare, furrowed eyebrows nearly fused together. Angela thought it would be a good idea to get to the point quickly.

"In short, we'd like to do an experiment with you and your customers related to our research." She explained the experiment briefly.

"Not interested. I don't want students messing around with my customers," she growled across the countertop. "Wanna buy some coffee?"

Alex and Angela looked at each other. "No, thank you," they said nearly simultaneously as they left and the door jingled behind them.

A couple of other attempts to connect with café managers that afternoon were met with slightly more genteel, but equally definitive, rejections.

They decided to try again the next day around midafternoon.

Another café on the list, the Blue Danube Coffee House, was only about a ten-minute walk from the university. Angela and Alex met on campus, situated on a large hill in the middle of the city. It was a nice day, yet they could see from this vantage point that an enormous fog bank loomed over the Pacific. The nice day was probably doomed in an hour or two. They walked west on Golden Gate Avenue past the university's large soccer stadium and blocks of charming row houses, then zigzagged over a few blocks to Clement Street, where they walked a few more blocks toward the ocean past strips of sundry small businesses long interspersed with ethnic restaurants, mainly Russian, Thai, and Vietnamese.

"Heard from anyone back in Huehue recently, Alex?"

"You mean, like Lourdes?" said Alex a little self-consciously.

"Maybe." Angela looked at him and smiled.

"We did exchange some e-mails, but then I was sending her an e-mail about three weeks ago and no response. She probably is busy with church things. I think she forgets about me."

"I doubt it, Alex. She's probably getting ready for the baby." She changed the topic to cheer him up. "Ever been to this place?"

"No, but I think a few of my friends have," he said. "They say that the coffee there is the boom."

"The *boom*?" Angela was puzzled. She looked over at Alex as they walked. "Do you mean they say it's the *bomb*?"

"Yes, I think that is what I mean." Alex seemed a little embarrassed and was silent for about half a block.

"Angela, tell me, why does one say the *bomb*? I do not understand the meaning of *bomb* in such a context. Does that mean to say that the particular coffee is very lousy?" They continued to walk. Angela found it was becoming more difficult for her to hold a grudge against Alex. They had been through a lot together. It was funny—she hadn't thought about The Debate for some time.

"No, no, Alex, it means exactly the opposite. It means that the coffee is great; it means it's awesome—it's to die for!" She looked at him and laughed.

"What does that have to do with *bomb*? I thought if a movie was a *bomb*, that meant it sucks really badly," Alex said, now sounding naïve and perplexed.

"Hmmm, yes, I can see that could be confusing," admitted Angela. They walked a little longer. "I guess it's a matter of the article in front of the noun *bomb*. You see, *the* bomb means precisely the opposite of *a* bomb."

"I don't understand all this about bombs and dying. Americans always have such militaristic ways of expressing," was the verdict Alex rendered as they arrived at the café. They walked through the front door and looked around at the walls. It was hip, but not "San Francisco strange." The Blue Danube had a mixture of clientele, men and women, older and younger, some University of San Francisco students living in apartments near the campus, some working people in on their lunch break. The shelves in front of the counter were stocked with tasty-looking treats. A smart-looking Asian-American man in his thirties stepped up to help them. He carried himself with some authority behind the counter, and he looked like someone who was more than an employee. He seemed like a good match for many of his customers: young, college-educated, and kind of cool.

"May I speak to the manager?" asked Alex.

"Yes, I'm the owner; name is Jimmy," he said, offering his hand.

"Yes, nice to meet you. I am Alex and this is Angela. We are graduate students working on a research project at the university." They ordered a couple of lattes from him as they began to talk. Angela explained the project while he fixed their lattes. Jimmy listened attentively as he poured the warm milk over his aromatic brew.

Angela explained, "You see, we're working on a project on fair trade coffee that follows coffee beans all the way from peasant growers in Central America to the coffee shop. Last week, we visited Java Joe's, a roaster in Oakland that imports coffee beans from the cooperative that buys from Huehuetenango, where we spent the summer with coffee growers. We're working on the part of the project that is trying to find out how much profit is realized at every link along the coffee value chain. And, uh . . . you're kind of the last link."

"Sounds cool, guys." He looked at them both back and forth.

"Would you now be willing to help us?" asked Alex.

"What do you need me to do?"

"We . . . would like to run an experiment," Alex said. Angela and Alex by now understood that café owners were wary of carrying out academic experiments with their customers, so he quickly added, "But it should be good for your business."

"What kind of experiment?" Jimmy seemed slightly puzzled now, but willing to listen. Angela was encouraged that he didn't say no immediately.

Alex responded. "See, surpluses occur at every intermediary in the chain. But the final part of this surplus is what we in economics call 'consumer surplus.' Consumer surplus is differences between what the consumers *would* pay for something and what they actually pay. We have designed an experiment to find out how much the people, like all your customers, are willing to pay for fair trade coffee."

"You mean how much more over the standard kind?" asked Jimmy.

"Yes, you are right," said Alex.

"Dude, for economics that's actually somewhat interesting. How does one . . . uh . . . find that out?" he asked.

Alex explained the experiment to him. It was pretty straightforward. Alex would stand at the doorway and pass out coupons that could be redeemed at one of two different discount levels for the two different types of coffee. The coupons had hidden marks on them so that different coupons could be handed out to men and women, and people appearing forty years old and over and people under forty, allowing the one compiling the data to identify choices between fair trade and standard by gender and some measure of age. The cashier's responsibility would be to mark on the coupon which type of coffee was chosen by each customer and collect all of the coupons in an old coffee can under the register. At the end of the day, Alex would see how many coupons were redeemed for each type of coffee at that day's price differential. The café would be reimbursed at the end of the day for all the discounts they had given from the coupons. Alex would try several different price differentials on different days. This would give them an estimate of how much people in rich countries were willing to help coffee growers in poor countries.

Jimmy seemed interested.

"We need to keep the time and day of the week on which we experiment constant so that we do not introduce a bias," said Alex.

"How about Saturday mornings?" suggested Jimmy. "I'm around that day and can give you a hand. We have a fair trade French Roast that we can offer alongside the standard."

"I will come here this Saturday at eight a.m.," assured Alex. "Don't worry. Dutch people never are late," he said solemnly, but then added, "Except on days when soccer is on television."

Jimmy laughed. "No problem, dude. The discount ought to give a little kick in the butt to sales, and the project sounds cool . . . I'm in."

They left the café practically skipping out the door.

"You did it, Alex!" said Angela. Alex grinned as they walked together back to the university. Angela's mission was to find whether the market took advantage of some consumers' greater willingness to pay for fair trade. She would undertake a random phone survey of cafés in the San Francisco Bay Area inquiring about prices they charged for their café products, both fair trade and standard coffee. After a little pilot investigation, she decided to focus on two main products, regular eight-ounce cups of coffee and medium-size lattes. These two drinks were found at nearly every café.

To try to obtain the broadest and least biased sample possible, she decided to go old-school and obtained several phone books that contained yellow-page listings for every part of the San Francisco Bay Area. She would look at the phone book listings in the "café" section and randomly call cafés to ask them their prices on four products: their standard eight-ounce cup of coffee, an eight-ounce cup of fair trade coffee, a standard medium-size latte, and a medium-size fair trade latte.

She began to make the calls from her apartment later that week. She started with Santa Cruz. That seemed like an easygoing place.

"Hello, ma'am, my name is Angela Lopez-Williams and I'm an

economics graduate student investigating coffee prices around the Bay Area. Could you tell me the prices you charge for a few of your products?"

"Are you from the competition?" a suspicious voice answered.

"No, ma'am. I'm a graduate student at the University of San Francisco."

"What do you study?"

"Well, as I mentioned, economics."

"Why are you calling about our prices?"

"Well, I could just pop in your door and look at your price board, but that would involve a lot of driving because the survey I'm conducting is fairly large."

"Okay," the voice acquiesced. Angela listed the products.

"We charge $1.75 for a small cup of coffee and $2.95 for the latte."

"What about for fair trade?" asked Angela.

"It's all fair trade. We don't exploit coffee growers here."

"Okay, great. Thanks so much."

"Bye."

She looked at the phone book for the next number. One down, 224 to go.

CHAPTER 23

Alex

ALEX ARRIVED PROMPTLY AT EIGHT A.M. THE FOLLOWING
Saturday at the Blue Danube with his experimental gear, which con-
sisted of a backpack full of coupons and a pad of paper for writing
down thoughts and observations. He checked in with Jimmy and took
his post outside the doorway. Only a few minutes later, a middle-aged
man turned to walk into the café with a *Wall Street Journal* tucked
under his arm.

"Having specials on French Roast today," announced Alex, pushing the appropriate coupon with the secret code for males over forty
toward him. "Seventy-five cents off our standard blend, and fifty cents
off the fair trade." The man took the coupon and regarded it curiously
in his hand.

"Hmmmph . . . ," he muttered to himself as he walked to the counter. The café was fairly quiet at that hour, and Alex was eager to see what
choice the man would make. Would he be willing to spend twenty-five
cents extra to join the fair trade cause? He waited anxiously. To Alex it
symbolized one of the great moral decisions of our time.

"Yes, I'll take the large French Roast," said the man. He handed
Jimmy the coupon.

"Would that be the fair trade French Roast, or the standard French Roast?" Jimmy asked casually. It was the moment Alex had been waiting for. He kept looking straight ahead down the sidewalk from the doorway but inclined his ear toward the counter. Jimmy was superb, Alex thought to himself. He kept his face completely deadpan as the customer decided. Alex was unsure if he himself would be capable of such self-control.

"Er . . . I'll take the standard," he mumbled.

Cheapskate capitalist, thought Alex.

Two women, both around thirty, approached the doorway. "Special today on French Roast. Seventy-five cents off standard blend, and fifty cents discount off fair trade," said Alex, greeting them happily. He handed each of the women a coupon.

"Oh, how nice," said one of them. They walked toward the counter.

"I just love his European accent," said the other as their voices began to fade. Alex blushed but pretended he couldn't hear. Both of them took the fair trade. It continued on like this throughout the morning. Slightly more of the women and, interestingly, the older customers chose the fair trade. Around one o'clock, things began to slow down, and Alex approached the counter.

"What have we here, Jimmy?" he asked, his voice revealing the anticipation.

"Dude, let's look." Jimmy reached down and grabbed the old coffee can full of the coupons. He dumped them out on the counter. A lot of people drank French Roast that day. They stacked the coupons in two piles. All in all, with the twenty-five-cent price differential, thirty-seven of the customers had chosen the *fair* trade French Roast, and twenty-five had chosen the standard, *free* trade French Roast.

"Very interesting behaviors," commented Alex scientifically as he scratched the short whiskers on his chin and pondered the two piles of coupons.

"Yeah. Lotta people willing to pay the quarter extra for fair trade. So what's next?"

"I think we must tempt people more away from fair trade. We will widen the gap. Let's try a dollar for the standard and keep twenty-five cents for fair trade."

"Wow, that's a big difference."

"Yeah, we see what happens. And maybe the time after that we try a fifty-cent difference."

"Sounds good. See you then, dude."

Alex paid Jimmy for the coupon discounts and strode away from the café toward his apartment, reflecting as he walked. He had learned something today: coffee drinkers, at least in San Francisco, were willing to pay more for their coffee to help the growers who grew their beans. But there was something else.

He began to reflect on how he had gone about developing an understanding of the world. Until this point he realized his academic effort had been devoted to a careful winnowing of the evidence in support of a foregone premise. It was just like his high school language teacher had taught him—to follow a thesis sentence in a paragraph with supporting material. But in a curious way, the experiment had positioned him in the business of truth-seeking. Somewhere along the way, and he wasn't sure where, he had begun to think less like an activist and more like a scientist. But the strange thing was that he felt no less passion for the truth; indeed perhaps more. And now he really wanted to know the truth: how much did the average coffee drinker care about coffee growers, and how effective was the current system in harnessing this goodwill?

CHAPTER 24

Rich

November 20, 2007

RICH SAT SWEATING AT HIS DESK SIXTY MILES SOUTHWEST OF San Pedro Necta. His office was in a trailer, the trailer was in a small World Bank compound in Pajapita, and Pajapita was a torridly humid agricultural village near the coast. The airy mountain breezes of the coffee project a few months before had been relegated to a pleasant memory. A small iron fan, resuscitated from being placed in storage somewhere back in the 1950s, sat on the floor as it squeaked rhythmically at each sluggish revolution.

Work on his fruit-export project would keep him in Guatemala for just another couple of weeks, after which he also would return to Berkeley. His project, funded by the Bank, was to help assess the impact of an agricultural transformation in the low-lying humid areas of the country. World Bank funding had helped convert large tracts of cattle pasture into tropical export crops: mangoes, pineapples, guava, and other tropical fruits. The director of the project, a Spaniard named Diego Vasquez, walked up the old plastic steps of the trailer into Rich's office.

Rich turned to him lethargically, unexcited. *"Hola,* Diego."

Diego looked slightly concerned as he regarded Rich's state. Darkened sweat patches covered the front of his shirt, the middle of his back, and his sides next to his arms as he was working on his computer. "Rich, do you need another fan? You are sweating formidably," Diego observed in English.

"No, Diego, I don't need another one of your fans. I need a freaking turbo-charged air conditioner and an enormous fridge full of cold drinks. What's up?"

"We need historical data on regional agricultural yields that are sitting in some file in a regional agricultural office in Huehuetenango. The data is old, covering the '60s through the '80s, and unfortunately it has not been electronically coded, only in hard copy. I don't trust the courier services here, and besides, someone needs to go through the files to make sure it's what we need. Would you mind heading up there in the next few days to get it?"

"I was just starting to run those estimations on the 1995 to 2005 production years. Why don't you send the *hormiga?"*

Carlos Jimenez, a.k.a. the hormiga, was a student from the university in Quetzaltenango. Viewed by all as a significant source of help on the project, he was also about four and a half feet tall. Aside from being short, even for a Guatemalan, he was also unusually skinny. Rich had nicknamed him *la hormiga,* or "the ant."

"Carlos has to be on data collection down at the coast this week, and anyway I would prefer to have you. You are more familiar with the data we need to complete the project."

"Okay, no problem, boss."

Only a few hours later Rich's cell phone rang. He looked down at the incoming number. It was someone from the United States. He answered it. "Rich Freeland."

"Rich, it is Alex."

"Lefty, *qué tal, amigo*."

"I am coming to Guatemala."

"What?" Rich asked, surprised. "When?"

"The day after tomorrow. Angela's coming with me."

"That's Thanksgiving!"

"Dutch people do not celebrate Thanksgiving, especially me. But they still allow me four days off. And Angela, her parents are on the East Coast visiting relatives for Thanksgiving and she had nothing to do and is bored. Her prof had postponed some assignment and she said she didn't trust me coming down alone anyway, but I think she was just joking. She said maybe she could help Fernando and Juana pick coffee during harvest this month. Anyway, we found online some cheap airplane tickets."

"Why are you coming down?"

"I want to see Lourdes. About Lourdes, I think I love her, Rich. And she has not been answering my e-mails recently."

"You love her?"

"Yes, Rich, I am believing so."

"Maybe she had the baby?"

"Yes, Rich, that is the point. Will you meet us at the Chinita?"

Rich reconsidered the cool breezes of Huehuetenango and the highlands, and realized that he had lapsed into a fleeting moment of insanity in his hesitancy to accept the work assignment from his boss in the first place. Now he had two reasons to go.

"No problem, Lefty. Believe it or not, got the director whippin' my hide to get some data up near there anyway. I'll get a seven thirty bus Thursday morning. Should be there around midday."

"*Gracias*, Rich. We will see you then."

—

Almost miraculously, the bus left on time that day and arrived sooner than expected in Huehuetenango. Rich quickly found the data at the agricultural office and hopped on a second bus for San Pedro Necta. He jumped off the bus with his backpack and walked over to the Hotel Chinita, where he checked in. Strange, the town seemed a little deserted. Must be the harvest. He made his way to the room, threw his backpack on the floor and himself on the bed. It was around one in the afternoon.

Not more than half an hour after he arrived, his cell phone rang. He glanced down at the number. It was Alex.

"We are embarking from the bus," he pronounced over the phone.

"What do you mean—you're getting on or getting off?"

"Off."

"Great, nice timing. Just got here myself," said Rich. "Y'all come on down, the price is right. I'm in room four."

CHAPTER 25

Alex

ALEX AND ANGELA ARRIVED AT THE INEXPENSIVE HOTEL, the host of many memories from the summer, and knocked on Rich's door. Rich greeted Alex with a firm Southern handshake, a man-hug, and a strong back-slap. He gave Angela a kiss on the right cheek.

"Rich, Angela, I would like to hike up to the house. Would you mind if I went alone first, and then we go together in the morning?"

Angela gave him a charmed glare with hands on her hips. "Oh, all right . . . I suppose we understand," she said in mock exasperation.

"No problem, Lefty. A man's got a right to privacy in matters of the heart." Rich stayed behind and settled in on his bed, apparently content with a pile of economics journals and the ensuing siesta.

Alex decided he could hike up to the house and make it back not too long after sundown. Carrying just a small backpack with some water in a canteen, he headed through the town toward the dirt road on the remote edge of town that led to the trail up into the mountains.

He passed by some of the little comedores, the little restaurants where he and the others had eaten so many meals. He noticed how few people were walking about the town today. It was unusual. Alex kept up a brisk pace as he passed a church on the left side of one of the main roads in the town. There was some kind of event happening at the church; people were dressed up.

He took a left at the intersection on the dirt road that led up into the mountains where Fernando and Juana lived. Horse manure littered the dirt road. After several hundred yards, the road narrowed and turned more steeply up the hill. Alex began to breathe a little harder from the increasing gradient of the road and the elevation. Even so, he was glad to be there. This felt good. A few of the growers they had met were working in their coffee fields. They waved to him as he walked by. He waved back, and Alex had a feeling that more people recognized his face in this tiny town in the western Guatemalan highlands than in his home city in the Netherlands. It was a funny thought.

He continued to hike as he slapped at a fly buzzing around his head. After a while it was time for a break, and he took the canteen out of his backpack and had several long swallows of cold water. He could see over the town now, the small adobe houses dotting the landscape beyond its center, each surrounded by a small field of coffee, the colorful cemetery in the background. Along the roadside, he could see that many of the coffee cherries that had been just little green dots when they had been there months before were now a large reddish-orange. School would be out now, and soon it would be time for the harvest. The children would help their parents in the fields. Fernando's whole family would join the picking crew, even the little ones. He wondered if he would be here long enough to help. Nothing he could think of pleased him more than the thought of helping Fernando's family pick their coffee during the harvest. He would pick next to Lourdes, and they would spend hours picking and talking until sundown. A wonderful feeling flowed through him merely at the thought. And after the harvest, Lourdes's family would have more money than they would have any other time during the year. They would be able to buy things they needed. He remembered what Sofia and Angela had told him about the Prisoners, and he hoped that the weather had been perfect here—and terrible in the rest of the world.

He continued up the old, pitted road, and after nearly an hour of hiking, he saw Lourdes's house in the distance. Fernando would be working outside preparing the fields for harvest, and Juana and Ema would greet him from the window, surprised to see him, and would ask him in for a meal. They would not have expected him to return. He knew they didn't approve of his tattoo, and he had had it painfully removed the week before. The tattoo had vanished from his right wrist, leaving a few laser burn marks that had yet to heal. But it would be a sign to them of his respect; he wanted them to be able to trust him with their daughter, and even their grandchild. They would laugh about the summer's happier events, and enjoy the special connection shared only by those who have bridged a friendship across income levels, language, and culture. He and Lourdes would talk, and he would share with her his thoughts about a book he had been reading in Spanish that she had given him. She would challenge every preconception he had about life and love and family, and he would listen to her. And they would pick coffee for hours together while Juana took care of the baby in the house. Maybe when they took a break, he and Lourdes would take a walk down to the creek. He approached the house smiling inside.

As he walked up from the cornfield in front of the dwelling, he saw no sign of anyone around the house. Usually the grandchildren and the nephews were playing soccer in the front or the little game they played with the hoops and sticks. The family must be out picking in the field. A dog barked in the side yard, but this didn't seem to attract the attention of anyone. He walked out to the field. The cherries were ripe for picking, but no one was picking them. He called for Lourdes. He checked in the field for Fernando and Juana.

Alex sat on the solitary concrete step leading up to the front door and waited. Even the neighbors seemed to be away. Time passed. Half an hour went by, then an hour. Disappointed, he decided to return to town. He retraced his path, descending down the dirt road about half a mile. A man who had seen him ascend called to him.

"*A quien buscas?*" he yelled across his small milpa field to Alex. Who was he looking for?

"*A Fernando Ixtamperic,*" answered Alex, now just happy to talk to someone.

"*No lo conozco,*" said the man. He didn't know him. Perhaps he was at the church with many of the others?

"*Okay, amigo. Gracias,*" Alex responded.

Alex descended down the dirt road back into town. From his location on the mountain path he had a view over the town, and he could see the church again. The words *Iglesia Pentecostes* were painted in purple under the eave. It was then that he remembered that this was the church that he had visited with Lourdes. It was her church.

People were filing out of the church now. Most were staring down at the ground. Many of those coming out of the church were young people—too young—he thought to himself. From the hill at a distance, he continued to watch the procession. More young people filed out of the church, and still more. How many could the church hold? Finally, a modest casket slowly appeared out of the front of the church, carried by six young pallbearers. It was a funeral. This was somebody who was too young to have died, he thought.

And then a sickening feeling overtook him.

Behind the pallbearers Alex spotted Fernando and Juana. Fernando was holding Juana's hand tenderly. They shuffled slowly behind the casket. Behind them other members of the family slowly walked, all looking at the ground. Behind the big casket, two other people carried a smaller casket. It was a tiny casket, the size of a treasure chest. Even from a distance Alex could see that many of the young women in the group were crying, and even some of the young men. The group stopped in front of a small pickup, which was decorated with ribbons and flowers to function like a hearse. It would carry the person in the big casket and the baby in the small casket to the cemetery of many colors, to lie together forever among the pastels. The pallbearers placed the caskets carefully together in the bed of the pickup, then stood back. Fernando and Juana each leaned over the big casket and gave it a kiss before it drove away.

CHAPTER 26

Angela

ANGELA AND RICH WERE WAITING FOR ALEX IN THE HOTEL room. When she had gone out to get lunch, Angela had learned of the bad news. Alex opened the door and silently sat down on the bed, drenched with sweat. He was perceptibly disturbed. Emotionally numb, his movements were like those of a zombie. His eyes were like a mannequin's, but his teeth and jaws kept clenching and unclenching as he stared straight ahead lifelessly. They were all silent for some time.

Angela sat down on the other twin bed across from Alex. "On the way to the comedor, I saw the procession. I was able to talk with one of her brothers."

Alex's eyes narrowed, and his lips were taut. He stood up and walked over to the window. He watched the last of the people lingering outside the church embrace, wipe away tears, and begin to return home. His lower lip began to quiver as he sat back down on the hotel bed. Angela sat down next to him with her hand on his shoulder. They were silent for several minutes before Alex spoke.

"What in hell happened?" he asked Angela finally, his expression tight and grim.

"It was some kind of brain hemorrhage related to her pregnancy."

Angela looked into his eyes and tried to say it as gently as she could. "Fernando and Juana don't really understand because the doctors don't really seem to know either. She wasn't even giving birth yet. I'm so sorry, Alex."

"And the baby?" he asked.

Angela shook her head dejectedly. There was no good news. "Poor little thing just didn't make it; they think maybe because of the loss of her brain function, but they don't know why. Would have only been born a few weeks early. Her brother said there were some signs that things were going bad. She started to feel very weak; then she became dizzy. They didn't have the money to take her to the hospital in Huehue. Thought it was probably just related to the pregnancy and might just go away. Then all of a sudden she lost consciousness, and they couldn't bring her back."

Angela looked at Alex's face, which was a virulent swill of emotions, frustrated, mad, and despairing in equal parts, but in all parts bitter. Tears came now, and his nose was running. Angela looked for a box of tissues, but there was just a towel. She handed it to him.

Rich sat down next to him and put his hand on the back of his neck. "I'm sorry, buddy."

Alex's body repelled the touch instantly and jerked away. He remained silent and brooding for a few moments. Then he turned to Rich and lashed out with a venom-laced tirade. "It's all just part of how it works for you, isn't it?" Alex glared at him. "Another coffee picker dies because her family didn't have the money for a doctor. But at least it is saving you five cents on your cup of joe."

Rich looked back at Alex, his face pained, without words.

"Can you now see, you stupid fool?" He was shouting now. "Can you see now how unfair this bloody world is of yours?" Alex rose up from the bed and stoically walked toward the window facing the church. Rich sat silent, staring at the floor.

"Please sit down, Alex," said Angela, trying to calm him, her voice shaky and on edge.

Alex regarded the church pensively through the window as a few more tears dropped down his cheeks. Then, without warning, he reared back and punched a hole through the window with his fist. Shattered glass flew everywhere, inside the room and crashing down to the sidewalk two stories below.

Rich dove for him and pulled him away from the window. Blood was pumping out of Alex's wrist in the inflamed area that formerly hosted the tattoo, and was soaking his clothes. Rich dragged Alex over to the hotel bed. "Help me hold him down!" he yelled to Angela. Angela held his legs and they forced him down on the bed.

Rich centered most of his formidable weight on Alex's chest to keep him from writhing. He checked Alex's wrist. Two large pieces of glass that had severed an artery were imbedded in his wrist and the muscle of his lower forearm. Blood surged from the wound, ran over the bedsheets, and puddled on the floor. Rich carefully removed the glass, grabbed the towel, and started to apply pressure to the wounds, elevating the arm. Alex began to turn a sickening white as the white towel quickly filled with blood. Then he lost consciousness.

A hotel manager ran to the door after hearing the noise and summoned a doctor.

—

Two hours later, Alex was lying in a hospital in Huehuetenango, alive and conscious, and with twenty-nine stitches in his right wrist.

Angela and Rich sat by his side at the hospital. None of them had spoken since their arrival. Rich looked down as Alex opened his eyes. "You're right."

Alex stared straight ahead and swallowed, then looked at Rich. "Which time?"

Rich turned toward him. "You're right. It's not fair."

CHAPTER 27

The young woman buried her face in the straw and wept silently for those inside the church as her baby lay by her side. The searing fire of the consumed church and its occupants burned down to a smoldering stench. Some soldiers fired shots into the embers. Did these soldiers have no respect even for the corpses of the innocent? Or could some have partially survived this inferno only to meet such a vicious end? Sadness, indignation, and fear consumed her mind. She did not understand why the army had come to their village to destroy, to destroy churches, and houses, and people. The people in her village were not garbage-eating rats. They were poor— poor people who had many problems—but people who always helped each other, sometimes even others out-side the village.

On the single television that existed in the village, they had watched the president explain the guerilla problem in a speech. She heard him say, "The guerrilla is the fish. The people are the sea. If you cannot catch the fish, you must drain the sea." This was better than the rats and the garbage, she thought, but she didn't understand the part about the sea. One can never drain the sea; she had seen it once, the Pacific, on a journey to deliver coffee to the coast. Didn't the president know that the people, the sea, neither could ever be drained? There will always be the people and there will always be the sea.

Soldiers ran to various locations in the village. They did not care to check every house. They seemed content to burn down the village. Within minutes she saw the lieutenant supervising two of his men sprinkling what she now knew to be gasoline around a house of a boy who used to be in her class at school. She did not know the boy well, but she remembered he was a good boy. He liked to play soccer, laugh, and chase girls around the school with the other boys. She watched one of the soldiers throw a match on the house, and saw the flames crawl up the walls to the roof.

The lieutenant and his men then turned their attention to Mildred and the other women. Many of them had become hysterical at the burning of the church and the houses, and they seemed to begin to understand their fate if they did not cooperate with the soldiers. The young woman knew what this meant, but she did not know which would come first: one of Mildred's friends would buy her life by telling about Mildred, or Mildred would buy her own life with information about the insurgency, Alberto, and perhaps the young woman.

Chaos was beginning to surround the group of women now. One of them pointed at Mildred, and Mildred shouted something back at her. The lieutenant grabbed Mildred by the hair and took her away from the group with some other men into the forest. She saw Mildred's face, panicked, sobbing, and red. Please, Mildred, tell them the stories you know from Alberto so that they will not hurt you. Do not argue with the soldiers. They have power over us, the power to take you away from me, and me from you.

The remaining soldiers made the other women stand up. They forced the women to march in a line behind some houses. The young woman ran to the other side of the barn to see what happened to them, but they were lost from view. She pounded her fist against the barn wall, for a moment not caring if it attracted attention. Then she sat down in a despairing silence.

After some minutes, she heard new noises outside. The lieutenant had returned from the forest. What she saw next caused her stomach to boil. She saw Eva approach the lieutenant, respectfully waiting for his attention several feet away as he finished directing three men toward some houses. She watched, sickened, as the lieutenant redirected his attention toward Eva. Hands held behind her back in deference, Eva was clearly informing her superior of something important he must know. The young woman's body began to shake as she saw Eva motion toward the barn as she talked. The lieutenant listened and then nodded, summarily dismissing her. Then he directed some men to grab a container of gasoline and follow him in the direction of the barn.

The young woman panicked as the group of soldiers began to walk in her direction. Clutching her child, she quickly moved toward the barn door, which faced away from the center of the village and was hidden from the view of the soldiers.

And she decided to run.

—

Angela

A couple of days later Angela, Alex, and Rich sauntered up the dusty mountain trail to the house to visit Fernando and Juana. It was a morose, silent trudge. Angela knew Alex's wrist still throbbed; he was hurting in every conceivable way. Rich seemed preoccupied with his own thoughts, and Angela, though melancholy herself, felt that attempts to cheer up either of them were likely to be ineffective, and anyway, she lacked the impetus to try. The relative gaiety of the summer had disappeared, replaced by a mood of confusion, tiredness, and despair.

They approached the house. Juana saw them approaching and walked slowly to greet them, looking tired. They each hugged her in turn. Angela looked over and could see that the shoulder of Rich's green Hawaiian shirt was wet with Juana's tears. Fernando left some other company in their house and came out to receive them, face drawn, eyes misty and forlorn.

They were introduced to other members of the family who had come to support Lourdes's siblings and parents. Everyone in the room appeared to be grappling with the loss, trying to explain it in a way that made sense. Angela thought, *How do you make sense of the senseless?* Lourdes had been so young. Even so, there was a kind of acceptance of death that was foreign to Angela. Here people over fifty died frequently of nothing in particular. Most families had either experienced the death of an infant or knew another who had. Death had not made himself a stranger in their village.

They had been there for over an hour when Fernando approached Angela.

"*Pues,* I am glad that you returned."

Angela studied his face. Despite his being grateful that they would be here to support them in one of their most difficult moments, she could tell that there was something else behind this. "What is it, Fernando?" she asked. "Why?"

"Because, Angela, I have one more story I must tell you."

—

October 1952

Friedrich and Ester established a new plantation in Mazatenango, not far from the old one owned by the Ehrlichmanns. Basilio, his wife, Marta, and some of his brothers and cousins took their families and headed a few hours north to another Mam-speaking region where new coffee land was being developed, in the province of Huehuetenango.

By this time people in Guatemala had suffered many years of military governments and had grown weary of dictators. Right after World War II, Guatemala democratically elected its first presidents, Juan José Árevalo from 1945 to 1951, and then Jacobo Árbenz from 1951 to 1954. These were good times in the country for coffee; local harvests were plentiful and prices across the world remained high.

The new democratically elected governments had to decide what to do with the German coffee land that had been annexed by the Ubico government—eighty thousand hectares of prime coffee land. Instead of returning it to its owners or their descendants, the Árbenz government converted the land into individual parcels under an agricultural reform law to be owned by the former mozos or managed as peasant-operated cooperatives.

Basilio worked for several years as a colono to a large coffee plantation owner as he and Marta established a home in the rural area around
San Pedro Necta. Beginning in the early 1950s, Catholic priests, some
of whom were Jesuit and Maryknoll missionaries from Europe and
North America, began to work among the indigenous communities
in the western highlands of Guatemala. Having compassion for the
plight of the indigenous coffee workers, they helped local communities organize themselves into cooperative agricultural associations. In
many cases new lands were cleared from the high jungle or forest to
create new areas for planting. To the consternation of many large coffee growers, some mozos left plantations to join the new associations,
where they believed they could avoid the drudgery and low wages of the
coffee plantations.

A winsome young Jesuit priest, Father Humberto Dias, who was
originally from Spain, approached Basilio about joining the cooperative. Father Dias taught the campesinos that the peasant associations
were part of the hands of Christ reaching down through the Church
to the poor and downtrodden to give them hope. They established a
communal coffee association under the leadership of Father Dias and
other leaders of the community, all sharing in the labor, as well as the
fruits of that labor.

It was not a perfect system. There were often conflicts over leadership and commitment to the work of the cooperative. Some workers left
the associations out of these frustrations; others stayed. But in a time
of high coffee prices, there was a sense of increasing communal prosperity. Probably more central to the objectives of the missionaries, the
associations created a sense of pride and economic opportunity in the
indigenous communities where they operated. The members of Father
Dias's community were generally happy.

Basilio worked in the campesino-operated cooperative with Father

Dias for several years until he and Marta managed to save enough from their involvement in the association to buy their own small parcel of coffee land. As he considered the purchase, he approached another indigenous coffee grower in the village who had accumulated a number of sizable coffee parcels, Adolfo Chuquahuit. He made him an offer on one of his parcels: four hectares of coffee land on a fairly steep incline, but good soil and tree cover. The deal was made, but shortly afterward a dispute arose between them over one of the boundaries on the plot. Basilio had been certain that the agreement included all the land adjacent to a small creek, with access to the water. Adolfo disputed the claim. It had never included access to the creek, he maintained. It led to a festering argument that was never entirely resolved.

But Basilio cultivated the entire area that he believed to be his own, and from this land he and Marta, especially in the good years, were able to feed and clothe their family. Over the decades they enjoyed a growing degree of leadership and respect within their Mam community. They had six children, including Emilio, the father of Fernando and the grandfather of Lourdes.

When Emilio was sixteen, Basilio's mare gave birth to a colt, which Emilio raised in the stable next to their small adobe dwelling. One night a thunderstorm frightened the colt out of its pen. A torrential rain swept through the village, flooding roads and homes. In brazen disobedience to the admonitions of his father to remain inside, Emilio stole away with the mare and rode it bareback up into the mountains to track down the colt. Vexed upon discovering that both Emilio and his mare had ventured out into the storm, Basilio grieved to Marta about the intransigence of his son. "Like something you might have done?" reminded Marta patiently.

In the moonlight Emilio returned on the back of the mare, leading the colt behind with a rope, all three soaked to the bone. Basilio ran from the house into the drenching rain, his frustration and worry forgotten, and helped his son down from the mare. He hugged and kissed him on the forehead, hair now plastered to it by the rain. "My son, you are very stubborn and disobedient, but also very, very brave. I am proud to be your father, and I am overjoyed that you are safe. Go inside and let your mother prepare dry clothes and some *atol* to warm you." Especially with his children, judgment for Basilio was usually trumped by heart.

Although it had supported the annexation of German-held coffee plantations at the beginning of the war, the United States government became concerned over the confiscation of private agricultural lands and their conversion into campesino-held lands, cooperatives, and nationalized agriculture. It smacked of communism. Perhaps most important, a significant portion of the nearly one million hectares annexed by the government was land held by the United Fruit Company. United Fruit had invested shrewdly in relationships with lawmakers in Washington DC. It made its complaint known plainly to Congress and to the Eisenhower administration. And the administration listened.

In 1954 the democratically elected Árbenz government was overthrown by a CIA-backed coup and replaced by a military government. A sequence of such governments ruled the country for most of the next four decades. In reaction to the dictatorial governments, a guerrilla war began in 1962. The guerrilla movement gathered momentum as multiple groups formed and initiated attacks in different parts of the country. By the mid-1970s, the government of Eugenio Laugerud García became determined to crush it. It was decided that the best approach was a counter-insurgency operation based on the United States military operation in Vietnam. The backbone of the operation was a network of civil patrols used to monitor villages believed to be hospitable to guerrilla activity. The civil patrols had strong ties to the military, whom they could call in as situations warranted. Lacking the support of a rural population, the guerrillas would be quickly annihilated.

The first massacres of indigenous villages under the García regime occurred in 1975, in the northernmost part of the Quiché province, Ixcán, less than ten miles from Huehuetenango. The Catholic-led agricultural communities in the region were viewed as sympathetic to local guerrilla movements, and their numbers had grown. Groups such as Acción Católica had grown all over the western highlands so that by 1967 there were 27,000 family representatives in their local associations. By 1975 the number had grown to 132,000 in over five hundred peasant associations. The communities had become a major movement among the local indigenous population. Coffee-plantation owners complained to the government about the cooperatives. They drew peasant labor away from their plantations during harvest, and on the supply side, the coffee from the associations competed with their own output. The complaints met with a receptive ear. The cooperatives were also viewed as insubordinate to the Guatemalan government itself.

The Guatemalan army's counter-insurgency units employed a standard methodology to crush the guerrillas. In order to inflict fear in a population accused of siding with the guerrillas, army units would arrive in a village. Aided by the civil patrols, they would identify local leaders accused of supporting guerrilla activity in the village, seize them out of fields and homes, and then execute them in the presence of village inhabitants. In villages where there was believed to be widespread guerrilla support, soldiers would then systematically burn houses, schools, and churches, all too frequently with residents locked inside. In many cases the military spared no one, neither children nor the very old. Those fleeing into the jungle were often hunted down and shot. Some escaped and sought refuge over the border in Mexico or fled through Mexico to the United States. The bodies of those unable to escape in such villages were either burned or dumped in mass graves.

As word of the massacres spread, resentment against the government began to intensify. The conflict spread from Quiché to other nearby provinces, and by the early 1980s, massacres were occurring in many parts of the provinces of Quiché, Huehuetenango, San Marcos, Chimaltenango, Alta Verapaz, and Sololá.

—

May 11, 1983

Basilio, now over seventy, did not support the guerrillas, nor did he support the army in its counter insurgency against them. Neither did his wife or children support either side of the conflict. But one night, a platoon of soldiers arrived in their village. Adolfo Chuquahuit and his wife, Eva, were leading members of the civil patrol.

They arrived at night at Adolfo's residence. A burly ladino lieutenant with a heavy mustache led a small group of soldiers to the house. The lieutenant and three of his soldiers walked into the house without invitation. He sat down and looked coldly at Adolfo. The right side of the lieutenant's unshaven face was severely disfigured. A scar from a crudely repaired gunshot wound extended from his temple to his nose. His right eye was missing, replaced by a glass eye that stared straight ahead, lifeless, like that of a fish, while his left eye stared at the occupants of the room. The life in the good eye was as cold and corpselike as the dead one.

"It doesn't seem that the patrol has been very effective at keeping the hearts of the village in line with their duty to the Republic, does it, Adolfo?" His voice carried little emotion. It sounded almost faintly bored, but it was clear that a wanton rage lingered just below the surface.

Adolfo shifted in his chair. "Lieutenant, I believe that most of the villagers are sympathetic to the cause of the Republic and its military effort, except for a few troublemakers, who by their words and actions have long communicated sympathy for the Marxist views of the guerrillas," replied Aldolfo. He continued, "Humberto Dias and his underling priests clearly are leaders in this regard. In the association he heads, they teach Marxist principles and claim that the government hates them and wants them to be poor mozos working on coffee plantations forever."

"Yes, of course. Dias and his guerrilla catechists must of course be eliminated. Who are his champions within the village?" Without having to be told, one of his subordinates was taking notes, calmly jotting down directions to their dwellings. It had all become routine, almost mechanized.

Adolfo casually mentioned several names, instantly sentencing them to death. He paused for a moment, reflected, and then decided to resolve a problem that had troubled him for some time. Following the previous list of names he added, "And of course there is Basilio Ixtamperic, one of Dias's earliest followers. He is old now, but still very respected by members of the association. His sons Emilio and Eduardo also command respect by members of the association, and their counsel is eagerly followed within the village."

"Are they traitors to the Republic?" asked the lieutenant.

Adolfo replied, "Never once have they indicated an interest in joining the civil patrol, despite my strong encouragement. I think you could say that . . . yes."

The subordinate calmly took down more notes and directions. This was the kind of information that was helpful to the soldiers. They shook hands with Adolfo and left the house.

Slightly before dawn, thirteen-year-old Fernando lay awake. Some of the farm animals were making unusual noises for this time of night, making it difficult to return to sleep. They sounded jittery. Perhaps a cat had crept in from the high jungle? A stray dog? He walked to the door of his house and opened it a crack. Across the rugged pasture in the dim light, he witnessed a group of six soldiers dragging his grandfather Basilio out of their house by his whitish-gray hair. His grandfather's face was almost completely covered with blood. His grandmother, Marta, was trying to scream, but her mouth was covered by one of the soldiers who jammed a pistol into her temple.

Panic and grief shot like twin shocks through his young body. He began to shake, his breath now coming in gasps. Somehow he found the strength to run and wake his father, Emilio, who bolted to a window. Watching the scene unfold, his father stood, biting down on one of his fingers, tears silently streaming down his cheeks. Fernando watched his father forced to decide in an instant if he was to die trying to save his own father's life. He seemed to understand that this would be suicide, and his attention swung to the survival of the rest of his family, now asleep in their beds. Emilio shook Fernando's mother, Gloria, as she lay in bed, his voice a sobbing whisper, barely under control. "*Mi amor,* we must leave the house quietly through the back door. They are here, Gloria. The soldiers—they have come to kill. *Apurate!*" Following his lead, Fernando ran to wake his younger siblings snuggled side by side in their shared bed.

Villagers in Huehuetenango lived in fear of the army and the civil patrols. Because of this, his father had prepared. Understanding that the soldiers often hunted down those who fled into the jungle, he had constructed an elevated platform in the densest part of the coffee field adjacent to their house, held up by wooden supports pounded into the ground next to the trunks of coffee plants. It was about seventy-five yards from the house. The platform itself was about four feet off the ground, surrounded by thick coffee plants. Fernando had helped build it with his father. It was virtually invisible, even in the daytime, unless someone happened to be standing right next to it. It was a well-camouflaged refuge. They even hid a few canteens of water there in case they needed to remain for days. An antiquated large-caliber Guatemalan army pistol that used to belong to Basilio's father hung inconspicuously from a nail on the bottom of the platform, protected from the rain.

Fernando helped his family grab what food and provisions they could, some tortillas wrapped in a cloth and a few pieces of fruit. They crept out the back as silently as possible, then fled into the coffee field. They arrived at the refuge. Huddling close together, the younger children whimpered quietly as volleys of shots and screams echoed intermittently from the village. They heard their grandmother sobbing hysterically, Emilio begging them in tears not to go to her.

Minutes passed as they remained breathlessly still, hearing the soldiers' profanity-laced tirade over the discovery of the escaped family. Then they heard their restless farm animals fall silent as the soldiers shot each of them methodically.

Hours passed. They saw smoke rising near the Iglesia Pentecostes on the west side of the village. They heard faint, muffled screams from the direction of the church. Smoke began to rise over several other parts of the village. There were more sounds of yelling and chaos. Smoke was now drifting into the coffee field. They smelled a pungent order that reminded Fernando of the time a neighbor's feed barn had caught on fire when it was full of mice. He pulled his T-shirt over his nose to quell the stench. More hours passed.

It was dusk when they heard the sound of someone running toward them. Through the coffee plants, they could make out a young woman holding a baby fleeing into the coffee field. Fernando recognized the woman; it was Mariela, one of his father's second cousins in the village.

Her baby girl had been born three months ago, and the family had attended the ceremony in which Father Dias had baptized the child only weeks before. They carefully watched Mariela. They were wary of calling her attention, unsure of who might be following and how close he might be. She was attempting to run, but unevenly, limping. The baby was crying. She stopped suddenly and as she turned to scan the field for a place to hide, they could see the gunshot wound in the left side of her abdomen. One side of her huipil was stained red, blood running over the carefully embroidered flowers. She was losing strength, trying to clutch both her wound and the baby.

Emilio put his hand over Gloria's mouth to keep her from calling out, and motioned sternly to Fernando and the other children with a tense index finger across his lips.

Before Emilio could restrain him, Fernando leapt off the platform suddenly, moving as noiselessly as possible through the coffee plants toward the young woman. He grabbed her hand and quickly led her back to the refuge. Her breathing was frenetic and had a wheezing, gurgling sound. She was shaking. Her face looked pale, her skin leathery and taut.

Emilio quickly embraced his son, took the baby and handed it to Gloria, and carefully pulled Mariela up on the platform, followed by Fernando. *"Dios les bendig . . . Dios les bendiga . . ."* She thanked them with a weakened voice in a whispered mantra. The baby began to cry louder, and Gloria tried to pass the baby back to her mother, but now that she had reached the platform, her mother suddenly appeared to lack the strength to take her. She began to lose consciousness. Dark red blood flowing from her abdomen began to puddle on the platform and drip off the side onto the soil. Gloria tried to bury the baby's head in her sweater between her arm and her chest to muffle the crying. Chaos and screams continued to echo from the village.

Who was following the woman? Fernando understood that if the baby continued to cry, they would soon know.

The baby was silent momentarily and looked at young Fernando, who somehow found the composure to smile back at her. Gloria began to help Emilio attend to Mariela, and she passed the baby hastily to Fernando. He held her in his arms. The baby began to smile quietly at him while he rocked her in his young arms as he had done so many times before with his younger brother and sisters.

The relative calm of the moment was interrupted by the crackling sound of another set of carefully placed footsteps. The group was hushed, the baby precariously awake but silent. Through the brush, Fernando could barely make out a beige lieutenant's uniform about fifty feet away, approaching through the coffee plants. Silently, he pointed at the figure to his father. As one hand of the uniform brushed coffee branches away, the other maintained a rigid grip on an automatic rifle. The uniform had a face: the scarred unshaven face of a lieutenant, emotionless as a pit bull. The uniform stalked deliberately, coldly, meticulously as its dead eye stared inertly ahead.

He appeared to be talking to himself under his breath, but then it became clear he was not talking to himself, but calling to his prey as he stalked her through the brush. He had wounded her as she had fled, and was following her drops of blood as a hunter tracks a wounded deer. *"Venga aca mi amor . . ."* Although young, Fernando understood what was happening, for he had heard stories from bigger boys in other villages. This soldier would use the woman for his pleasure before executing his task and returning to his unit.

Emilio gently pushed the heads of the family down as low as possible on the platform. He motioned to Fernando, who was closest to being able to reach for the pistol. He quietly handed the baby back to his mother. Fernando's arm slowly reached down under the platform for the old pistol hanging below it. His finger reached the handle, but he was having difficulty because the trigger guard was caught on the nail head. He fumbled with it, causing the handle to knock against the wood. Wincing and clenching his teeth at the noise, he twisted his shoulder even farther to release the pistol from its crude clasp. He could not adjust his body any farther without making noise or pushing somebody else off the platform. He could now hear the soldier's movement through the coffee branches even with his head down as he grappled for the pistol. He extended his arm one last time to reach another inch underneath him. The roughly hewn edges of the plywood cut into his bicep. The pain in his arm was becoming unbearable, but in this last attempt, he was able to free the trigger guard from the nail. Finally the pistol was free. He grasped it with his hand and slowly passed it to his father.

Fewer and fewer coffee branches obscured the view between the walking uniform and the refuge. The group was harder to see in the murky dusk, but still visible if someone were close enough. The uniform turned and headed directly toward them. Perhaps he had heard the noise? Fernando watched his father gradually raise the ancient weapon through the coffee branches, his shaking hand lining up the bead of its hefty barrel between the menacing eyebrows that stalked them in the dusk.

The lieutenant saw the family when he was less than fifteen feet away from the hideout. The sight of the huddled group of villagers took the lieutenant by surprise; he was expecting just the woman. It also could have been that the limited world which he viewed through the solitary eye may have hindered his perception and encumbered his response. But in the extra split second it took for him to raise his automatic weapon, Emilio pulled the trigger. The ancient pistol fired, resounding like an antiquated cannon, as gray-white smoke erupting from the weapon enveloped the platform. Its fat bullet struck just above the lieutenant's eyebrow just above the dead eye, removing his officer's hat along with the top part of his head.

Fernando hoped that the platoon back in the village would confuse the shot with the myriad others that were coming from the arms of those chasing down villagers in the forest. But this was an officer. They would come looking for him.

Emilio motioned to his son. "Come, Fernando, we must bury the body."

Fernando, still shaking intensely, jumped off the platform, helped drag the body away from the area near the platform. Emilio and Fernando quickly dug a large hole with sticks to bury the lieutenant's body between the base of some coffee plants, throwing trash over the top to disguise the freshly dug dirt. They kept the officer's automatic rifle. If a group of soldiers discovered them now, they would pay with heavy casualties.

Fernando returned to the shelter and held the baby girl once again in his arms. Crying loudly after the solitary gunshot, she was quiet and at peace now. Thin black hair curled around the bottom of her tiny ears with their petite gold earrings. She wore a pink dress and white socks with little yellow ducks on them, and tiny white shoes. A delicate collar adorned with flowers encircled her neck, and her blouse was buttoned up to the top button. She was an endearing little baby, oblivious to hate and violence around her, an island of grace. Fernando brought her up to his face and rubbed noses with her, making her smile.

He gazed down at her, noticing the birthmark in the shape of a crescent moon running from her eye down to her chin, the only blemish on a cherubic face. Remembering her name from the baptism, he cooed to her in a quiet whisper, *"Angela, Angela, nuestra pequeña angelita. Está bien Angela . . . nada mas te va a lastimar . . ."*

Gloria cradled Angela's mother in her lap as Emilio worked in vain to stem the flow of blood from the wound in her side. Fernando prayed as his parents tried to save her life. A doctor may have been able to save her, but it was beyond the knowledge of a peasant couple from the campo. Mariela, young woman of the coffee plantation, appeared to know that she was not going to live to raise this child. *"Que cuiden la nena por favor . . ."* She wished them to care for the baby. And then, in stuttered whispers, she told the family her secrets as they bent down to listen. She seemed to want someone to know so that perhaps her baby might one day know. Mariela lapsed in and out of consciousness a few more times over the next hour. Finally, Angela's mother lay motionless, her lifeless eyes staring up at the coffee branches hanging overhead and the clouds behind them.

⁓

Angela sat in her wooden chair and looked at Fernando, stunned and speechless. Tears flooded down her cheeks. By this time a sizable crowd had gathered on the floor around Fernando to listen. The others in the room were equally astounded.

"My . . . *mother?*" asked Angela, her voice a hoarse whisper.

Fernando nodded slowly.

She looked at Juana, and around at the little adobe house in which they were sitting, and at the colorized portrait on the adobe wall of Basilio and Marta in middle age, proud, wise, and content, gazing down on them through the picture's timeworn wooden frame.

"You knew it was me from the beginning."

"Sí," said Fernando. "Yes. I believed it to be true when we met. Now I am certain."

It was obvious how he had known, and the irony of it was not lost on Angela. "But why didn't—"

"*Pues*, only if I knew you would love your past would I tell you that it was yours."

"And *your* family took me to the orphanage?" she asked, just wanting a few of the details.

"Yes, your mother's husband, Domingo, and many of the other men in the village were killed with my uncle Eduardo in the forest. They were found in a mass grave. Some people told my parents of an orphanage in Guatemala City that was making adoptions to the United States for orphans who were victims of the war. My father believed this would be best for you—to leave this place. So he and my mother brought you there. It was difficult. The army wanted to kill them, and they had to be very careful."

"Your mother and father were brave and kind."

"Indeed, they were, as were my grandmother and grandfather, who were both killed that same day, my grandfather, who was a faithful colono to coffee plantation owners for so many years." Fernando paused. "Angela, that day seventy-five people were killed in our village. Father Dias from Spain, who had spent twenty-nine years in the village working and living among us, was killed. He and all of his priests were killed, and their bodies were dragged into the center of the village as an exhibit for a lecture by the lieutenant about the consequences of friendship with the guerrillas. Thirty people burned inside the Iglesia Pentecostes."

Juana hugged Angela, who cried on Juana's shoulder.

"Your father a guerrilla fighter. I am finding myself exceptionally jealous," said Alex.

Angela laughed and smiled at him through her tears. "You never give up, do you, you crazy idiot," she said as the two of them embraced.

"Angela, there is something I would like to do—when you are ready," said Fernando.

"What is that?" She wiped more tears off her face, then nodded. Fernando took her hand and led her to a short, middle-aged Mayan couple across the room, a decade or so older than himself. The woman was plump and slightly stooped, with eyes that had wrinkles on the sides developed from a lifetime of warm smiles. She wore a faded but intricately colored Mayan corte and huipil and her hair was adorned by beautiful blue and white cloths that intertwined with her graying braids. Her husband donned a thin weathered mustache and slim straw cowboy hat. They smiled at Angela.

"This is my father's second cousin, Belinda, and her husband, Octavio. Belinda is your mother's sister. They are your aunt and uncle."

CHAPTER 28

Rich

RICH'S INTERNSHIP AT THE WORLD BANK CAME TO AN END. It was time for him, too, to return to California. He finally landed at San Francisco International Airport via a plane route that had to be redirected through Miami and Indianapolis. From the airport he took the commuter train, the BART, across the Bay to Berkeley. He slogged up the two flights of stairs to his apartment on University Avenue. It was only five in the evening, but he was exhausted. Why did his flights always get redirected two thousand miles out of his way? A little jolt of caffeine would keep him going until bedtime. His apartment was only a few doors down from his favorite café, Au Coquelet.

A friendly barista strode up to him.

"*Hola*, amigo Juan," he said to the barista.

"Hey, Rich, you been gone forever, man!" Juan smiled, glad to see him.

"Gimme the strongest espresso shot in the house," he said. "The one that cures jet lag."

"How many time zones?" asked Juan, measuring the proper dosage at the machine.

"Well, just two actually," admitted Rich.

"That's nothing, man," Juan chided him.

"Hey, y'all want some spare change in your little tip jar or not? Been traveling so much last two days, back end's sorer than a dummy's butt on report card day."

Juan grinned. "Rich, you always got a million of them, man."

"Yeah, yeah . . . How's that espresso coming?"

Rich stood at the counter and his eyes wandered to the menu he had gazed over on many previous visits. For the first time, he noticed the price difference between the standard coffee and what they charged for fair trade: $1.75 for regular coffee and $2.00 for fair trade. $3.15 for a regular latte and $3.65 for fair trade. *Whoa,* he thought to himself, remembering Angela's survey.

"Hey, Juan, how many cups of coffee do you get out of a pound of beans?" Rich yelled across the cafe to Juan, who was working on the espresso.

"About forty," he yelled over the loud gurgling sound of the machine. "You think our coffee's too weak?"

"No, it's fine, forget it."

He did some elementary math in his head. Twenty-five-cent difference times forty—that's ten bucks, a bit more than the cost of a bag of regular old beans. No way a bag of fair trade cost the café more than double the price of good ol' *free* trade. He had his espresso, got a bite to eat, and thought about it some more. Even bigger price differential with lattes. It was troubling, and he couldn't stop thinking about it. There was something significant here.

He returned to his apartment upstairs and sifted through a pile of old mail and magazines. He had forgotten to cancel his subscription to the *Economist,* and the issues had piled up behind the mail slot in his door while he was away. The espresso was kicking in now, giving him a little more energy. He had some time before settling down for the evening, and figured it might be as good a time as any to call

Sofia. He punched her name on his cell phone, and they talked for a while about Rich's return and setting up a time to meet with Angela and Alex across the Bay.

—

December 15, 2007

Rich had a car in Berkeley, a 1978 Chevy Impala that he had driven out to California from his parents' home in rural Georgia. During his time in the field, it had been garaged at his friend Stuart's place up in the Berkeley hills. Stuart was a grad student friend of Rich's who had stumbled upon a cushy house-sitting assignment for a professor at UC Berkeley. The professor was in the physics department, and a year before, he had initially left for Europe as a visiting scholar on an ostensibly short-term research project. In the meantime, it seemed that he and his collaborators had made a breakthrough where they found themselves continually on the cusp of identifying some kind of new particle. As a result, the physics professor was perpetually extending his European assignment and Stuart's house-sitting job, which was by no means a problem for Stuart.

Rich strode up through a rose-lined walkway to the lovely house and greeted his friend. Stuart opened up the garage door for him.

"The old war wagon," uttered Rich to himself as he set eyes on it again for the first time in many months. As he fired up the aging Impala with the white vinyl top, blue smoke spewed out of the car's rear, filling the garage. Stuart hid his nose and mouth in the collar of his T-shirt and fled to the front yard. It must have been due to the car's inactivity, thought Rich. He backed it out slowly, revealing a large oil stain on the professor's otherwise pristine garage floor, courtesy of the Impala. Rich and Stuart worked for a while, trying to scrub out some of the oil stain with Ajax. Then Rich drove away to pick up Sofia.

Sofia and Rich chatted and listened to an oldies station on the Impala's grainy AM radio as they drove the car over the Bay Bridge to San Francisco. They had the windows rolled down, and Sofia hung her arm outside of the passenger window. It was a nice day, especially for December, and a warm California breeze blew through the car. One of her boots rested on the cracked dashboard in front of her as they talked.

The Bay was a light steely-blue, and the late afternoon sun reflected off the ripples in the water, creating a ballet of dancing pinpoints of orange. A curl of fog rolled between the towers of the Golden Gate Bridge, and a large container ship loaded with imports from Asia passed under the bridge as they passed over it in the Impala. Another container ship, not quite as heavily loaded, made its way out of the gate, sailing toward Asia. Sofia and Rich joked about the difference. It was the trade deficit in action.

They met up with Angela and Alex at a seafood restaurant down by the marina, a favorite of Angela's. Rich gave her a friendly hug and a Latin kiss on the right cheek. Alex offered his left hand to Rich with a sheepish grin. His right wrist remained ensconced in a white bandage. Rich hugged him with the embrace of two men who have been through adversity together, then so did Sofia.

"Let me see that wrist," she asked gently.

Alex carefully pulled back the bandage to reveal the long, reddish scar still adorned with a pattern of stitch marks that looked like the seams of a badly sewn baseball.

They discussed more of what they had learned about Lourdes's death, which wasn't much, even though Rich had one other opportunity to talk with Fernando and Juana before he left. It was a difficult topic for everyone, especially Alex. They moved on to Angela and Alex's second-year development economics classes, Rich's and Sofia's plans for the academic job market, and the trials of research. There was a pause in the conversation when Sofia spoke.

"There's going to be a meeting in Berkeley next month."

"What kind of meeting?" asked Angela.

"About bringing together the different parts of the research from the project. We think we may be getting close to having some conclusive results about the impact of fair trade coffee on the growers," she said. "Do you two think you could give a presentation to the group on your work? I must tell you, there will be some fair trade association executives present at the meeting and at least one faculty member who is a committed fair trade activist. Things could get a little heated, but we thought it important that they attend."

Angela and Alex looked at each other.

"I think we could be ready for that," said Alex. Angela agreed.

They left the restaurant and walked back to Rich's car. Rich thought he had been lucky and found a free parking spot, but apparently it had been free because it was in a loading zone. The Impala now sat forlornly in its parking space in the marina with a ticket tucked under its windshield wiper. Rich opened the envelope. "What, seventy-five bucks? What do they think I am, freakin' King Midas?" He muttered to himself, "Probably next to nothing for folks who live in this neighborhood . . . buy a new yacht each time the old one gets wet . . ." The muttering faded away as he opened the heavy door of the Impala and settled down in the tattered driver's seat.

The others piled into the car, and they headed toward the university. The weather was pleasant that evening, and there seemed to be more to say. They decided to take a walk in Golden Gate Park. Rich parked the car, this time in a legal parking space. In the park a gentle wind was blowing through the coastal pines. It smelled like the pines and the sea. Sofia and Alex talked as they walked along the path through de Laveaga Grove. Rich and Angela, walking behind them, listened.

"I'm so sorry about Lourdes." Sofia put her arm on Alex's shoulder.

Alex hesitantly asked, "Sofia, do you believe in God?"

"Yeah . . . I do."

"If he is supposed to be good, how does he allow Lourdes to die for being willing to carry the baby of the man who violated her?"

Sofia's face became troubled. "To be honest, it is hard to conceive of anything less fair, Alex. But perhaps in some mysterious way, he may even be able to use even the worst tragedies like this for good."

"Yes, something like this she told me before too. But even her baby has died. What kind of good will come out of this, Sofia?"

"I don't think anyone who knew Lourdes will be the same after knowing her. That makes for a lot of possibilities." She looked at him with a hopeful smile, and they continued to walk side by side in front of Angela and Rich as they passed the Conservatory of Flowers.

"She was so genuine, Sofia, maybe the most genuine person I have known. It was like she could see colors that I could not see. And simple in her thoughts, in her faith—a simple faith, Sofia, but no, I would not say simplistic. Like why does she forgive that man? He does not deserve to be forgiven. And did you know even that she told me she prayed for your snakes fear? Can you believe—"

It was only upon saying this that he remembered the story Angela had told him later about the barba amarilla at the shrine of Pascual Abaj. "Were you . . . ?"

"I was startled, to be sure, Alex, but surprisingly not scared, at least as before. Then we stepped back and watched it wind its way into the woods."

"You would not pretend to me, Sofia."

"No, Alex, I would not."

Alex laughed softly to himself and hung his head.

Sofia took a deep breath and reflected for a moment. "We think we have everything to give to the poor, and nothing to receive. Unfortunately, sometimes they may see it that way too. But I can't imagine what is more valuable than what Lourdes gave to those who knew her."

Alex could sense Sofia looking at him as they walked, and as he glanced back at her, she spoke softly to him and said, "Perhaps there was a part of Lourdes that was always meant to develop more fully in you."

They had walked in a long loop and had returned to the Impala. They piled back into the aging car, and Rich and Sofia dropped Alex and Angela off near their apartments, which were next to the campus.

"Don't forget about the meeting," reminded Sofia. "March fifth—Wednesday."

Angela assured them, "We'll be ready."

CHAPTER 29

Alex

January 24, 2008

ALEX WAS AN ACTIVE MEMBER OF THE INTERNATIONAL
Justice Club at the university, which held its meetings on Thursdays
during the noon hour. The club was populated primarily by undergraduates, but Alex didn't feel too old or too wise to be out of place. The
club met weekly to discuss international economic, political, and environmental issues and to present forums on these issues to the campus
community. The president of the club was Genevieve Wilkins, a senior-
class student from Sausalito majoring in peace and conflict studies.

The club had organized a debate between two of their professors. One of the professors had taken a stance against sweatshops in
developing countries. The other had argued that despite its flaws,
international investment promoted economic development. It had
been a civil debate, but there was no question regarding the victor in
the eyes of the club members. The antimultinational professor had
won the debate with a barrage of anecdotes documenting the use of
child labor in multinational firms. The promultinational professor
had lost badly. He could neither match his opponent's gloomy stories

with an equal number of happy stories of his own, nor match the other professor's charisma. It was a blowout, and the club members went home satisfied.

The next day, Alex was lying on the lawn in front of the library doing some of his class reading. It was January, a month that in San Francisco has some fair-weather days that catch even its long-term residents by surprise. In his reclined position on the sunny lawn, Alex was having a hard time staying awake. As he read, the sentences became blurrier and blurrier, and the angle of the book drooped lower and lower. Finally, as he closed his eyes in the warm afternoon, *A Modern Introduction to Econometric Analysis* settled gently and harmlessly on his chest.

His vulnerable position made him a prime target for Genevieve, who spotted him snoozing on the lawn as she strolled across campus. She quietly leaned over Alex, put her legs on either side of his waist, and tickled him hard on both sides of his ribs. "IT'S TIME FOR THE TEST!" she shouted playfully, eighteen inches from his face. Alex sprung up like a jack-in-the-box and let out a yell that caught the attention of some nearby students, who laughed, but nowhere near as loudly as Genevieve.

"Oh, why do I make friends with the undergraduates," said Alex, after he recovered. "You are like puppies; you don't know boundaries."

"Puppies, huh?" Genevieve started to tickle him again. She tickled hard, apparently sharing the same unrestrained passion for tickling as she did for social justice, which was quite extensive. Alex suspected that she also may have had a bit of a crush on him.

"No more, please . . . Genevieve . . . okay . . . now I am officially begging you at this moment to stop . . ." She finally relented.

"You can make up for calling me names by telling me what an awesome debate I organized last night." She proposed the deal with a puckish grin. Alex looked at her. It was not the first time he noticed she was a very attractive girl.

"Genevieve, I commend you for hosting a most excellent and enlightening debate," said Alex, injecting mock formality into his congratulation.

They began to talk about the evening. "Can you believe those stories about Nike plants in Indonesia? What supervisors do to those workers . . ."

"Yes," said Alex. "Indeed, it is clear that Nike sucks very much."

"No question," she agreed fully. "And not just Nike. We should ban all of them, Alex. Every one. I swear, I want to commit my life after college to making sure every last one of those multinational factories in poor countries is boarded up."

Alex thought about this. "Every last one?" he asked, to see if she was exaggerating simply to make a point.

"Yep," affirmed Genevieve, staring straight ahead and nodding determinedly.

"Hmmm . . . I think an across-the-board ban probably wouldn't be the best idea."

"What do you mean? Why would you want to go halfway in fighting exploitation?"

"Because it's good to work for economic justice, but you have to think carefully about how things impact people," said Alex.

"Freeing people from virtual slavery seems like a pretty worthwhile cause, don't you agree, Alex? Remember, $1.35 a day?" she recalled to him from the debate. "$1.35 a day, Alex. That's a crime."

"I know, it is terrible," agreed Alex sincerely. "But if you were to ban all multinationals in poor countries, this would indeed create first a lot of unemployment, and then lower wages because you are in actuality removing capital from the country while flooding the country with unemployed labor. I don't say that we shouldn't monitor multinationals to put stops to worker abuses, but you have to consider effects on people of removing all these jobs, even if they are jobs that neither you or I would ever want."

"I still think no job is better than a horrendous job with terrible wages," she said.

"Unfortunately, Genevieve, I'm not sure the people in the factories would agree. They could always have no job if they wanted to. They could just quit. Since they don't quit, they must prefer that job to no job." He was listening to himself speak, and the logic he was using sounded like something coming from Rich, a thought he found a little disturbing. Thank God Rich wasn't around. It would have been embarrassing.

"What about those kids they talked about last night? You think it's okay for those thirteen-year-old kids to be working in the factory instead of going to school?" she asked.

"I hate that those kids are working in the factory," said Alex. "I sincerely do hate it. I wish all of the kids had chances to go to school. We need to do way more to help them go to school. I even think that in most cases, children should be banned from working . . ."

Genevieve interrupted, aghast. "*Most* cases? Alex, what do you mean, *most* cases? Obviously, *all* child labor should be banned!"

"Look, Genevieve, I am not for two seconds saying that I am voting for child labor. But I have to tell you something: for poor people there are even worse things."

"Worse things? Like what?"

"Like starvation."

These were strong words, and Genevieve was silent for a moment. Alex continued. "What if a child has to work so that the family will not starve? It is better to miss school than to starve to death. Before saying such a thing, you have to think. I don't like child labor, but what would be the impact of banning all of child labor everywhere? No child labor on farms for the coffee harvest, no teenagers working in shops to feed their younger brothers and sisters, no kids shining shoes in the market to earn extra money for their family . . . I agree every kid should be in school, but in some cases imposing simplistic solutions could make matters worse."

Genevieve got up and said, "Sorry, Alex. I think your arguments about 'impact' just add confusion to issues that are pretty much clear to everyone except egghead economists. I'm not really concerned with impact. I just want to do some *good* in this world."

She left Alex and stormed off to the library.

CHAPTER 30

Angela

March 5, 2008

IN PREPARATION FOR THE MEETING, ANGELA COMPILED THE data from her survey, and Alex worked on writing up the results of his experiments. They were eager to share the results with Sofia and Rich and the faculty members at Berkeley working on other phases of the project. The meeting was to be held at the UC Berkeley campus.

That morning Angela arrived punctually at Alex's apartment. To her dismay, he was still putting the finishing touches on his presentation slides. "Alex, we can't be late!"

Alex kept his eyes on the screen. "Five more minutes. I must finish the last two slides only."

Angela waited for several minutes, each one like an epoch, staring down at the rug of the bachelor pad littered with beer bottles and video game controllers.

"What have you been doing all week? We've got to catch the BART train!"

"Okay, okay. So sometimes I have a little bit of procrastinator problems."

"Bring your laptop and finish it on the train." She reached over and slammed the lid on Alex's laptop, cramming it into his backpack. They ran to the Muni stop just in time to watch the bus that would take them to the BART station pull away.

"We can't wait for the next one. I'm going to call a cab." The wait for the cab felt interminable, but finally one came for them that dropped them off at the Civic Center BART station where the train would take them to Berkeley.

A frenetic debate about the order of Alex's slide presentation was temporarily drowned out as the train loudly plunged into its tunnel running underneath the San Francisco Bay. The train reemerged from its undersea voyage and made a few more stops. Only seconds before the train arrived at the Berkeley station, Alex clicked *File, Save.*

They scurried up the escalator to the street level and ran two blocks east toward the campus. The meeting was due to start several minutes ago. Angela withdrew the now sweaty map out of her pocket that Sofia had e-mailed them to locate the proper building. The sweat had blurred the words and lines on the map to the point that they fumbled to decipher it. "You should have printed with laser jet, not ink jet," remarked Alex, nearly out of breath.

"You should stop playing with your joystick and get your work done," Angela retorted.

"Video games give me relief from being around stressed-out people as yourself."

"You always say Dutch people are never late," panted Angela.

"Except when there is soccer, and last night I played an outstanding Super Nintendo World Cup match against my—"

"I can't believe we're late because you played some video soccer game last night with your roommate instead of getting your presentation ready," she bellowed, out of breath.

They stared at the map and made out the title of the building, Giannini Hall, named after the Italian-American founder of the Bank of America.

"Angela, look—this is the way!" Alex pointed uphill to the north, and they sprinted in the direction of the building.

"I think I'm going to pass out," said Angela.

"You must harness your Mayan mountain-trekking stamina," shouted Alex as they ran.

They stopped, even more winded and sweaty, outside the building. Taking a moment to catch their breath, they opened the door and were greeted by a stern gaze from the marble bust of A. P. Giannini. The front doors let into a striking marble foyer with a twenty-foot ceiling. A portrait of an important-looking man in a blue suit hung on the wall. A wide, winding staircase to the right led up to faculty offices and classrooms on the second and third floors. Their footsteps echoed in the marbled vestibule as they proceeded up the staircase.

On the next floor, they were immediately greeted by Sofia, who quickly motioned for them to join the meeting in the conference room. The others were already seated. She gave Angela a quick hug and felt the sweat on her back. "Running a bit late?" She smiled. Angela rolled her eyeballs and silently jerked her head in the direction of Alex.

They entered the conference room, which was filled with Berkeley professors, graduate students, a few undergrad research assistants, and executive directors of fair trade coffee associations. Among the faculty were two of their own professors from the University of San Francisco, Rich and Sofia's advisors at Berkeley, Rudolph Goldhard, a professor in the political science department, and another professor collaborating on the project who had flown up from the University of California at San Diego for the meeting. Sofia's advisor introduced them to Norman Blowner and Josefina Reyes, executives from fair trade associations in the United States and Europe, and ushered them to two seats on one side of the conference table.

Shelves of academic journals surrounded them, interspersed with black-and-white photographs of some of the department's founding faculty members and economics Nobel Prize winners at the university, commemorative plaques, and other awards won by faculty and students. Some of the participants in the project were loading slides onto a laptop from their flash drives to project their results onto a screen at the end of the table. After they had finished, conversation died down and the room quieted.

"We are grateful to you for your assistance on this project," said Rich and Sofia's advisor, who was apparently directing the meeting. She directed her comments to Angela and Alex. "And it's wonderful that you can use some of this for your thesis work."

"We will begin with Alex and Angela. Please, would you tell us what you have found?"

Alex walked up to the projector and loaded his slides, encountering a temporary compatibility problem with the operating system, which was quickly fixed with the assistance of one of the other graduate students. Angela fidgeted in her seat during the awkward start as Alex glanced around at the serious, inquisitive faces around the table.

He began by reviewing the experimental design with them, and then he launched into the results. "My experiment tries to determine how much more consumers are willing to pay for fair trade coffee. I carried it out at a café in San Francisco on three Saturdays." His feet shuffled a little bit, and all of a sudden he looked a little unsure of what to do with his hands. He glanced at his faculty advisor from San Francisco, who offered an encouraging smile. "Well, I began on the first Saturday of the experiment by handing to our subjects, the café customers, coupons for French Roast coffee at the door. The coupons offered a choice on the first day of fifty cents off for standard French Roast and twenty-five cents off for fair trade French Roast."

"And so what happened?" asked Sofia from her seat around the table, eager to know.

"Well, when we counted coupons in the container at the end of the session, thirty-seven of the customers had redeemed the coupon for fair trade and twenty-five for the standard coffee. So the next Saturday I changed the values of the coupons so that it made the standard French Roast much more attractive to them. It gave the customers a dollar off for the standard and twenty-five cents off fair trade."

"Quite a substantial differential," one of the professors noted, fingertips pressed together under his chin.

"Yes, I know it," nodded Alex. "At that seventy-five-cent differential, forty-one chose the standard, but still sixteen opted for the fair trade." The professors nodded in affirmation. Made sense—prices matter.

"The third Saturday I split the difference, offering coupons with seventy-five cents off the standard and twenty-five cents off fair trade. At the end of the day, basically it was a tie: thirty-three of the customers chose the fair trade French Roast and thirty-two chose the standard French Roast."

"That was lucky," interjected Sofia. "You didn't even have to interpolate."

"Yes," grinned Alex. "To make it a short story, it appears that the median café patron, at least in San Francisco, is willing to pay fifty cents more for a cup of fair trade coffee over free trade."

The room buzzed with conversation, many surprised at the hefty premium customers were willing to pay to buy fair trade. Norman Blowner and Josefina Reyes, the fair trade executives, glanced at each other and at Rudolph Goldhard approvingly. The professor thanked Alex. He sat down, hastily running his shirtsleeve across his forehead.

"Angela, what are the results from your survey?" the Berkeley professor asked.

Angela brought out a folder and gave everyone around the conference table a handout with the printed results from her slides. It had results from her survey of cafés around the San Francisco Bay Area. She met the eyes of the group, cleared her throat, and began.

"I surveyed 225 cafés around virtually every part of the Bay Area by telephone, getting phone numbers from the yellow pages, where I felt I could get the most complete sample. The average price of a fair trade cup of coffee is $1.70, and for the latte it is $3.20. I examined the average price difference between what the cafés charge for *fair* trade and the standard *free* trade coffee using two easily comparable products: eight-ounce cups of coffee and twelve-ounce lattes. As you can see, the average markup for fair trade coffee overall came out to approximately 15.2 cents."

"Do you get the same result when you control for other variables? For example, fair trade may have a higher markup because it's frequently organic," one of the professors pointed out.

"Yes. Even when we run a regression analysis controlling for other variables, we find that fair trade adds almost exactly the same markup on the price," Angela responded. The faculty sat back in their chairs, now more willing to accept the results of her study.

"Well, of course fair trade coffee is costing the cafés slightly more than the standard coffee," Norman Blowner quickly pointed out.

"Yes, we found that roasters often charge between fifty cents and a dollar more per pound for fair trade to cafés for wholesale coffee," said Angela. "That seems a lot considering they pay only around twenty cents more for the beans. I think I understand why the markup in general is so high at the roaster level; the roasters have some significant costs in the form of high domestic wages, insurance, and other things. But does it cost any more to roast fair trade coffee?"

It was obvious to everyone at the table that of course it didn't. Cafés were clearly marking up prices of fair trade coffee because the consumer market was willing to pay more for it. Norman Blowner and Josefina Reyes were murmuring something to one another. "Thank you, Angela," said Rich and Sofia's advisor. Feeling relieved that her part was over, Angela returned to her seat next to Alex, where they quietly exchanged fist bumps.

"Mr. Freeland, do you have something for us?"

Rich had been relatively quiet, taking notes throughout the discussion, comparing these figures with what they had found over the summer. Rich stood up and opened his slides on the laptop. A colored graphic opened up on the screen that broke down the entire value chain from a cup of coffee.

"So our data from the summer indicate grower costs at $1.02 for the 7.8 pounds of coffee cherries that become a pound of roasted beans. For this our fair trade–certified farmers received $1.29 per pound since only a quarter of their crop is actually sold as fair trade. The uncertified coffee growers got about $1.26. Just covering its costs, the nonprofit fair trade exporter sold to the importer-roaster at $1.48. The roaster sold the roasted fair trade beans wholesale to cafés and store retailers at $5.25, and the grocery store retailers sell this same pound of beans for about $9.00. The cafés brew up the pound of fair trade beans to make forty eight-ounce cups of coffee that they sell at an average of $1.70 a pop, so the beans in a single cup of coffee cost the café only 13.1 cents. Clearly a lot of this markup goes to cover electricity, rent, and the salary of our friendly neighborhood barista. But this pound of coffee bought from wholesalers for $5.25 creates about $68.00 of retail coffee."

There didn't seem to be any questions, so he continued. "So if it might please the present company, I would like to draw several noteworthy conclusions from our data: First, because the certified growers received $1.29 per pound and the uncertified growers received $1.26 per pound, once you subtract the annual three-cent cost of certification, our fair trade coffee growers end up with what the little birdie left on the rock."

Blowner stood up, his bald head turning pink. "This is, frankly, an absurd set! We know that fair trade coffee offers myriad benefits to our coffee growers! We see them in the field every time we visit them. You can never tell us that what we do has no impact on them."

Josefina Reyes and Rudolph Goldhard nodded profusely in affirmation.

"You see because you want to see," Rich replied, unintimidated by the outburst. "But that is not what the data say. The *fair* trade growers are no better off than the regular *free* trade growers, at least as a result of growing fair trade coffee. Based on this year's crop, they both have a profit margin of twenty-four cents per pound of roasted coffee. And the profit to both on a $1.70 cup of coffee is only about $0.006, or barely over half a cent."

That the profit to growers from a cup of coffee was so low was shocking to just about everyone, including the professors and the students who had been doing the fieldwork. The professors remained silent during the exchange, extend closed lips and raising their eyebrows in the well-known scholarly gesture indicating surprise but nonoverreaction.

Rudolph Goldhard interjected, "Mr. Freeland, I was there during the coffee crisis. I saw what belonging to the fair trade network achieved for our growers. Saw with my own eyes, rolling up my sleeves with the coffee pickers. I find your presentation to be highly misleading and of dubious academic value."

"Fortunate you brought up the coffee crisis, Rudolph," said Rich. "Nice segue into my next slide. You're right that this is the time when fair trade brings maximum benefit to the growers. During the coffee crisis when prices fell to half of the fair trade price floor, once you subtract the cost of certification, the added profit to a grower who sells a quarter of his crop as fair trade is about one-third of a cent on a cup of coffee." Some of the graduate students quickly checked this basic arithmetic. It was correct.

"Now according to the presentation by my illustrious colleague from San Francisco"—he motioned toward Alex, who smiled sheepishly at the group—"the added willingness to pay for a cup of fair trade coffee by consumers in this liberal, conscioussness raised metropolis in which we live, appears to be about fifty cents. As economists, we count consumer surplus as an important benefit in a market. People feel better about consuming fair trade coffee because they think they are helping coffee growers, and they are clearly willing to pay through the nose for it, maybe to make themselves feel better, who knows. Understanding this, cafés mark up fair trade prices and take about 15.2 cents of this willingness to pay per cup, while the roasters seem to take about two to three cents of it."

Rich definitely had the attention of the group, and Blowner and Reyes looked on helplessly. Angela was sitting next to Goldhard, watching him doodle a series of daggers on his notepad as Rich charged on to his key point. "So to summarize, even in the *worst* of times, when coffee prices are in the tank and fair trade coffee offers its greatest relative benefit to growers, the consumer, the café, and the roaster together *benefit 150 times as much* as the producer from a cup of fair trade coffee.

"So, everybody, let's see how many of y'all are smarter than a fourth grader: Even in a coffee price crisis when fair trade has its maximum benefit at a third of a cent per pound, guess how many fair trade lattes it would take to buy $100 of education for Guatemalan kids?" A few people around the table grinned and tried it on their open laptops. It was $100 divided by $0.0033 and then multiplied by the forty lattes per pound of coffee.

An undergraduate proudly responded before most people finished: "1.2 million lattes."

"You got it, Junior. That's about four million bucks spent on fair trade lattes to buy $100 of education for the *niños*. Yes, folks, I think we've somehow stumbled upon it—the most inefficient development program ever devised by mankind."

Rich sat down. Angela glanced around. There was an awkward quiet in the room. It was a large number of lattes. Josefina Reyes and Rudolph Goldhard sat in dumbfounded, staggered silence. The heat rising from Norman Blowner's forehead rendered the conference room radiator redundant. He spat, "I trust that you will not be applying to FairCaf after graduation, Mr. Freeland."

"Wouldn't dream of it, sir," said Rich as he pulled his flash drive from the computer.

One of the senior professors involved in the study spoke for the first time, his large mane of gray hair reflecting a crown of wisdom that had accrued over years of studying the myriad failures and comparatively few successes of antipoverty efforts. "The research Sofia will present will likely explain why you have these results. What we are seeing here is the product of well-intentioned people creating a faulty institutional mechanism that unfortunately undermines its attempt to help coffee growers. The flaw is a bit subtle, so I'm going to tell a story that illustrates what is happening."

The professor began the story. "Once there was a rich man who wanted to help people in a poor country. The people there were so poor that all of them earned only one peso an hour from their labor in the field. The rich man flew down to the country and established a small office in the countryside where he would sit behind a desk and hand out a peso at a time to each who came. People would wait in line to get their peso, which they would receive after filling out a small amount of paperwork. Then the next person in line would get his peso.

"One day an economist was visiting the area and asked what the man was doing. 'I am helping poor people,' said the rich man. 'I have given away much of my wealth—one peso at a time—to thousands who have come to me for help.' And the rich man was not lying. Indeed, he had given exactly what he said.

"But the economist then turned to the person at the front of the line and asked him how long he had been waiting for his peso. 'About an hour,' said the man, who now had reached the front of the line. 'The line is always about that long. I should know; I've been through it several times now.' And this was so, for every time the line was less than an hour long, it was worth it for one of the villagers to stand in the line to get his peso. If the line ever became longer than this, people would realize the wait was no longer worth it, leave the line, and go back to work.

"The rich man asked the economist why he was talking to the people in his line. 'Because you haven't helped anyone,' said the economist. The rich man responded, 'That's not true—I have given away hundreds of thousands of pesos to these people!' But the economist replied, 'Yes, but since everyone can get a peso, the opportunity cost of these people waiting in line to get the peso has been equal to the peso they were given.'

"Now a few people overheard the conversation between the economist and the rich man. Coming to their senses, they realized that there was nothing to be gained from waiting in the line to receive the peso. But when they left, the line became shorter, and thus it became worth waiting in line for the peso again. So the people returned to the line. The rich man, now frustrated with the situation, decided to increase his giving: instead of giving people a single peso, from then on he would hand out ten peso bills. But as soon as people found out the news, the wait in the line increased dramatically—to ten hours. The economist left and went back home, because he didn't have the heart to tell the rich man that he was doing no more good for the people than before."

The professor smiled at his story. So did the others around the table, except for Goldhard, Blowner, and Reyes.

"Correct me if I am wrong, but I think I understand the parable," said Angela to the others around the table. "It's a problem of free entry into fair trade certification. Because the market for fair trade is limited, the more coffee growers around the world that become certified for fair trade, the lower the percentage of the crop the cooperatives are able to market as fair trade coffee, so that the people who are supposedly helped by these well-intentioned efforts in the long run are no better off than anybody else."

"Yes," said the professor. "It is an unsettling paradox."

"Sofia, would you present the results we have obtained?" asked her advisor.

"We obtained the most recent thirteen years of coffee-grower data from a large fair trade association in Guatemala. We have reason to believe that it may closely represent the industry as a whole."

Everyone studied the projector screen. "As you can see, the data from our research show that in the years the benefits to being a fair trade grower increased during this thirteen-year period, the fraction of growers' crops actually marketed as fair trade coffee became smaller. For example, during the worst year of the coffee crisis in 2002, the fraction of the crop able to be marketed as fair trade fell to 15 percent. Even when the price of coffee marketed as fair trade was sixty-two cents *higher* than the market price of sixty-three cents during these years, the average grower who was fair trade certified never received more than a twelve-cent premium per pound."

Sofia continued. "As coffee prices have risen, the share of fair trade–certified grower's crop marketed as fair trade has gone up again. This is consistent with what we would expect with free entry and exit into any industry where there are extra profits to be made. Free entry into the fair trade coffee marketing channel has essentially driven out all of the surplus benefits to coffee growers accruing from fair trade. In years of low coffee prices, the growers gain a little bit from being in the network, but when coffee prices are higher, they lose from the cost of certification."

Sofia looked around the room and gave the final word "Our conclusion after examining the data carefully is that on average over the last thirteen years, the monetary premium to growers from participating in the fair trade network has been essentially zero."

"Zero?" asked several of the students together, incredulously.

"Yes, unfortunately. *Zero.*"

The veins running down Blowner's temples looked as if they would imminently explode. "You have data from one cooperative and you claim that this pitiful result generalizes to the entire fair trade coffee industry?" he argued loudly.

"Mr. Blowner," replied Sofia, smiling, "do you think that coffee farmers in Africa or Asia would be less rational, less eager to improve the lives of their families than those in Guatemala?"

Blowner had no answer to this. He looked to Goldhard for support, who also came up empty.

The students looked at the Berkeley professors, who slowly and sullenly nodded their heads in agreement with the results. The findings merely reflected a fundamental law of microeconomics: free entry drives out surpluses in markets. They were satisfied with having discovered something important and not obvious, but disappointed with the finding itself. These were people who did not want to see well-intentioned efforts fail. A morose silence hung over the room.

Josefina Reyes quickly broke it. "But what about the social premium? What about all those schools and projects that have been built as a result of fair trade? You can't say that people haven't benefited from the fair trade program. In my view one of the best things about fair trade is not necessarily the higher income but the work in the villages."

The professor from UC San Diego responded to her. "The schools are a good thing. It's like all the money the rich man gave away. You could point to all the wonderful things people bought with it. However, you would be ignoring opportunity costs. The growers not directly, but *indirectly*, paid for those schools with the cost of their certification. You raise a good point though. To the extent that the fair trade program can channel money from growers that might have been spent on things less valuable than schools, it has been helpful. However, I don't think the main point of fair trade coffee has been to redirect how the growers spend their money. But you are probably right that one of the best things about fair trade is the social work in the villages—because there doesn't seem to be any long-term benefit from better coffee prices."

"Obviously the problem is that the market for fair trade coffee is too small," interjected Goldhard. "If people just became more conscious of the issue and bought more fair trade coffee, the market would be bigger, and growers would prosper."

Angela and Alex's advisor from San Francisco responded. "But, Rudolph, it's just like the parable when the man increases his giving to ten pesos. Even if the market for fair trade coffee grew, or the fair trade premium increased, more coffee growers would direct their crop into fair trade until eventually the benefits of it dissipated."

The professor from San Diego spoke again. "Yes, that is correct. Even if all the beans in the world were miraculously purchased as fair trade, the higher return to coffee would lure new production into the market, starting the process all over, and the benefit would again dissipate unless the consumer market for coffee were to keep infinitely increasing, which is a silly proposition."

"It would seem that the only way to create surplus benefits to coffee growers would be to limit access to fair trade certification," said Sofia. "You could create sustainable artificial surpluses to a limited number of growers by preventing new growers from becoming fair trade certified—just like the man giving the money could limit the length of the line."

Alex jumped in. "You shouldn't have a group of coffee growers who are arbitrarily privileged over others. That would be unfair."

"This is the rotten apple in this whole approach to helping coffee growers," Rich interjected. "The last thing we should be doing is giving incentives for people to produce more coffee."

Sofia recalled to her advisor, "While we were in Huehuetenango, we visited Jennifer evaluating the microfinance program making loans to coffee growers. She said some borrowers had expanded their other businesses enough that they were backing off coffee production. Rich's comment reminded me that if we're going to intervene in the market, we should be giving people incentives to grow *less* coffee, to raise prices for all the remaining growers."

Angela glanced at Blowner and Reyes and was happy to see that they were beginning to take some notes.

Sofia looked over at them across the table. "I don't think any of us regards fair trade coffee as a scam, but it clearly represents a missed opportunity, and a very unfortunate one. Here are a huge number of comparatively wealthy coffee drinkers who on average appear willing to transfer fifty cents a cup to a coffee grower in a poor country. But over the last ten years they've been transferring less than a tenth of a cent. Think of the benefits that could have come from all of this willingness to transfer income to the poor."

"Better just to put a kitty on the coffee counter," added Rich. "Have people contribute directly to a school fund in a coffee country. Work better if even half the spare change ever made it down there."

"Yes," said Angela, "one could do a lot to harness this willingness to help coffee growers. Cafés could sponsor coffee-growing villages, using money to build fresh-water wells, vaccinate kids, pay for school tuition. Educating kids would increase their opportunity cost of being coffee growers and then reduce the coffee supply so prices would naturally trend upward in the long run."

"Yes, and other mechanisms could be designed that mitigate the effects of coffee price volatility on the growers," commented another professor.

After others contributed their own ideas, the meeting was adjourned for lunch. Angela stood up from the table and her eyes met Sofia's across the room. She knew Sofia was proud of her; this meant a lot.

Before she could leave the room, the hand of Josefina Reyes touched her shoulder. "May I have a word with you, Angela?"

"Of course."

"We're looking for some bright young minds to work with us on . . . er . . . some of these issues. Do you think you might be interested in perhaps . . . talking with us?"

Angela smiled.

———

Angela, Sofia, Rich, and Alex walked together from Giannini Hall to a café called Brewed Awakening on Euclid Street north of campus. Angela and Sofia ordered mochas, Alex a tall latte, and Rich his standard double espresso. Roaming through the room filled with coffee-fueled academic discussion groups and graduate students cramming for examinations, they found an empty table and sat down.

"So how do you like advanced econometrics?" Sofia asked the two master's students as they blew on their beverages. The class was one of the last they had to take before graduation in May.

"It gives me a sore head," replied Alex. "But I am liking it mostly." Angela studied Alex for a moment as he talked about what techniques they were studying. As he raised up his latte, his shirtsleeves slid toward his elbows, exposing the wounds on his wrist. They had healed, but left behind a series of jagged scars.

"Ditto," Angela added to Alex's thought. "Discontinuity designs, nonparametric estimation, maximum likelihood estimation—all important, but not the friendliest beasts to tame."

Angela looked at Rich and Sofia. "I had a question for you guys."

"Sure. What's up?" said Sofia.

"I've been thinking about today. Do you think all the money and effort that is spent to aid people in poor countries does any good?"

"Part of it does," Sofia answered. Rich seemed to at least grudgingly agree to the statement.

"Which part?" asked Angela.

"We've got our best people working on that one," said Sofia, trying to discreetly wipe off a mustache left by her mocha.

"I don't understand how so much money can be wasted on poverty programs that don't work," said Angela.

"Because the reasons people give to the poor are mostly unrelated to what actually helps," said Rich.

"That is a depressing thought."

Sofia responded, "Yes, but you have to understand that a lot of it has been our fault, economists I mean. We wasted decades developing elaborate theoretical models that helped us to explore a fantasy world of perfect markets that had little practical use in solving the world's most pressing problems. Now the profession has woken up and is doing much more applied work that tries to answer practical questions like what kinds of programs actually help people."

Rich added, "You know, economics is probably at the caveman stage physics was at before Sir Isaac came along. And social behavior is more complicated than apples falling out of trees, maybe more complicated than the movement of light and particles. Matter can't reason; light can't strategize. Got a long road ahead before important breakthroughs filter down to the folks who are doing the giving."

"But we must know that *some* things work," reasoned Angela.

"Yes," said Sofia. "Last week I was at a seminar that documented the big impact of clean water in villages. They presented some convincing evidence that providing fresh water to villages reduces infant mortality by up to half for something like ten dollars a person per year. There are other efforts that have similarly big impacts relative to the cost, like providing mosquito nets to families in areas with malaria, and annually administering a fifty-cent dose of deworming medicine to children. Many programs that focus on children—supporting their education, their health, their goals and aspirations—have also demonstrated big impacts—the younger the children, the better. These are things that governments and people can support, knowing that it's probably making a difference."

Rich added, "And sometimes it's just better to give 'em cash. Let people themselves decide how to use it best instead of giving them cows and pigs, or having them participate in some fair trade system that doesn't work anyway. Bucketloads of funding going down that road now; finding big impacts in randomized trials."

In reflecting on all of this, Angela almost forgot to ask Sofia an important question. "I heard about your offer to be an assistant professor at MIT. Have you accepted it?"

"Yes, I did, actually. Just last week," she said.

"Nerd alert!" shouted Angela playfully, rocking back in her chair. "That's so cool."

Sofia smiled. "How about your doctoral applications?"

"I wanted to tell you guys. I've been admitted to a few programs in California, but I just found out a few days ago—I made the wait list for MIT," she announced proudly. She had been waiting to tell Sofia. "I was hoping you were going to be there!"

"Angela, that is very awesome," said Alex, congratulating her. "The top economics program in the world. Will you let me come and be your apartment cleaner?" he teased.

"I'll be looking for a research assistant next year," Sofia said to Angela. "Any interest?"

"Are you kidding?" said Angela. "I'll do it for free if you can just kick their butts a little to let me in."

"Obviously I'm a rookie and don't have much clout, but I'll try to identify the right butts and do my best to kick them in just the right way," Sofia promised. Angela smiled, grateful.

"Well, I have also to report some good news," said Alex, blushing a little. "I found out yesterday I am beginning an internship with the World Bank in July —their Latin America division."

"The World Bank—" responded Angela. "You got it? I can't believe it. *You?*"

"The Bank has become more interested in working with faith-based development organizations, did you know? And they like my experimental study. They said it was 'original,' whatever means *that.*"

"Oh my gosh, the sympathy I'm feeling for the World Bank now," exclaimed Angela.

There was only one left. "And what about the Mr. Rich?" inquired Alex.

"Still weighing my options, Lefty."

Sofia looked at him and shook her head. "Rich just accepted a job doing health program evaluation with a small nonprofit based in Bolivia."

Rich glared at Sofia.

"What are you ashamed of?" she asked him.

"I thought you might end up staying at the Bank," Alex said. He looked as surprised as Angela felt.

"Well, let's just say I find business suits a little itchy around the neck area."

Alex looked down at his latte and shook his head, saying nothing, smiling to himself.

Angela looked at him. "I think that's awesome, Rich."

CHAPTER 31

Sofia

January 17, 2014

THE TELEPHONE ON SOFIA'S DESK RANG, INTERRUPTING HER thoughts as she was editing an article for the MIT Press that someone had submitted to the *Review of Economics and Statistics*. She fumbled for the receiver, barely taking her eyes off a puzzling sequence of equations she was trying to reconcile.

"This is Sofia." As she listened attentively, she continued to ponder how the author's proof satisfied equations 17(b) through 21(c).

A voice with a European accent on the end of the line introduced himself politely. He was hoping to contact Ms. Lopez-Williams, who had failed to reply to several e-mails.

"I'm afraid Angela isn't at the university anymore. She filed her dissertation last May. Actually, you can congratulate her. She is now Dr. Lopez-Williams."

More talking and explaining followed on the other end. He was a faculty member at the University of Bonn and hoped that Angela would present a paper from her dissertation at a conference there that month. Naturally, travel and per diem would be provided.

"She is on leave, deferring her new faculty position until the following fall."

More talking.

"That's wonderful that her article has won the award, but I'm almost sure it will be impossible for her to come present her findings at the institute in Bonn anytime within the next few weeks."

The voice persisted.

"You see, Angela and her husband have been living in Central America since September. They have been expecting a baby, and she thought it important that her baby be born in Guatemala."

How interesting. Why was that?

"Perhaps it would be best if I let her explain the story to you."

—

Angela's fingers flowed smoothly over the coffee plant as the morning sun made its way through the shimmering green leaves, creating a dancing pattern of light on her face. The coffee cherries were nestled together close to the branch in little clusters of about eight to twelve. Their hard, smooth exteriors felt cool against her palm as she dropped them into the burlap sack that was hanging in front of her colorful *traje*. Carefully but methodically, she worked her way around one coffee plant, moving to the next. She had been a good student of coffee picking; Juana had taught her well. The sack was filling quickly with fire-engine-red coffee cherries. It would be a good harvest this year.

Angela felt one of the little fruits bounce off her shoulder. From two plants away she heard a repressed giggle, which of course was teenage Ema. Having the baby wrapped around her back made it impossible for Angela to give chase, making her an even more appealing target than usual for Ema's little pranks.

"*Ven aca, mi pequena bromista,*" she called to Ema, who emerged from behind a neighboring plant. The Spanish had become easy now; it flowed effortlessly through her mind, to her tongue, and over her lips with the easy, stiletto-like precision of a native speaker. Ema scurried over to Angela and hugged her, putting her bronzed arms around Angela's huipil. Then she pulled back the *mantel* wrapped around the sleeping infant on Angela's back and peeked down into her face.

"*Se parece su papa, no a ti!*" She looked like her dad, and less like Angela.

"*Solo porque es guera,*" replied Angela casually. Ema laughed. It was only the blond hair, because the rest of her looked exactly like her, in her own modest opinion.

Angela responded, "*Mira la piel, la negrita es la mia, por cierto.*" There was no doubt that baby Mariela had her own rich amber skin, not the fairer skin of her father.

She and Ema picked side by side for a while, Ema using the ladder to help her with the cherries located in the high spots. They shared stories and laughed together in the cool morning dew. Angela looked at her and in a flashing moment saw Lourdes in her face, Lourdes who would miss so many of life's opportunities in a young life unnecessarily cut short. She would make sure that Ema had those opportunities; yes, she would make sure of it, personally, and would soon have the means to do so.

Angela whimsically asked Ema if there were any cute boys at her school. Ema's weight shifted on the ladder as she instantly turned to repel the question with a flying coffee cherry. But at this, the ladder began to sink in a patch of soft mud under one of its supports, and between the burden of the baby on her back and weakness brought on by laughter, Angela proved increasingly ineffective at steadying it.

"*Ema, bajate, se hunde la escalera!*" Angela yelled.

It was too late and it all fell toward the ground like a slowly wilting flower, resting on a neighboring coffee plant, with Ema tangled up in the branches, legs kicking at the clouds.

Unfortunately, the entire series of events transpired at the moment of Fernando's arrival.

Fernando indeed appeared curious about what they might be doing to his coffee plants. With the patience of a father toward a beloved youngest child, he helped Ema extract herself from the coffee branches.

He brought news that Victorina, an older woman living on the other side of Seis Cierros, had come to the house to see Angela. Apparently it was about some gifts that she had; probably for the baby, Angela thought. That was nice. It was good timing; her sack was getting full and the little peeps emanating from the cocoon signaled that Mariela needed changing anyway. She gave Ema her sack and walked through the coffee field toward the house, Mariela still bundled on her back. Perhaps her father might help with this one.

"Alex, would you change the baby while I make a visit with Fernando?" called Angela into the house. "Alex?"

Alex staggered slowly out of the back room. His mood seemed relatively upbeat, but he looked unshaven and disheveled from being up much of the night with Mariela, who at three weeks had not yet synchronized her waking and sleeping schedule to the day/night routine that is standard for older humans. He gently untied the red and yellow blankets that secured Mariela to Angela's back and lifted his daughter above his head as his sleeves fell to his elbows, revealing traces of the old scars on his wrists. He nuzzled Mariela close to his unshaven face.

"Oh no!" he laughed as he held her tiny face a few inches above his. "Daddy's princess makes little dumplings? . . . Daddy makes stinky-poos all better . . . ," he cooed as he began the changing ritual on a makeshift diaper table. "Angie, have you the diaper bag?"

—

Angela followed Fernando and Victorina down the dirt road passing in front of the house.

"Your daughter is *muy bendicida*, Angela," remarked Fernando as they walked.

"Blessed with a father who changes diapers?" she replied.

"Far stronger than I in this way," Fernando admitted sheepishly. "*Es buen hombre*, Angela." A good man.

"Thank you, Fernando."

They continued to walk down a path through some trees to a collection of ramshackle adobe dwellings. Outside chickens chased each other, and an old rusty mountain bike lay in the dirt on its side, and Victorina spoke.

"I knew your mother well," she explained. "But not as well as did my younger sister. Your mother was my sister's best friend. My sister's name was Mildred."

They walked inside one of the modest houses, and Victorina led Angela to a small wooden box. It looked old, probably made out of some kind of native wood, clearly hand-carved with inlays of Mayan jaguars, archers, stars, and new moons.

"The box was a present from my father to Mildred when she was nine, but she kept it her whole life. She died the same day as your mother, Angela, the day the soldiers entered the village. But when they were friends, they would give each other gifts." The three, who had each lost family that horrific day, sat down together on some humble chairs, and Angela and Fernando watched as Victorina opened the wooden box. She pulled out a light blue ribbon made of handwoven cloth.

"Your mother gave this cinta to my sister for a birthday when they were little to wear in her hair." Angela had seen many Guatemalan women with the cinta intertwined through their braids.

"For you to have," she said.

Angela took the cinta in her hand. It was maybe forty years old now, yet still very elegant.

"Thank you, Señora Victorina. I will treasure this."

She handed Angela several other items from the box, a few cards and letters from her mother to Mildred, and a metal comb with a bone handle that had a woman's figure engraved in it.

"They always wanted each other to be beautiful," she said.

The last item she drew out of the box was a small wooden crucifix on a copper chain. "From your mother to my sister, after her confirmation," Victorina explained. "Now it is for your baby, perhaps to give at her baptism."

Angela sat down on one of the beds in the room and held the cross with the forlorn figure of Christ hanging on it, regarding it in the palm of her hand. The hand-carved figure on the cross looked different than similar figures she had seen before. The face had Mayan features.

She stared at the Mayan-looking figure on the cross, and her mind began to trace the remarkable path of her life: her birth in San Pedro Necta, her rescue by Fernando and his family, adoption, growing up in California, insecurities about her birthmark and her identity that never seemed to abate, the seemingly impossible odds of discovering those who knew her as a child. The path since her return to Guatemala: accepted from the wait list at MIT the last week before school started, spending five years studying under Sofia, writing what some of the faculty at MIT called one of the finest dissertations that year.

Then she reflected on the day when she and her friend Alex became more than best friends. This was followed by the two breakups, the two getting-back-togethers, and the decision that if they were going to fight like an old married couple, they might as well be one someday. It was that day during one of their return visits to Guatemala, when they hiked together to the peak of the Santa Maria, that he told her he loved her and could not live without her, getting down on one knee and asking her to marry him. Then came the difficult periods when he was away with the Bank, working in a faraway country as she toiled at her consulting job in DC, Alex then leaving the Bank to enroll in seminary, then the founding of the nonprofit together.

Despite the path taken by Alex, inwardly she never regarded herself as a deeply spiritual person; it was only at this moment that she began to feel that something had guided her life, or at least had accompanied her, through its valleys and peaks all to reach this very day, and what lay beyond. Angela began to caress the delicate figure in her hand.

Some of the valleys she did not understand. She did not understand the death of Lourdes and her baby, although she couldn't help but see how her own life had been dramatically altered because of it. And though her understanding of poverty had grown through her studies, she did not understand why so many of her relatives had to live without knowing anything other than being poor. Then she thought of her mother, and she began to see her mother's death in the Mayan-looking figure on the cross. How ironic, she thought, that her mother's death had given Angela all of the advantages that never would have been hers had it not been for a singularly gross act of brutality.

Angela put the items in the pocket of her traje, except for the crucifix, which she placed around her neck, tucking the figure under her huipil. She thanked and hugged Victorina, and she and Fernando walked back to the house, where Juana and Ema greeted them. Ema smiled and put her finger to her lips, motioning to the porch where Alex lay asleep out front in a chair, dozing peacefully with his hat over his face and the baby Mariela asleep on his chest.

POSTSCRIPT

THE RESULTS OF THE STUDY BY MY COLLEAGUES FROM THE University of California on the impact of fair trade coffee, now pending publication in the *Review of Economics and Statistics*, were surprising to many academics, and perhaps even more surprising to the fair trade coffee industry. Yet as researchers on the project presented the findings in seminars at research institutions, other economists began to see the flaw in the design of the fair trade certification system, and it became clear how it was impossible for the system to yield long-term price benefits to growers.

One of the researchers mentioned that in a seminar at the RAND Corporation, after researchers in the audience understood the fair trade certification process, they predicted the ensuing zero-impact result even before seeing the data. This was because the fair trade coffee mechanism, as it has been practiced to date, attempts to violate one of the most fundamental laws of economics: where surplus profit can be obtained, it will be sought after, driving the benefits out of the system.

The flaws in the fair trade coffee system should not discourage us from more effective efforts to help the poor in developing countries. A recent poll I undertook, among top development economists specializing in the study of program impacts, listed the provision of fresh water as yielding the largest benefit per dollar among the antipoverty programs to which ordinary people frequently contribute. (Drinking fair trade coffee finished second to last, ahead only of handing out free laptops to children in poor countries.) Giving money to organizations that work in preventative health, especially among children, is highly effective: deworming, antimalaria campaigns, vaccinations, nutrition programs for expectant mothers, and so forth. My own research on international child sponsorship indicates that sponsoring a child, particularly girls, and particularly in sub-Saharan Africa, has tremendous impacts on the future education, vocation, and adult income of beneficiaries. While microfinance has shown somewhat disappointing impacts in random-ized controlled trials, recent efforts to channel cash grants directly to the poor have shown remarkable impacts in many parts of the world. Researchers find that the vast majority of these funds are not wasted, but rather spent on food, clothing, schooling, and building up house-hold assets like animal herds and small business capital.

While the economics and the research study discussed in this book are real, the characters in this book are mainly fictitious with the excep-tion of two. Jimmy, the owner of the Blue Danube Coffee House in San Francisco, is a real person, a really wonderful person, and we thank him for allowing us to carry out behavioral experiments on his coffee cus-tomers. Lourdes Asusana Guitz Alva was a wonderful young friend of our family living in a Quiché village in western Guatemala, whom my wife and I had the pleasure of sponsoring through Mayan Partners as she attended secondary school, and who inspired her character in this book. In November 2009 Lourdes died unexpectedly of a pregnancy-related brain hemorrhage at the age of twenty-one, and we dedicate this book to her memory.

Reading Group Guide

1. Based on your own experience and views on poverty and globalization issues, which character in the novel can you identify with most closely?

2. At times do you feel guilty about living in a rich country when so many in the world live in poverty?

3. If you have traveled to a developing country, how did the contrast between your lifestyle in your home country and what you experienced there make you feel? Can you relate to Angela's feelings when returning to her country of birth for the first time?

4. Do you believe globalization is generally a good thing for the poor in developing countries, or do you believe it hurts them? Why?

5. What is the responsibility of people in wealthy countries to those living in poverty in developing countries? What forms the base of your values that dictates your relationship toward the poor? Spiritual? Secular?

6. Consider Alex's debate with Genevieve about sweatshops. What do you believe about multinational investment in

developing countries? What is our best ethical response to it as consumers?

7. Do you drink fair trade coffee? What might be a better way to help coffee growers in poor countries than the traditional fair trade mechanism?

8. Can you think of other ways people give to the poor overseas that may make them feel good about themselves but may not be very effective in helping the poor?

9. What is one idea you have to help a poor family or individual in a developing country? How do you know it would genuinely help them as opposed to merely making you feel less guilty about living in a wealthy country?

10. Moving forward, would you be willing to commit to taking one concrete step of action that would support the plight of the poor to live with economic security and dignity?

LIST OF REFERENCES BY CHAPTER

THE TEN LARGEST COFFEE-CONSUMING NATIONS ON A PER capita basis in order are Norway, Finland, Denmark, Sweden, the Netherlands, Switzerland, Germany, Austria, Belgium, and France. The United States ranks twelfth. (Data is from the Global Market Information Database, published by *Euromonitor*.) The ten largest coffee-producing nations in order are Brazil, Vietnam, Colombia, Indonesia, Mexico, India, Ethiopia, Guatemala, Honduras, and Peru. (Data is from the Food and Agricultural Organization.) Figures on per capita income, infant mortality, and education come from the World Bank and the Millennium Development Goals database.

CHAPTER 5

The references to Sofia's dialogue on economic growth are from Daron Acemoglu, Simon Johnson, and James Robinson (2001), "The Colonial Origins of Comparative Development: An Empirical Review," *American Economic Review* 91 (5)5: 1360–1401; and Daron Acemoglu and James Robinson (2006), *Economic Origins of Dictatorship and Democracy* (New York: Cambridge University Press).

CHAPTERS 8-10

The data from the study of the fair trade coffee value chain come from Rosangela Bando and Gonzalo de los Rios (2007), "The Coffee Value Chain in Guatemala: A Case Study of Fair Trade," and Rosangela Bando and Elizabeth Sadoulet (2012), "Understanding the Coffee Value Chain in Guatemala: A Case Study," USAID-BASIS Brief (March).

CHAPTER 11

Many of the references to the early history of coffee are from Regina Wagner (2001), *La Historia del Café de Guatemala* (Bogota, Colombia: Benjamin Villegas y Asociados); Nina Lutinger and Gregory Dicum (2006), *The Coffee Book* (New York: New Press); Inernational Coffee Organization, "The Story of Coffee" (www.ico.org/coffee_story); and Gordon Wrigley (1988), *Coffee* (New York: Wiley).

CHAPTER 13

The story of Guatemalan immigration is taken from an experience I had during fieldwork, where most of the men from the households I needed to interview had left and were working as busboys in Houston. It was claimed in the (relatively small) village that five hundred men were currently living there, many of them in the same apartment complex. An excellent international economics text with outstanding data on immigration and foreign investments is Appleyard, Field, and Cobb (2010), *International Economics*, 7th ed. (New York: McGraw-Hill/Irwin).

CHAPTER 15

References used in creating the backdrop for Guatemalan coffee history are principally taken from David McCreery (1994), *Rural*

Guatemala (Stanford, CA: Stanford University Press), and William Roseberry, Lowell Gudmundson, and Mario Samper Kutschbach, eds. (1995), *Coffee, Society and Power in Latin America* (Baltimore: Johns Hopkins University Press). Also see Steward Lee Allen (1999), *The Devil's Cup: A History of the World according to Coffee* (Toronto: Ballantine).

CHAPTER 17

Amy L. Sherman (1997), *The Soul of Development: Biblical Christianity and Economic Transformation in Guatemala* (New York: Oxford University Press), is an excellent resource on the emergence of evangelical Christianity in Latin America generally and Guatemala specifically. See also David Stoll (1990), *Is Latin American Turning Protestant? The Politics of Evangelical Growth* (Berkeley: University of California Press).

The seminal work on World Systems Theory is Immanuel Wallerstein (1976), *The Modern World-System: Capitalist Agriculture and the Origins of the European World-Economy in the Sixteenth Century* (New York: Academic Press). See also Fernando Henrique Cardoso and Enzo Faletto (1976), *Dependency and Development in Latin América* (Berkeley: University of California Press).

For academic papers that have indicated economic openness to be linked to growth, see Jeffrey Sachs and Andrew Warner (1995), "Economic Reform and the Process of Global Integration," Brookings Papers on Economic Activity, no. 1: 1–118, and Romain Wacziarg and Karen Horn Welch (2008), "Trade Liberalization and Growth: New Evidence," *World Bank Economic Review* 22 (2): 187–231.

An excellent review article that examines the impact of globalization on inequality is David Richardson (1995), "Income Inequality and Trade: How to Think, What to Conclude," *Journal of Economic*

Perspectives 3:33–55. See also Ann Harrison and Gordon Hansen (1995), "Trade, Technology, and Wage Inequality," *National Bureau of Economic Research*, working paper no. W5110.

A great article on the impact of Protestant missions on the development of democracy in poor countries is Robert Woodbury, "The Missionary Roots of Liberal Democracy," *American Political Science Review* 106 (2): 244–74.

The seminal article on the economics of identity is George Akerlof and Rachel Kranton (2000), "Economics and Identity," *Quarterly Journal of Economics* 115 (1): 715–53, and the same authors give a discussion of identity and poverty traps in Akerlof and Kranton (2005), "Social Divisions within Schools," in *The Social Economics of Poverty*, ed. Christopher Barrett (New York: Routledge).

CHAPTER 18

Data from Bando and de los Rios (2007). The historical references to US–Latin American coffee relations and the International Coffee Agreement draw from Mark Pendergrast (1999), Uncommon Grounds: The History of Coffee and How It Transformed Our World (New York: Basic Books), and Nina Lutinger and Gregory Dicum (2006), *The Coffee Book* (New York: New Press). The information about fair trade coffee is taken from the online resources of Global Exchange, www.globalexchange.org. Much of the background on the origin and structure of the fair trade coffee industry comes from Antony Wild (2004), *Black Gold: A Dark History of Coffee* (London: Harper Perennial).

CHAPTER 19

The new innovations in the study of causal effects have revolutionized development economics. Excellent references for this material are Esther Duflo, Rachel Glennerster, and Michael Kremer (2007),

"The Use of Randomization in Development Economics: A Toolkit," in *The Handbook of Development Economics*, ed. Dani Rodrik and Mark Rosenzweig; and Shahidur R. Khandker et al. (2010), *Handbook on Impact Evaluation* (Washington, DC: World Bank and Oxford University Press).

CHAPTER 23

The experiment and data collection described in chapter 23 were carried out by graduate students at the University of San Francisco. Data from the experiment presented in the story is actual data.

CHAPTER 27

The story of the massacre was taken from personal interviews with rural Guatemalans who suffered through the genocides of the early 1980's and a compilation of accounts from a number of books that recount specific episodes of this tragic time, including Ricardo Falla (1994), *Massacres in the Jungle: Ixcán, Guatemala, 1975–1982*, trans. Julia Howland (Boulder: Westview Press); Gonzalo Sichar Moreno (2000), *Masacares en Guatemala: Los Gritos de un Pueblo Entero* (Guatemala: GAM); and Beatriz Mans (2004), *Paradise in Ashes: A Guatemalan Journey of Courage, Terror, and Hope* (Berkeley: University of California Press).

CHAPTER 29

The research on child labor that Alex refers to is Kaushik Basu (1998), "Child Labor: Cause, Consequence, and Cure," *Journal of Economic Literature* 38: 1083–119. For an excellent study on the unintended consequences of child labor pooling, see Prachant Bharadwaj, Leah Lakdawala, and Nicholas Li (2014), "Perverse Consequences of Well-Intentioned Regulation: Evidence from India's Child Labor Ban" (working paper, University of California at San Diego).

CHAPTER 30

A key study on the shift in income shares from producers to consumers is John Talbot (1997), "Where Does Your Coffee Dollar Go? The Division of Income and Surplus along the Coffee Commodity Chain," *Studies in Comparative International Development* 32 (1). Consumer trends for coffee consumption can be found at the National Coffee Association USA website at www.ncausa.org.

The fair trade coffee impact study described in chapter 30 is Alain de Janvry, Elizabeth Sadoulet, and Craig McInstosh (2010), "Fair Trade and Free Entry: The Dissipation of Producer Benefits in a Disequilibrium Market" (working paper, University of California at Berkeley, Department of Agricultural and Resource Economics, with grand funding through BASIS-USAID). Other data is taken from Bando and de los Rios (2007).

Other studies have also examined problems of over certification, including Margaret Levi and April Linton (2003), "Fair Trade: A Cup at a Time?" *Politics and Society* 31: 407–32, as well as the problem of low transfers to growers, for example, Marc Sidwell (2008), "Unfair Trade" (London: Adam Smith Institute). Other studies, such as Utting-Charmorro (2005), "Does Fair Trade Make a Difference? The Case of Small Coffee Producers in Nicaragua," *Development in Practice* 15: 584–99, claim positive benefits from fair trade to coffee growers. Yet these and some other more recent studies suffer from statistical identification problems that render them unable to identify the causal impacts of fair and some other more recent trade coffee. Another recent study using rigorous impact identification is Raluca Dragusanu and Nathan Nunn (2014), "The Impacts from Fair Trade Certification: Evidence from Coffee Producers in Costa Rica," (working paper, Harvard University), which finds small positive impacts on the most skilled producers but none for the majority of fair trade coffee producers in the study.

ACKNOWLEDGMENTS

I WOULD LIKE TO ACKNOWLEDGE MY FRIENDS AND COLLEAGUES at the University of California at Berkeley, Alain de Janvry and Betty Sadoulet, as well as Craig McIntosh at the University of California at San Diego, for their outstanding research on the fair trade coffee project. All of us involved in the project would like to thank Rosangela Bando, Gonzalo de los Rios, Owen Ozier, Seth Morgan, Josh Schellenberg, Jerlin Hurtado, and Victoria Fontillas for their outstanding fieldwork in Guatemala, and Elizabeth Katz at the University of San Francisco, who organized and supervised much of this fieldwork. Rosangela and Gonzalo carried out the careful initial work that investigated the free trade and fair trade coffee value chains on which this story is based. For outstanding collaboration in survey work related to this book, I owe my deep gratitude to master's students at the University of San Francisco, especially Ben Buttorff, Sire Diedhiou, Eric Fischer, Quinn Keefer, Kate Hereford, Frank Hoffman, Patrick Madigan, Ram Rajbanshi, Laine Rutledge, Kittiyaratch Thanakornmonkkonchai, Raj Thiagaraj, Tim Van Vugt, and Skyler Wilson. Phillip Ross, my former research assistant at the University of San Francisco, now a doctoral student at Boston University, worked tirelessly on some of the data compilation and experimental research for this project. Many thanks also to Jimmy

Hsu, the owner of the Blue Danube Coffee House in the Richmond district of San Francisco, for his generous cooperation with our project. I would like to thank members of my faculty book club at the University of San Francisco, especially Tom Cavanaugh, Cornelia Van Cott, Casey Flaherty, Catrina Hayes, and Sunny Wong, who along with Stephanie Antalocy, Kathy Berla, Tracy Seeley, Debby Wilbur, and Max Zeigler, read over the entire manuscript at different stages, offering constructive comments that chipped the edges off a rough manuscript and helped shape it into a novel. This book was substantially improved by the edits and suggestions of contracting editors Dave Lambert and Nicci Jordan Hubert. Nobody could ask for a more helpful and encouraging editor than mine at Thomas Nelson, Ami McConnell. Thank you, Ami, for your insightful comments and passion for the book. The title originates from the thoughtful creativity of Thomas Nelson's wonderful publisher, Daisy Hutton. Jeremy Milford and Diana Milford helped with the design process. I want to express my deepest thanks to my agent at the Agency Group in New York, Sasha Raskin, for believing that an economics professor could write fiction and for immensely helpful comments on the original manuscript. Thank you to all the members of Mayan Partners here in the US and in Guatemala, and to Max Bixcul, Juan Ajcoc, and Vicenta and Diego Navichoc in San Pedro, Guatemala, for so many great stories about coffee-growing. A special thank-you to my parents, Richard and Judy Wydick, who taught me how to write and gave detailed comments on early drafts. Finally, I would like to acknowledge and thank my daughters, Allie (9) and Kayla (4). It may not always have seemed like it at the time, but those little interruptions in the office were peace for my soul. Above all, I would especially like to thank the Lord, who gives so much grace every day. And last I am so grateful for my favorite coffee drinker of all, my beautiful wife, Leanne Wydick, who has exhibited the patience of Job with me as this book has slowly come to fruition.

About the Author

Photo by Karly Loofbourrow

BRUCE WYDICK IS PROFESSOR OF ECONOMICS AND INTERNA-tional studies at the University of San Francisco. He has published academic articles in leading economics journals on the impact of development programs such as microfinance and farm animal donation, and was the lead investigator of the worldwide impact study of Compassion International's child sponsorship program. He also writes a regular column on economic issues for *Christianity Today*.